PARLIAMENTARY DEMOCRACY IN CRISIS

In November 2008, as the economic decline was being fully realized, Canada's newly elected minority government, led by Conservative Stephen Harper, presented a highly divisive fiscal update in advance of a proposed budget. Unable to support the motion, the Liberal Party and New Democratic Party, with the backing of the Bloc Québécois, formed a coalition in order to seek a non-confidence vote and to form a new government. In response, Conservative cabinet ministers launched a media blitz, informing Canadians that the opposition was mounting a 'coup d'état.' Ultimately Governor General Michaëlle Jean allowed Parliament to be prorogued, the coalition fell apart, and a budget was accepted by the House in January 2009. However, widespread public uncertainty and confusion about the principles of government evident during the crisis revealed a grave lack of understanding about the mechanics and legalities of parliamentary democracy on the part of Canadians.

With a foreword by former Governor General Adrienne Clarkson, *Parliamentary Democracy in Crisis* brings together journalists, political scientists, and leading constitutional experts to analyse the crisis and to discuss the nature of Canada's democracy. The contributors bring perspectives from both French and English Canada and cover all aspects of the crisis, including the prorogation of Parliament, the role of the governor general, the proposed Liberal-NDP coalition, the challenges of minority parliaments, and the now-evident rifts in the culture of Canadian democracy.

Knowledgeable and comprehensive but still highly accessible, *Parliamentary Democracy in Crisis* provides a reasoned and timely response to Canada's parliamentary crisis of November 2008.

PETER H. RUSSELL is a professor emeritus in the Department of Political Science at the University of Toronto.

LORNE SOSSIN is a professor in the Faculty of Law at the University of Toronto.

EDITED BY PETER H. RUSSELL AND
LORNE SOSSIN

Parliamentary
Democracy in Crisis

UNIVERSITY OF TORONTO PRESS
Toronto Buffalo London

© University of Toronto Press Incorporated 2009
Toronto Buffalo London
www.utppublishing.com
Printed in Canada

ISBN 978-1-4426-4076-4 (cloth)
ISBN 978-1-4426-1014-9 (paper)

Publication cataloguing information is available from Library
and Archives Canada.

University of Toronto Press acknowledges the financial assistance to its
publishing program of the Canada Council for the Arts and the Ontario
Arts Council.

University of Toronto Press acknowledges the financial support for its
publishing activities of the Government of Canada through the Book
Publishing Industry Development Program (BPIDP).

Contents

Foreword

THE RIGHT HONOURABLE ADRIENNE CLARKSON,
PC, CC, CMM, COM, CD

Twenty-Sixth Governor General of Canada

Dispelling ignorance should be the first duty of the intellectual. This series of essays is an analysis of what has just transpired in the governing of our country, and the information should be available and absorbed by every Canadian at this juncture in our history.

In November/December 2008 there was an enormous interest in the functioning of our political system accompanied by an abysmal lack of knowledge about the system. The idea that we were in crisis is something that I personally take with a grain of salt; just because a resolution has to be found does not mean that the situation is a crisis. We have a viable way of governing ourselves: it has been tested through our history since responsible government became the norm in 1848, nineteen years before confederation, with Robert Baldwin, Louis-Hippolyte La-Fontaine, and the governor general of the time, Lord Elgin. What was set in place has stood us in good stead and, if its principles are understood, can stand us in good stead for the future.

During my mandate as governor general, the subjects dealt with in this book were on my mind, not only at the time of elections but every time it was my duty to deliver the Speech from the Throne or to give royal assent to bills in the Senate. These occasions were accompanied by some pomp and justifiable ritual, precisely because they are part of the structures that we must have in order to continue our tradition of parliamentary democracy.

When I studied Canadian history in my last year of high school, we concentrated a good deal on the evolution of our system of government from the Royal Proclamation of 1763 through the Quebec Act of 1774, right up to the Statute of Westminster of 1931 and the Letters Patent of 1947. This last document – the Letters Patent – is of vital importance and set in place the contemporary powers of the governor general which it transferred from the monarch. Yet it is virtually unknown to the general public. We also focused heavily on the King/Byng crisis of 1926; our entire class, contrary to most current opinion, thought that Lord Byng had done the right thing! Perhaps we were all influenced by Eugene Forsey, whom our teacher quoted reverentially as the greatest authority on Canadian parliamentary and constitutional matters. Certainly, Forsey disagreed with the view that a constitutional crisis occurs when a government faces defeat; he emphasized that the confidence of the House gives legitimacy to our form of responsible government, and that any defeat of a government and what followed was simply part of a constitutional process.

High school students today do not get the opportunity to learn Canadian history as I and my generation did. This is not only regrettable but shameful. A country that does not know its past can only stumble through the present and will need a Braille map for the future. In the recent heated discussions of November and December 2008, most people and much of the media did not understand that we do not have a presidential system in Canada. We do not vote for a prime minister. Perhaps some of this has to do with the fact that we were observing closely and vicariously a most historic and exciting presidential contest in our elephantine neighbour. A mixture of vicarious envy and delight seemed to wash over us and probably did not help in our understanding of our own unique and vivid narrative. Even if we are mouse-like in comparison, we do have an old, continuous, fully articulated organic system – a strong skeletal infrastructure of institutions, healthy flesh due to a constant democratic diet, and an intriguing triangular personality. What could be more interesting than that? Canadians should learn to live in their own moment.

The events of a few months ago should be a rallying cry for all of us to examine the interpretations of our parliamentary democracy and to convey our knowledge and experience about them. This book helps in its various ways to do this; its readers can become part of an informed public which will be knowledgeable about the democratic machinery to which we have made refined interventions.

It's important for all of us to know that our citizens elect members to legislatures, that we vote for individuals who will carry the message of the political party whose banners they wear. And it is up to them, the elected members, to choose a leader and form both a government and an opposition.

As governor general, I felt that the office was intricate, essential, and steeped in constitutional right, customary convention, and practical usage. I often discussed the governor general's duties and reserve powers with some of the scholars in this book. In this parliamentary system that we originally inherited from the British and have reshaped to fit our very different reality, we all must approach the sophisticated reading of our processes with a minimum amount of anxiety.

These writers come from across the country. Ottawa is not the country. Ontario is not the country. Quebec is not the country. The country is composed of ten provinces and three territories, differing in tradition, history, and physical make-up and geographic anomaly. In travelling the country for years as a journalist, I was always struck by how different all the parts of the country were and yet how my study of its history from the time I was a child until I graduated from university helped make my understanding of it more profound and more interesting. I was glad to be prepared by my discovery of this geography through my working career and I can honestly say that it helped me to understand what otherwise would be dry legalese in the functions of the office of governor general. I also came to understand in six years that there are ways in which our institutions can be usefully reformed and rendered more transparent and comprehensible in order to ensure not only the integrity of our purpose as a nation but also the vitality of our vision as a leading democratic country in the world.

Our constitution is one of the oldest in the world: the French have had five in the time that we've had ours. We don't change our minds; we just tend to refine things in a continuing and stable manner. When I became governor general, somebody mentioned to me a principle that one of the essayists in this volume repeats: the governor general, like a physician, should first of all 'do no harm.' This is all very well, but it must not be interpreted to mean 'do not do anything.' This would be a betrayal of our constitution and of parliamentary democracy as it continues to develop in this country.

There is so much misunderstanding about our system and of the functioning of every part of it that we are in serious danger of losing the good things that we have and of not understanding when bad things happen. This book is an attempt to come in on the side of the good things. I urge you to read it because of that. Canadians deserve no less.

Introduction

PETER H. RUSSELL AND LORNE SOSSIN

The presentation of the Harper government's economic and fiscal statement in the House of Commons on Thursday, 27 November 2008 set off a political explosion in Canada's parliamentary life, the likes of which have not been seen since the King-Byng affair of 1926. Two features of the explosion were immediately evident. First, it engaged Canadians politically at a level not matched since a decade or so ago when the continuation of confederation was at issue. Second, in the ensuing deluge of debate and discussion, it became apparent that Canadians were not well schooled in the principles and rules of parliamentary democracy.

It was those two features of the political eruption that inspired John Yates, the president of the University of Toronto Press, in the early days of the political storm, to inquire if we would be interested in organizing and editing a book about it. At the time John approached us, though the course the crisis would take was far from clear, public interest in the issues it was raising could not have been clearer. The day after the governor general's decision granting Stephen Harper's request to prorogue Parliament, the Asper Centre for Constitutional Rights at the Faculty of Law, University of Toronto, hosted a public noon-hour forum on the crisis. A large and aroused crowd of students, faculty, politicians, members of the general public, and journalists jammed the law school's hall, flowing out into the reception area and down the corridors of the building. A glance at newspaper headlines and television screens or a few minutes of talk radio showed similar levels of engagement across the country.

To those of us who participated in public fora and media interviews on the crisis and who teach and write about the parliamentary side of our constitution, it was equally apparent that the Canadian public's knowledge of the constitutional foundations of parliamentary democracy was very low. It was obvious to us that there was a great and immediate need for accessible scholarly writing about this 'unwritten' part of Canada's constitution. John Yates did not have to twist our arms to respond positively to his suggestion.

The book we have organized and edited in response to John Yates's invitation has three aims. First, it is intended to provide contemporary accounts of how political events that will become legendary in Canadian history were experienced and debated at the time. Second, by obtaining contributions from leading Canadian scholars in constitutional and parliamentary studies, we hope to reduce the knowledge deficit that became so evident in the crisis. Third, many of the contributions are forward-looking, anticipating the role that coalition governments might have in Canada's future and charting the evolution of constitutional conventions.

In selecting colleagues to contribute to the volume, we were not looking for a single point of view. We were looking for Canadian scholars who have been teaching and writing about Parliament and its constitutional foundations for a considerable period of time. We also wanted an experienced and respected journalist to provide a chronicle of the main events of the crisis. We were delighted with the positive and quick responses we received to our invitation. The contributors are a strong, country-wide group of Canada's leading scholars and writers in the fields of constitutional and parliamentary studies. When we approached them in early December, we knew that a new session of Parliament was scheduled to open on 26 January 2009 and that the confidence of the House of Commons in the Conservative government would likely be tested that week. With that in mind, we asked our contributors to complete final versions of their chapters by the end of the first week in February 2009.

We are most grateful to our authors for their willingness to set aside other projects in order to meet our deadline and to write in a way that makes their ideas and knowledge accessible to all Canadians interested in learning more about the crisis and the issues it raised. Many of the authors also took time to comment on one another's drafts and cross-reference other chapters in their own contribution. We appreciate the way this interaction makes for a more coherent collection.

Although our authors left us relatively little editing to do, we could not have assembled the book and prepared it for publication without the help of our editorial assistant Colette Langlois, a masters student at the University of Toronto's Faculty of Law. Colette's administration of the project and editorial acumen gave us the steady and knowledgeable hand at the wheel that was essential to completing the project in the short time we set for it. We are grateful for the additional research assistance provided by University of Toronto JD graduate Vasuda Sinha. We are indebted as well to Daniel Quinlan, the law and political science acquisitions editor at the University of Toronto Press, for the advice, support, and encouragement we received throughout the project. Once again, UTP has shown its ability to publish in a timely and accessible way the thinking of Canadian scholars on topics of great public interest.

We owe a very special note of appreciation to our former governor general, the Honourable Adrienne Clarkson, for taking time in the midst of an extremely busy 'post-retirement' life to read all of the chapters of the book and write a Foreword for it.

The book begins with two narratives. The first by Michael Valpy, the *Globe and Mail*'s lead writer on the crisis, provides an account of events from the election of Canada's fortieth Parliament on 14 October 2008 until the decision of the new Liberal leader, Michael Ignatieff, at the end of January to support the Harper government's budget. The second, by Gary Levy, a seasoned observer of Canada's parliamentary scene, provides an account of developments in preceding parliaments which planted the seeds of the crisis that erupted in the early days of the fortieth Parliament.

The second section of the book examines the governor general's decision to prorogue Parliament. The rules on whether, and in what circumstances, the governor general should grant a request to prorogue Parliament are discussed in 'To Prorogue or Not to Prorogue: Did the Governor General Make the Right Decision?' by C.E.S. (Ned) Franks. Franks discusses the possible precedents that support both the granting of the prime minister's request to prorogue (for example, no governor general has ever refused a prime minister's request for prorogation) as well as the precedents for denying such a request (it is well established that the governor general should not allow a prime minister to use dissolution of a Parliament to escape facing a vote of confidence in the House, so why should the request to prorogue be any different?). He believes, in the end, that the governor general made the right decision.

Andrew Heard takes a decidedly different view of the governor general's decision. In 'The Governor General's Suspension of Parliament: Duty Done or a Perilous Precedent?' he argues that, based on the precedent of this governor general's decision to prorogue Parliament, future prime ministers can claim that they are entitled to suspend Parliament at any time, for any reason. By this single action, Heard concludes, the governor general has risked the only meaningful hold that our elected representatives have over the government of the day – the threat to vote non-confidence.

Lorraine E. Weinrib examines the prime minister's request for prorogation as part of 'a pattern of disregard by Harper of a number of deeply embedded constitutional principles and practices.' She also raises a particular concern regarding the government's appointments to key posts (the Senate and the Supreme Court, for example) during the prorogation period. She concludes that this episode reflects the weakness of Canada's constitutional safeguards and structures.

The third section of the book examines the role of constitutional conventions and the governor general in Canada's constitutional system. Brian Slattery draws on the Supreme Court of Canada's landmark decisions in the *Patriation Reference* of 1981 and the *Secession Reference* of 1998 to consider the relationship between Canada's written and unwritten constitution. His analysis shows how the governor general serves as the ultimate guardian of the constitutional order.

In their essay, Lorne Sossin and Adam Dodek argue that, while constitutional convention circumscribes the role of the governor general, it does not extend to preventing her from justifying her decisions to the public. In a constitutional culture increasingly tied to an 'ethos of justification,' Sossin and Dodek conclude that it is not tenable for the governor general to remain silent in the face of the parliamentary crisis of 2008.

Jean Leclair and Jean-François Gaudreault-DesBiens also believe that constitutional conventions must evolve. Specifically, they argue that constitutional conventions need to be informed by and consistent with the broader unwritten constitutional principles that animate Canada's constitution. Democratic legitimacy is one of these principles, and it falls to the governor general to safeguard this value. In so doing, she becomes a constitutional 'actor' rather than a constitutional 'object.'

The fourth section of the book considers the coalition government and the challenges facing parliamentary government in Canada. Lawrence LeDuc looks at the politics and the process of building coalitions and the way in which coalitions vary across democratic jurisdictions. His discussion shows how coalition building lies at the very heart of democratic politics. Peter Russell links coalition building to the distinctive dynamics of minority parliaments. Because minority parliaments have become so frequent and are likely to remain so in the future, Russell argues that it is high time that Canadians became more savvy about how best to live with them. Russell concludes that the lack of political consensus in the wake of this crisis suggests there is much work to do before Canada learns to live with the minority parliaments it is likely to keep producing for the foreseeable future. Finally, Graham White laments the demise of the proposed Liberal-NDP coalition as a lost opportunity for serious parliamentary reform. White's enthusiasm for the coalition is linked to the signal it sent about the possibility of real parliamentary change without abandoning the principles of responsible government that have long served Canada well.

The fifth and final part of the book addresses how the crisis reflects deep tensions in Canadian politics and democratic culture. Grace Skogstad explores the vigorous and visceral reaction of western Canada to the prospect of the Liberal-NDP coalition bringing down the Harper government. Skogstad provides an account of why western Canada opposed the coalition and why most people in that region preferred an election over an intra-parliamentary transition as the route to installing a government in Ottawa. Skogstad concludes by assessing the implications for parliamentary democracy of western Canada's response to the events. Jennifer Smith's chapter analyses the fundamental cleavage between parliamentary democracy and populist democracy. She argues that Prime Minister Harper 'has undermined the right conduct of parliamentary democracy, first by taking deliberate steps in the direction of populist democracy and second by creating confusion about the role of the House of Commons in sustaining or dismissing the government of the day.' Smith concludes that the real legacy of this crisis is the weakening of Canada's tradition of responsible parliamentary government.

David Cameron, who has the final word in this volume, concludes that while Canadian parliamentary democracy experienced some very troubling moments during the crisis, in the end it weathered the storm. Canada's system of parliamentary government ultimately asserted itself, imposing accountability on the key players and showing its capacity to impose the will of a constitutional people on all who seek power.

We agree with David Cameron's assessment. While some of the contributions to this volume show how the crisis of the winter of 2008–9 highlighted the fragility of Canada's parliamentary traditions, constitutional safeguards, and public understanding of our parliamentary democracy, we believe that the book as a whole points to an optimistic conclusion. The crisis has renewed interest in, and critical reflection

about, our political and constitutional system. The esoteric act of prorogation became a central concern for all Canadians. The remote figure
of the governor general became the subject of unprecedented scrutiny.
This crisis has served as a spark that we believe will rekindle public
debate, public understanding, and ultimately public confidence in Canada's parliamentary democracy.

PART ONE

The Events and Their Background

1 The 'Crisis': A Narrative

MICHAEL VALPY

What has been an itch in my mind since early December 2008 is the word 'crisis.' Was it a parliamentary crisis when our country's constitution – shaped through centuries of inherited and home-moulded evolution – worked precisely as it should, however baffling the machinery appeared to most Canadians (let alone foreigners)? Was it a crisis, or an empurpled drama created by politicians and the news media? Or was the machinery by which we govern ourselves as a twenty-first-century progressive, liberal democracy revealed to be flawed and inappropriate, or perhaps merely in need of tweaking, a dash of transparency added here, some new rules and different players added there? The purpose of this book is to address those questions. My task is to set down the narrative of events that transpired.

Canada's system of governance is that of a constitutional parliamentary monarchy. The governor general – the monarch's surrogate, personifying the people of Canada and sitting above the fray of politics as the 'dignified' function of government – must have ministers who can govern as the 'efficient' function of government: they must, in other words, enjoy the confidence of Parliament, have the support of a parliamentary majority. To avoid a vote of non-confidence in the House of Commons that almost certainly would have resulted in his minority Conservative government's defeat, Prime Minister Stephen Harper asked the governor general to prorogue Parliament (terminate the parliamentary session that had begun just a few days earlier), a questionable but not entirely unprecedented act. The governor general's reserve powers – powers she can exercise without the approval of another branch of government – gave her the discretion to accept or reject the prime minister's request. She thought it over, considered the implications, and said yes. Full stop. That is the summary of what happened. The country at no time was at risk of tumbling into bedlam and anarchy. Whatever the governor general's decision, someone would have been given her nod to govern Canada legally; unless, of course, no political party or group of parties could claim Parliament's confidence, at which point she would have authorized another election to be called. That is how the system works.

The crown's role in the machinery of Canada's constitutional monarchy rarely sees daylight. Only a handful of times in our history has it been subjected to glaring sunshine, unfortunately resulting in a black hole of public understanding as to how it works. It is an ignorance that Canadians share with Australians and New Zealanders whose systems are largely the same. I have a personal illustration of imperfect comprehension. I was assigned by my *Globe and Mail* editors through early December to explain the governor general's constitutional role. Of six articles I wrote, two required next-day published corrections and the accuracy of a third was politely but unambiguously challenged by one of the authors of this book. The scandal-sheet *Frank* magazine, now departed, claimed 50 per cent accuracy in its articles; one would think the *Globe and Mail* could do better.

But to return to that word 'crisis' ... one definition of 'crisis' offered by the *Concise Oxford Dictionary* is 'a time of danger or suspense in politics.' Whether there was danger depends upon one's perception of events. However, there was suspense, marked by an abundant presence of the unpredictable and the unfamiliar. Opinion polls can presage election outcomes but not the reasoning of a governor general in the employment of her reserve powers. And the unfamiliar elements of the constitution led to explanations in the news media that were often as much hindrance as help, my favourite being the headline on a blog in the online magazine *Slate*: 'Chaos in Canada: What Happens When an Unelected Royal Official Closes Parliament,'[1] along with former official languages commissioner Keith Spicer's bizarre assertion that Canada was looking like 'Zimbabwe run by the Queen.'[2]

So let's call it a crisis.

The October Election

My narrative of events begins on 15 October, the day after Canada's fortieth general election.

Claiming that the 39th Parliament had become dysfunctional and that he needed a stronger electoral mandate to manage the economy in difficult times, Prime Minister Stephen Harper asked Governor General Michaëlle Jean to dissolve Parliament on 7 September, which she did, clearing the way for an election.

The outcome on 14 October was predicted accurately by almost every public-opinion poll: a strengthened plurality (the largest number of votes cast and MPs elected, from 127 to 143 seats in the 308-member House of Commons) for Harper's Conservatives but still less than a majority; a disaster for the Liberal Party under Stéphane Dion (a decline from 103 to 77 seats, and the party's worst popular-vote result in history); a negligible decline in seats (from 51 to 49) for the Bloc Québécois led by Gilles Duceppe; and an increase (from 29 to 37 seats) for the New Democratic Party (NDP) under Jack Layton. In addition, two independents were elected. A number of political commentators observed that the country had been put to an election that changed nothing. This was not true.

The campaign was one of the most uncivil in modern Canadian history, marked by the Conservatives' personal attacks on Dion as a man unfit to lead Canada's government. It revealed deep fractures in the country's polity: only one Conservative was elected in Canada's three largest cities; only two Liberals were elected between northern Ontario and the city limits of Vancouver; the sovereigntist Bloc Québécois elected almost twice as many members in Quebec as the three national parties combined; and the voter participation rate – 59.1 per cent – was the lowest on record. All major parties, except the Greens (who did not win a seat), received fewer votes than they had in the previous election of 2006, although the percentages of the popular vote shifted only slightly: the Conservatives went up 1.4 points; the Liberals dropped nearly four points; the Bloc and the NDP stayed pretty much the same; and the Greens went up 2.3 points. In addition, the public-opinion polls consistently showed that Canadians were not enthusiastic about the leaders of either of the two major parties, Harper or Dion. If anything, the quality of leadership was the election's ballot-box issue: Dion was seen by a significant portion of voters as not leader-like (poll-takers said he lacked sufficient masculine presence) and Harper, while clearly preferred over Dion, was unable to overcome substantial doubts as to his trustworthiness, doubts aggravated by campaign missteps, chief among them being the Conservative leader's apparent misreading of the onrushing financial crisis in the United States and its impact on Canada. Three of his statements – that collapsed stock prices presented a good opportu-

nity to pick up bargains, that the government already had done everything necessary to deal with the situation, and that economic stimulus
through deficit financing was out of the question – became shackled to
him like the chains on the ghost of Jacob Marley.

What was different about Canadian politics after the 14 October election was, first, an awareness that, after three campaigns as Conservative leader, Stephen Harper had failed to persuade Canadians to give
him a majority government, and, second – and not unrelated to the
first proposition – that the three opposition parties would not be as
easily intimidated by the prime minister as they had been in the previous Parliament into supporting government bills and budgets largely
out of fear the Conservatives would trounce them at the polls if the
government fell and an election were called. That was particularly the
case for the Liberals, seeing the end of their credibility as a potential
governing party unless they stood up to Harper with plausible vigour
(the accepted orthodoxy within the Liberal caucus being that the party
had suffered from its lack of militancy against the government in the
previous Parliament).

In the campaign's immediate aftermath, Harper, after two and a half
years of leading one of the most pugnacious governments in memory,
seemed to understand both the electorate's take on him and Parliament's altered political dynamics. In his election-night victory statement in Calgary, he pledged to fulfil his party's election platform, but
also to govern for Canadians who had voted for other parties. And he
offered cooperation with opposition MPs. 'This is a time,' he said, 'for
us all to put aside political differences and partisan considerations and
to work cooperatively for the benefit of Canada. We have shown that
minority government can work, and at this time of global economic
instability we owe it to Canadians to demonstrate this once again. We
stretch out a hand to all members of all parties, asking them to join together to protect the economy and weather this world financial crisis.'[3]

With the government's books showing bleeding red ink – $1.7 billion
in August alone, as revenue stagnated and spending ballooned – and
the looming spectre of a budgetary deficit, Harper reminded his party
at its policy convention in Winnipeg that the Conservatives must avoid
an ideological approach to governing. 'We will have to be both tough
and pragmatic, not unrealistic or ideological in dealing with the complex economic challenges before us,' he said. 'We must work hard to
keep Canadians' trust and earn it again. We must listen to all voices,
whether they supported us or not.'[4] He had the same message for his

cabinet and parliamentary caucus, advising them to shelve aggression and take the high road; be firm in facing the opposition but also be fair. He replaced the fiery and relentlessly combative Peter Van Loan as House leader with the less partisan British Columbia MP Jay Hill, who told reporters: 'On our team's part, we certainly want to see a new tone [in Parliament]. There seems to be a consensus that we want to be very serious in how we approach everything that flows from the economic instability facing our nation and indeed facing the planet right now.'[5]

Harper drained some of the testosterone out of his cabinet by appointing more women. One party source quoted anonymously in the *Globe and Mail* said that the prime minister cited women members of his caucus as models to emulate, because they were good at verbally sparring with opposition members without coming off as too combative.[6] Political scientist Antonia Maioni, director of the McGill Institute for the Study of Canada, declared: 'Stephen Harper is realizing that he is a minority government prime minister. I think he realizes that he has to find new strategies to govern. He may be coming to terms with that as a political leader.'[7] Peter Donolo, a partner with the polling firm Strategic Counsel, agreed: 'There's a lot to be said for a charm offensive, particularly at a time like this.'[8] As Parliament got back to work on 18 November, opposition members quickly noticed the new mood. Toronto Liberal MP Bob Rae called it cozy.[9]

The mood in Rae's party was something else. With the opinion polls darkening like scary black storm clouds over the Liberals' election campaign, Stéphane Dion had plodded on towards the 14 October finish line 'kind of like the little engine that could,' in the words of campaign co-chair Mark Marissen.[10] He had said forty-eight hours before voting day: 'I will never quit. I will stay for my country. I'm the leader. I am the leader. And I'm working to win. I'm not a quitter.'[11]

But a week after the votes had been counted, he announced that his tenure would end at a party policy convention morphed hurriedly into a leadership convention, scheduled for the beginning of May in Vancouver. The party's parliamentary caucus had trod on his fingertips-hold on the office and declared that it did not want to travel with him any further than necessary. 'I wish I had succeeded, of course,' he said. 'But you need to accept in democracy the result and move on. That's what I'm doing. The past is the past.'[12] First New Brunswick MP Dominic LeBlanc, then Toronto MP Bob Rae, and finally Toronto MP and deputy leader Michael Ignatieff indicated their desire to replace him. There was no enthusiasm in the party for a longer list of candidates.

The Opening of Parliament

When Parliament opened, a senior government official told journalists that the prime minister intended to push potentially divisive issues to the back of the legislative agenda and focus on finding common ground among the political parties to fix the faltering economy.[13] The official said the economy would dominate the Speech from the Throne – the traditional statement of a government's legislative intentions, read by the governor general – while secondary issues would be moved down the list of priorities. 'Canadians want their government not squabbling about secondary issues. I think they want them finding a consensus and agreement on the large issues around the economy and that is what we're going to do,' the official said. Jay Hill, the new Conservative house leader, underscored the theme of the peaceable kingdom, going so far as to suggest that the Conservatives might 'govern collectively' with the opposition parties.[14] 'I'm hopeful that we're not going to try to fight the election campaign all over again right at the start of this Parliament,' he said. Liberal House Leader Ralph Goodale said that he had already noticed a positive change in his dealings with Hill. 'So far, the essential message that [Hill] is sending, if I'm reading it right, is a message of greater flexibility and sensitivity on the part of the government.'[15]

As heralded, the Throne Speech on 19 November focused on economic measures and held out a collegial hand. The *Globe and Mail* reported:

> There are clear attempts in the speech to woo support from all three opposition parties, acknowledging the fact that Canadians elected another minority Parliament. Some of the pledges are similar to promises made by the Liberals, Bloc Québécois and New Democrats during the election campaign. In what could be seen as a nod to the Liberals, the government pledges to continue working with provinces on plans for securing Canada's economy and to find savings by reviewing programs. For the Bloc, the government promises a Charter of Open Federalism allowing provinces to opt out of any national program that is in exclusive provincial jurisdiction. On issues regularly raised by the NDP, the government is promising to increase incentives for energy-saving home retrofits, legislation banning all bulk water exports to the United States and expansion of federal programs dealing with homelessness and affordable housing.[16]

The speech also contained references to potentially politically divisive measures such as a series of justice initiatives, including added penalties for offences related to youth crime, organized crime, and gun violence, but, as the *Globe* went on to report, 'earlier this week, the prime minister's office signalled that it would not be aggressive in pushing through its agenda on non-economic issues like crime.'

NDP Leader Jack Layton called the proposals 'very timid' and said that his party would vote against the Throne Speech. Bloc Québécois Leader Gilles Duceppe said that his party also would vote against the speech because it offered nothing for Quebec. But Liberal Leader Stéphane Dion said that, while the speech fell short of what was needed to revive the faltering economy, it would be irresponsible to plunge the country into another election over it. Thus, the Liberals would support it and the government was in no danger of falling. As the Liberals' Bob Rae stated: 'The throne speech is no big deal. The throne speech is simply a set of intentions – good intentions or bad. There's nothing much in the throne speech to tell us where the government really wants to go.'[17]

What is evident from this post-election narrative is that all – or almost all – the signals from the governing Conservatives and the three opposition parties were the same: signals of awareness that the fractiousness of the 39th Parliament should not be carried over into the 40th Parliament and that Canadians, although they had not elected a Parliament from which a majority government could take office, wanted a legislature that would work constructively to address the country's deepening economic problems.

All the more baffling, therefore, is what happened next.

The Fiscal Update

It has become the practice for the government to place before Parliament a fall fiscal and economic update, sometimes a corrective mini-budget, that informs Canadians how predictions on government spending and revenue made in the spring budget are working out. Finance Minister Jim Flaherty scheduled such a statement for Thursday, 27 November. By the 25th, rumours were circulating on what it contained: the government's intention, inter alia, to suspend the right of federal civil servants to strike until 2011, to suspend the right of women federal employees to seek legal remedy on pay-equity issues, to raise money through a major sell-off of crown assets, and to eliminate political parties' subsidies of $1.95 for each vote they received.

The rumours proved correct: all of those provisions were indeed in the minister's financial statement. Further, while national governments elsewhere were assembling stimulus packages and promising bailouts for sinking economic sectors, Flaherty – having already announced that the government would present no major stimulus program before the spring budget of 2009 – portrayed the government as guiding Canada through the economic storm with low taxes, modest spending increases, and balanced books, going so far as to predict a small budgetary surplus over the next two years, eliciting expressions of disbelief from most economists.

A political uproar ensued. Or, in more prosaic language, all hell broke loose.

The government's plans to suspend women's rights to seek legal redress on pay-equity issues and the right of federal civil servants' to strike were seen as unalloyed ideological actions. Only two days earlier, the country's largest public-sector union, the 100,000-member Public Service Alliance of Canada, had announced that it would accept the government's offer of a 6.8 per cent pay raise over four years despite having earlier rejected it, a decision praised by Treasury Board President Vic Toews as 'very responsible' and 'a fair agreement for both employees and the taxpayer.' The plan to eliminate the political parties' vote subsidy – worth $27 million a year out of Ottawa's $245-billion annual budget – was labelled provocative and a partisan attack aimed primarily at the money-straitened Liberals, far less successful than the Conservatives at raising money from their supporters. 'Instead of an immediate stimulus package to attack the recession, this government is apparently going to attack democracy,' declared NDP Leader Jack Layton. All of these 'zingers,' *Globe and Mail* political columnist Jeffrey Simpson reported, were concocted in the Prime Minister's Office, sent over to the Finance Department at the last moment, and not presented to the Conservative cabinet or parliamentary caucus for prior discussion.[18]

The question of why it was done rests in the realm of speculation. The conventional wisdom of political pundits and observers was that an aggressive prime minister and his inner circle saw a safe opportunity to shaft the Liberals – $3 million in debt with an unpopular, lame-duck leader – by cutting off two-thirds of the party's revenue (as well as a hefty chunk of the financial resources of the Bloc and the NDP through a subsidy that was not popular with voters) and they did not believe the three opposition parties would unite to vote the government down on the issue. Defence Minister Peter MacKay boasted to the Halifax *Chronicle-Herald* on Thursday that, when the subsidy measure came before Parliament, the opposition would blink. 'When they play chicken,' he said, 'they wind up looking like chickens.'[19] Except they didn't.

The Coalition

Layton asked former NDP leader Edward Broadbent to telephone former Liberal prime minister Jean Chrétien on Thursday morning and discuss with him what coordinated response the two parties might make. The party leaders – Layton, Dion, and Duceppe – met one-on-one several times during the first part of the day and quickly determined there was both a willingness and the opportunity to overthrow the Conservative government. The opportunity was twofold: first, Flaherty declared that elimination of the vote subsidy was part of the government's fiscal framework and therefore would be subject to a parliamentary confidence vote when the government introduced enabling legislation on Monday, 1 December; second, Monday was the Liberals' opposition day in the Commons, which they planned to use by introducing a non-confidence motion to defeat the government on grounds that it had failed to offer economic stimulus. By early afternoon, the three parties had begun coalition talks.

The talks continued into Friday and the weekend. It was reported that Governor General Michaëlle Jean, on an official visit to Eastern Europe, had made contingency plans to cut short her trip and return to the capital.

The prime minister's initial public response – as senior Conservatives began catching which way the opposition wind was blowing – was to use the government's power to delay any confidence motions by one week, until Monday, 8 December, and to challenge the legitimacy of a coalition government led by Stéphane Dion, the head of the Official Opposition. 'The opposition has every right to defeat the government,' Harper said, 'but Stéphane Dion does not have the right to take power without an election. Canada's government should be decided by Canadians, not backroom deals. It should be your choice – not theirs. They want to install a government led by a party that received its lowest vote share since Confederation. They want to install a prime minister – prime minister Dion – who was rejected by the voters just six weeks ago.'[20] Thus, the prime minister introduced a constitutional element into what had been until then solely a political mêlée: if the minority government, elected only forty-six days earlier, was defeated by a vote of confidence in Parliament, did a coalition of opposition parties led by the leader of the Liberals have the right to form a government without an election being called? Interestingly, the same question, framed differently, was being asked within the Liberal caucus: Did its members want to be part of a coalition led by the unpopular Dion, who had been pushed by his own party into pledging to step down in five months' time?

On Saturday, 29 November, the government dropped its plan to eliminate political party subsidies, although it had insisted Thursday and Friday that there would be no backdown. On Sunday, 30 November, it cancelled its intention to ban public-sector strikes and announced that Flaherty would deliver a budget on 27 January, 'the earliest date in modern times,' said the finance minister. On the same day, the media obtained a memorandum written by Guy Giorno, the prime minister's chief of staff, urging Conservative MPs to take to the airwaves to oppose the coalition and to get their supporters to call into radio talk shows.[21] Significantly – raising questions about the stability of the proposed coalition – the media further reported that the Liberal caucus was divided on whether Stéphane Dion or some other member of the party should head the coalition on an interim basis until the party's leadership convention in May, or whether the leadership convention should be advanced and a new, permanent leader chosen quickly. Moreover, the Canadian Press said that Michael Ignatieff, the acknowledged front-runner in the campaign to replace Dion, was cool to the coalition plan, was being advised by key supporters to distance himself from it, and was inclined to accept the concessions that had been wrung out of the government and not vote to defeat it.[22] His major opponent, Bob Rae, strongly supported the original plan, a coalition with Dion as interim leader.

On Monday, 1 December – with the U.S. National Bureau of Economic Research declaring the United States to be officially in recession – the Liberal, New Democratic, and Bloc Québécois parties unveiled a formal accord setting out a Liberal-led coalition with the NDP that would govern with the support of the Bloc on confidence matters until the end of June 2010. The Liberal-NDP accord would last until 30 June 2011. Dion would be prime minister until he was replaced as Liberal leader. The parties promised a multi-billion-dollar stimulus package. The three party leaders also made public a letter to the governor general saying that the prime minister and his party had lost the confidence of Parliament and the coalition was ready to take over the government. '"I have respectfully recommended to Her Excellency that she should, at her first opportunity, exercise her constitutional authority and invite the leader of the Official Opposition to form a new government with the support of the two other opposition parties,"' said Dion.[23] At a press conference, Dion and Layton urged Harper to accept his fate and not destabilize the country by fighting tooth and nail against the inevitable demise of his government. Ignatieff, Rae, and the Liberals' third leadership contestant, Dominic LeBlanc, endorsed the accord.

Prorogation

On Monday afternoon, for the first time, a Conservative cabinet member, Environment Minister Jim Prentice, dispatched by the prime minister to meet reporters, raised the possibility of the government requesting Governor General Jean to prorogue – suspend – Parliament until January. The step was all but unprecedented in Canada. In 1873 Sir John A. Macdonald, Canada's first prime minister, had asked the governor general, the Earl of Dufferin, to prorogue Parliament so that Macdonald could halt the work of a committee investigating his improper acceptance of campaign funds. Lord Dufferin only reluctantly agreed. But he set a firm time limit on the suspension – ten weeks. And when Parliament resumed, Sir John A. accepted the handwriting on the wall and resigned before a vote of censure could be held – to be replaced, without an immediate election, by Alexander Mackenzie and the Liberal Party.

On Monday evening, Harper told Conservatives at their annual Christmas party: 'We will use all legal means to resist this undemocratic seizure of power. My friends, such an illegitimate government would be a catastrophe, for our democracy, our unity and our economy, especially at a time of global instability.'[24] The media pointed out that Harper himself, in 2004, with a minority Liberal government at risk of being defeated in the Commons, had sent a joint letter with Layton and Duceppe to then-Governor General Adrienne Clarkson, urging her to 'consider all your options' if the government fell on a confidence vote. Their letter had said: 'We respectfully point out that the opposition parties, who together constitute a majority in the House, have been in close consultation.'

In Europe, Governor General Jean said in a CBC-TV interview that she had received the opposition leaders' letter and was cutting short her visit to return to Canada. '"I received [the] letter, and the message in the letter is clear. I think that my presence is required in the country.'"[25] Asked what she would do if Harper requested prorogation, Jean replied: '"Before I can answer this question, I have to see what the prime minister has to say to me, and what he is actually thinking of doing. I don't know exactly anything about his intentions yet."'

By Tuesday, 2 December, the government was indicating that prorogation would be the route it would follow. The exchange that day between Harper and Dion in Parliament's Question Period was explosive, with the prime minister focusing on the inclusion of the sovereigntist Bloc in the coalition pact and at one point accusing Dion of removing the Canadian flags from the room before signing the accord with Layton and Duceppe. Thus, to a political and constitutional uproar, the prime minister now added a third element: national unity. (News organizations took several photographs that clearly showed there were two Canadian flags, as well as the flags from all the provinces, directly behind the leaders as they read their statements – along with a third, separate Canadian flag behind the table where they signed.)

The issue engulfed the news media, the radio call-in programs, and Canadians' conversations with one another. Pro- and anti-coalition rallies were held across the country. Public opinion varied widely by region – with western Canadians strongly opposed to a coalition and Quebecers tending to support it. Constitutional and parliamentary scholars were besieged by the media for their analyses of the governor general's options and their views on precedents. What became starkly apparent was that most Canadians were ignorant – at the very least uncertain – of how their constitution worked, of what the role of the crown was, and of what discretion the governor general had in the use of her reserve powers.

On Wednesday, 3 December, Harper and Dion – but not Layton and Duceppe – were granted air time by the television networks to address the nation. The prime minister told Canadians that the opposition parties, instead of waiting for the government to bring in a budget that would confront the country's economic worries, 'propose a new coalition which includes the party in Parliament whose avowed goal is to break up the country.

Let me be very clear: Canada's Government cannot enter into a power-sharing coalition with a separatist party. At a time of global economic instability, Canada's Government must stand unequivocally for keeping the country together. At a time like this, a coalition with the separatists cannot help Canada. And the Opposition does not have the democratic right to impose a coalition with the separatists they promised voters would never happen. The Opposition is attempting to impose this deal without your say, without your consent, and without your vote. This is no time for backroom deals with the separatists; it is the time for Canada's government to focus on the economy and specifically on measures for the upcoming budget. This is a pivotal moment in our history.[26]

It was immediately noted that, while Harper said 'separatist' in English, he said 'sovereigntist' in French.

Dion, in a clumsily video-taped response, declared that the prime minister and his government had refused to propose measures to stimulate the Canadian economy and had instead introduced a mini-budget – the 27 November economic statement – that 'demonstrated that his priority is partisanship and settling ideological scores.' He then went on to talk about the parliamentary issues at stake:

The Harper Conservatives have lost the confidence of the majority of Members of the House of Commons. In our democracy, in our Parliamentary system, in our Constitution, this means that they have lost the right to govern.

Canadians don't want another election, they want Parliamentarians to work together. That's our job. Canadians want their MPs to put aside partisanship and focus on the economy. The Liberal Party and the New Democratic Party are ready to do this. Jack Layton and I have agreed to form a coalition government to address the impact of the global economic crisis. The Bloc has agreed to support this government on matters of confidence. The Green Party has also agreed to support it.

Our system of government was not born with Canada. It is ancient. There are rules that govern it and conventions that guide it. Coalitions are normal and current practice in many parts of the world and are able to work very successfully. They work with simple ingredients: consensus, goodwill and co-operation. Consensus is a great Canadian value. In this spirit, we Liberals have joined in a coalition with the NDP. We have done so because we believe we can achieve more for Canadians through co-operation than through conflict. We believe we can better solve the challenges facing Canada through teamwork and collaboration, rather than blind partisan feuding and hostility. Our coalition is a consensus to govern with a well-defined program to address the most important issue facing the country: the economy. It is a program to preserve and create jobs and to stimulate the economy in all regions of the country. The elements of the program need to be spelled out and this is what we will do if we are allowed to present it to the House of Commons.[27]

The Governor General Decides

The following morning, Thursday, 4 December, the prime minister and Canada's top civil servant, Clerk of the Privy Council Kevin Lynch, arrived at Rideau Hall to meet with Governor General Jean and her secretary, Sheila-Marie Cook. They gathered in the same oak-panelled study where, eighty-two years earlier, Governor General Lord Byng had been requested by Prime Minister W.L.M. King – facing defeat in the Commons – to dissolve Parliament and clear the way for an election. Byng refused dissolution and called on Conservative leader Arthur Meighen to form a government.

The meeting lasted more than two hours. By convention, what transpires between a prime minister and the sovereign, or her surrogate, is not made public. But the *Globe and Mail* reported that they discussed the state of Canada's economy, the viability of an alternative coalition government, and the mood of Parliament and the country. At one point, the *Globe* said, the governor general and Cook left the prime minister and the clerk and went to a nearby room to consult with her adviser, constitutional law scholar Peter Hogg. They then rejoined the two men and the governor general granted the prorogation request. Again, by convention, no reasons were disclosed.[28] Parliament was closed down until 26 January.

The Liberals Change Leaders

Over the 6–7 December weekend, Michael Ignatieff launched a campaign to have the party's parliamentary caucus elect him immediately as interim leader, to be confirmed – or not confirmed – at the May convention in Vancouver. His organizers reported Sunday that he had the support of fifty-five of the party's seventy-seven MPs. The party's executive set aside objections from Bob Rae and recommended that the two-stage process be accepted. On Wednesday, 10 December, Stéphane Dion was ousted and Ignatieff replaced him as leader of the Official Opposition.

The New Session Opens and the Crisis Ends

When Parliament resumed on 26 January, the Throne Speech read by the governor general declared, contritely, that 'the government's agenda and the priorities of Parliament must adapt in response to the deepening crisis. Old assumptions must be tested and old decisions must be rethought.' It spoke of the government assembling its budget 'in a spirit of open and non-partisan co-operation.' And it lifted phrases from an Ignatieff speech in promising a budget that would 'protect the vulnerable [and] protect the jobs of today while readying the economy to create the jobs of tomorrow.'

The NDP and Bloc Québécois said they would vote against the speech; the Liberals said they would support it. The next day Jim Flaherty introduced his budget. It projected deficits of $85 billion over five years and offered a stimulus package that included $12-billion infrastructure spending over two years, $20 billion in personal tax cuts, $13 billion to lubricate credit, $3 billion for home renovations, and other government spending. The NDP and Bloc again declared they would vote against it. The Liberals' Ignatieff announced: 'We're putting this government on probation.'[29] He said that he was prepared to 'swallow hard' and support the Conservative government, provided it agree to table regular updates outlining how it was living up to the commitments outlined in the federal budget. As a result, the NDP's Jack Layton declared the coalition plan dead and said Stephen Harper would remain prime minister for a considerable amount of time thanks to the Liberals' support.

The drama was over.

NOTES

1 *Slate* magazine, 5 December 2008, http://www.slate.com/id/2206040/.
2 Keith Spicer, 'Zimbabwe Run by the Queen,' Ottawa *Citizen*, 15 December 2008.
3 Campbell Clark, 'Harper Bets the House, Wins Another Minority,' *Globe and Mail* online, 15 October 2008.
4 Steven Chase and Bill Curry, 'Harper Warns Tories to Avoid "Ideological" Governing,' *Globe and Mail* online, 13 November 2008.
5 Tim Naumetz, 'Speeding Reform, Better Decorum Issues in Commons Speaker's Race,' Canadian Press, 16 November 2008.
6 Brian Laghi and Steven Chase, 'Facing a Crisis, Harper Instructs MPs to Be Less Confrontational,' *Globe and Mail*, 20 November 2008.
7 Ibid.
8 Ibid.

 9 Bob Rae, Symposium on the parliamentary crisis, University of Toronto Faculty of Law, 13 January 2009.
10 Jane Taber, 'Dion Must Go,' *Globe and Mail*, 15 October 2008.
11 Ibid.
12 Les Whittington and Bruce Campion-Smith, 'Dion Out, Liberals Party,' Toronto *Star*, 21 October 2008.
13 Brian Laghi, Bill Curry, and Gloria Galloway, 'Harper Pushes United Front in Economic Battle,' *Globe and Mail*, 18 November 2008.
14 Ibid.
15 Ibid.
16 Bill Curry, 'Throne Speech Warns of Deficit,' *Globe and Mail* online, 19 November 2008.
17 'Rae Has the "Scars" and the "Experience" to Lead the Liberals,' *Canada AM*, 20 November 2008.
18 Jeffrey Simpson, 'After the Storm: The Convulsion Has Left a Weakened Government, a Nervous Opposition and a Legacy of Miscalculation,' *Globe and Mail*, 6 December 2008.
19 Michael Valpy and Daniel Leblanc, 'Harper Blind to Bloodlust in Opposition Ranks,' *Globe and Mail*, 29 November 2008.
20 Brian Laghi, Steven Chase, Gloria Galloway, and Daniel Leblanc, 'Harper Buys Time, Coalition Firms up,' *Globe and Mail*, 29 November 2008.
21 Les Whittington, Tonda MacCharles, and Bruce Campion-Smith, 'Tories Blink First in Showdown,' Toronto *Star*, 30 November 2008.
22 Bruce Cheadle, 'Tories Toss Policy, Release Secret Tapes to Dodge Defeat,' Canadian Press, 1 December 2008.
23 Bruce Cheadle, 'Liberal-led Coalition Asks to Form Government,' Canadian Press, 1 December 2008.
24 Ibid.
25 Juliet O'Neill, David Akin, and Andrew Mayeda, 'Governor General Returning to Ottawa to Face Brewing Political Storm,' *Canwest News Service*, 2 December 2008.
26 'Full Text of Stephen Harper's Televised Address,' Canadian Press, 3 December 2008.
27 Ibid.
28 Michael Valpy, 'GG Made Harper Work for Prorogue,' *Globe and Mail*, 6 December 2008.
29 Campbell Clark and Jane Taber, 'Ignatieff Okays Budget, with Conditions,' *Globe and Mail*, 29 January 2009.

2 A Crisis Not Made in a Day

GARY LEVY

The origin of the December 2008 parliamentary crisis is variously attributed to a conspiracy among opposition parties to overturn the results of the 14 October election, a devious plot by Prime Minister Stephen Harper to weaken the opposition, or an inadequate, unacceptable, and overly ideological economic statement by the finance minister on 27 November 2008.

This chapter argues that the unusual prorogation of Parliament by the governor general after thirteen sitting days and in the face of a non-confidence motion was really the culmination of repeated abuse of the most important principle of responsible government, the confidence convention. The crisis forces us to reflect upon whether we still have Westminster-style responsible government in any meaningful sense.

Playing Fast and Loose with the Confidence Convention

Simply stated, the unwritten confidence convention provides that, if defeated in the House of Commons on a confidence question, the government is expected to resign. The prime minister may ask the governor general for dissolution of Parliament and a general election but, of course, the governor general does not have to accede to every such request. In her memoirs Governor General Adrienne Clarkson wrote: 'The question arose during Paul Martin's minority government of whether or not I as Governor General would grant dissolution and allow an election to be called if the prime minister requested it. After considering the opinions of the constitutional experts whom I consulted regularly, I decided that, if the government lasted six months I would allow dissolution. To put the Canadian people through an election before six months would have been irresponsible, and in that case I would have decided in favour of the good of the Canadian people and denied dissolution.'[1]

There is nothing magical about the first 180 days. Dissolution is at the discretion of the governor general before or after a six-month period. Similarly, there is no hard-and-fast rule about what is a question of confidence. It is widely accepted that certain traditional motions – namely, the motion to adopt the Throne Speech, the motion to adopt the budget, and the Appropriation Bill (government estimates) – are automatic votes of confidence.

There is less agreement on other areas related to confidence. What would happen if a government refused to resign when it had lost confidence? Does defeat of an important government bill always constitute a vote of confidence? Can procedural motions be considered matters of confidence? Can a government claim to have lost confidence without being defeated in the House?[2] The failure of successive minority parliaments, starting with Paul Martin's, to find the right answers to these questions led to the December 2008 crisis.

When Martin took over as leader of the Liberal Party in November 2003, he inherited not only a majority Parliament (won by Jean Chrétien in 2001) but also a report by the auditor general on a case of financial mismanagement which came to be known as the sponsorship scandal. All the problems had occurred under the Chrétien government but Prime Minister Martin decided to launch a public inquiry headed by Justice John Gomery to get to the bottom of the affair. He also called a snap election for June 2004, well before the Gomery Commission could report.

The sponsorship scandal dominated not only the election campaign but the entire Martin minority Parliament which began in the fall of 2004. The opposition used bodies like the Public Accounts Committee to make the point, over and over, that the Liberals lacked the political, ethical, or moral basis to continue to govern the country.

In February 2005 Martin presented his first budget, which appeared ready to go down to defeat. The Martin strategy was to avoid an election until the final report of the Gomery Commission (scheduled for February 2006). He expected that this report would exonerate him personally from any responsibility for the scandal. Thus, in April 2005, Martin addressed the nation and took the extremely unusual step of promising to tie the next election date to an external event. He said that he would call an election within thirty days of the Gomery Commission's final report. The opposition parties were aghast at this idea and decided to use one of their upcoming supply days to introduce a non-confidence motion in the government.

On 18 April the Official Opposition gave notice of a motion that, if adopted, would have designated dates for the remaining six opposition days, the timing of which is exclusively within the purview of the government. Martin responded by postponing every opposition day and the government house leader went as far as to undesignate an opposition day that had already been set. To counter this manoeuvre, the opposition tried to attach a non-confidence motion to a committee report and then moving concurrence of that report. This series of events led to 'The Curious Case of May 10, 2005,' as Professor Andrew Heard called it. After much procedural wrangling and Speaker's rulings, a vote was held and the non-confidence motion attached to a committee report passed by a vote of 153 in favour and 150 opposed. The government ignored the vote, claiming that it was on a procedural motion only. Yet Heard and others concluded that, by any meaningful definition, this had been a valid non-confidence vote: 'All three opposition parties had stated well in advance that they believed this vote to be a test of confidence. While the wording was convoluted the content still clearly inferred that supporters of the motion were in favour of the Government's resignation.'[3]

The government did hold a second and 'definitive' confidence vote nine days later and it survived, but only after inducing Belinda Stronach to defect from the Conservative Party, thereby creating a 152–152 result which was broken by the casting vote of the Speaker. When the House resumed in September 2005, the government once again postponed opposition days, this time until mid-November. (Also in September the three opposition party leaders, Stephen Harper, Jack Layton, and Gilles Duceppe, wrote to the governor general suggesting that they were prepared to form a government if she received a request for dissolution.)

On the first opposition day, 21 November 2005, a New Democratic Party (NDP) motion was carried by a vote of 167 (representing all three opposition parties) to 129. It called on the prime minister to wait until the week of 2 January and then ask the governor general for an election to be held on 16 February so as to avoid a Christmas campaign. The NDP motion was rejected by the government – and rightly so from a traditional point of view. You cannot at the same time say you have no confidence in the government and then ask it to stay in office for a few more weeks or months.

But the motion does raise the question of whether Canada has taken too parochial an understanding of confidence. The Westminster model is not the only approach to making and unmaking governments. Some countries have provisions for caretaker governments after a vote of non-confidence. Others require a constructive vote of confidence, meaning that you cannot simply defeat a government and force an election but must also propose an alternative government.

In any case, a few days later, on a Conservative opposition day, the government was defeated on a simple non-confidence motion. The election was held on 23 January and returned the first Harper minority government.

Fiddling with a Fixed Election Date

The Harper government had a plan to end the constitutional improvisation of its predecessor. Following the lead of certain provinces,[4] it enacted legislation fixing the date of the next federal election for October 2009 and every four years thereafter. Of course, none of these provinces had minority governments or bicameral chambers. But it was not a matter of simply underestimating the complexity of federal politics. The fixed election date was smoke and mirrors from the very beginning.

First, in a system of responsible government, the date of an election cannot be absolutely fixed as it is in the United States. Elections are still required if the government loses confidence and, legally, the prime minister could still ask for dissolution at any time.[5] The law explicitly stated that nothing in it 'affects the powers of the Governor General, including the power to dissolve Parliament at the Governor General's discretion.' More important was the cynical way in which the law was adopted and used. The Official Opposition was reluctant to agree to the legislation although it was eventually passed in the House of Commons. The Liberal-dominated Senate appeared ready to hold it up indefinitely in committee. Witnesses who appeared before a Senate committee, including Professor David Smith, argued that fixed election dates fit neither the theory nor the practice of parliamentary government. 'Fixed election dates do not give the public greater voice in politics. In fact, the partisan motivation and potential for engineering defeats within the House shifts the focus of attention even more than at present from constituents to the party leaders in the House.'[6]

In March and April 2007 polls suggested the Conservatives were surging ahead of the Liberals, even in the crucial province of Ontario.

Rumours abounded that the prime minister was about to call an election. Candidates were told to be ready and election machines were put into gear. The Liberals, unprepared for an election, promptly returned the fixed-date election bill from the Senate to the House with a minor amendment adding 'referendums' to the clause that allows the chief electoral officer to change the date in case of a conflict with a provincial or municipal election or with a day of 'cultural or religious significance.' The government rejected the amendment and, when the Senate decided not to insist, the law came into effect in May 2007.

It soon became apparent that the new legislation did not create an equal playing field as suggested by its proponents. Instead, it basically transferred the responsibility for setting the election date from the prime minister to the leader of the opposition. On several occasions, the government, with an eye on the polls, challenged the Official Opposition to bring it down. Instead, the Liberals repeatedly spoke against government bills and then abstained from voting to avoid an election.

Following the Throne Speech to start the second session of the 39th Parliament, the prime minister stated that virtually every vote on government business was going to be a matter of confidence. The result was more abstentions by the Official Opposition. The government, for its part, even took the unprecedented step of using the confidence convention to impose closure on the Senate. On 6 February 2008 the minister of justice appeared before the Senate Legal and Constitutional Affairs Committee studying an omnibus amendment to the Criminal Code. He gave the committee an ultimatum. Pass the fixed-date election bill by 28 February or else. 'I do not believe I would have any choice except to advise the Prime Minister that I believe that this is a confidence measure and I will put the matter in his hands.'

Of course, the Senate is not a confidence chamber. The defeat of a bill by the Senate does not bring down the government, although past governments have used defeat or delay by the Senate as a reason for calling an election.[7] That would be much harder to do with a fixed-date election law. So the next day a motion was introduced in the House calling on the Senate to report the bill to the House by 1 March 2008. The opposition maintained that this motion was 'subversive of everything we have done under our Constitution involving two Houses in this Parliament ever since day one.'[8] However, with the Liberals abstaining, the motion was adopted by a large majority.

The Senate did return the bill before 1 March, thereby averting a possible constitutional crisis. This single incident can be put down to political brinksmanship but the precedent, taken to its logical conclusion, has profound implications for our system of government.

Some observers, such as Norman Spector,[9] suggested that the idea of fixed election dates was a mistake. Prime Minister Harper himself came to this view in August 2008 when he met with his caucus to consider the upcoming fall session. He decided to ignore the legislation and declared that Parliament had become unworkable. To bolster his argument, he met separately and briefly with the leaders of the other three parties and asked them for assurances they would cooperate in making Parliament work during the fall session. When he failed to receive such assurances, he declared that Parliament had lost confidence in his government and asked the governor general to dissolve Parliament and set the election date for 14 October 2008, one year earlier than required under his own fixed-date election statute. No vote of confidence took place in the House.

A court challenge was launched against the prime minister for breaking his own law although, in a purely legal sense, there was nothing wrong with what he did.[10] The initial days of the campaign were characterized by much criticism of the prime minister for violating the spirit if not the letter of his fixed-date election law. But this criticism needed to be set alongside the fact that the three opposition parties (all of whom claimed to support the legislation and had voted for it) did not even consider proposing to the governor general an alternative government to serve out the remaining year of the mandate envisaged by the fixed-date election statute. Nor did the governor general suggest to the prime minister that, in light of the fixed-date election legislation, he needed an expression of the House's will before he could claim that there was no confidence in his government.

The Financial Statement of 27 November and Its Aftermath

That is the background to the government's financial statement of 27 November 2008, which resulted in two separate issues of confidence and two more examples of how some politicians seem to have lost sight of the way our institutions are supposed to work. The first confidence issue was the economic statement itself, and the question to be asked is how in the world a ministerial statement came to be a matter of confidence. Of course, the government can consider anything to be a matter of confidence and that was the clear impression given to the other parties.

In a more procedural sense, we are talking not about the statement itself but about the ways-and-means motion that would follow. But, properly understood, every ways-and-means motion should not necessarily be a question of confidence. It is really just notice to the House that financial legislation will follow. Surely a government is entitled to give notice to bring in any legislation it wants. Only after the legislation is debated and voted upon should the question of confidence arise, and even if financial legislation is defeated it need not be a matter of confidence.

To be sure, the opposition was outraged by the contents of the financial statement. Since the election, the opposition had been told that all its questions about a fiscal-stimulus package would have to wait for the financial statement. But in fact there was no stimulus in the statement. Instead, there were proposals to limit public subsidies to parties, introduce a ban on public-service strikes, change the pay-equity process, and sell government assets to raise money, none of which had been mentioned in the election campaign. Facing an outraged and united opposition, the government agreed to withdraw the objectionable items. But it was too late. Beyond the proposals or non-proposals in the financial statement, the prospect of never-ending confidence threats had turned the parliamentary battle into a political and a constitutional crisis.

The second confidence issue came about because the Liberals, being unwilling to abstain as they had in the last Parliament, said that they would use the supply day scheduled for 1 December to introduce a non-confidence motion. They also formed an alliance with the NDP, supported in a limited way by the Bloc Québécois, to make sure they had the support to form an alternative government. The opposition parties then informed the governor general of their accord.

The government reacted by postponing the vote on the opposition day for a week. In doing so, it was following the precedent set by Paul Martin and procedurally was on solid ground. But surely we have to ask whether this is the proper way to deal with non-confidence motions.

When supply motions were originally introduced into the rules, they were not even 'votable.' Supply days were to be used by the opposition parties to discuss any matter they wanted, in keeping with the tradition of 'grievance before supply.' Slowly over the years, a few supply motions became votable and now virtually all of them end with a vote. But supply days are scheduled by the government. It is obvious what happens when there is a non-confidence motion on a supply day. It has happened twice and the results are not pretty. Desperate things are said and done as people wait for the guillotine to fall.

Before the non-confidence motion could come to a vote, Prime Minister Harper asked the governor general to prorogue Parliament, thus ending the first session and eliminating the non-confidence motion. The correctness of this decision is discussed elsewhere and will be debated for years.[11] But it was not the governor general's decision as much as the government's logic that is really worrying.

During the more than two hours it took the governor general to come to a decision, the following exchange took place between CBC journalist Don Newman and Transport Minister John Baird, who defended the government's position that a coalition depending on support from the 'separatist' Bloc Québécois would be illegitimate.

John Baird: And I think what we want to do is basically take a timeout and go over the heads of the members of parliament, go over the heads frankly of the Governor General, go right to the Canadian people. They're speaking up loudly right across this country in a way I've never seen.

Don Newman: So you now think the House of Commons is illegitimate. That the Governor General is illegitimate and – well no. Now but John you are a Conservative. You have always been a Conservative, and you live in a British parliamentary system and in a British parliamentary system, it is only legitimate for the government to be the government if it can sustain the support in the House of Commons, and to say now you're going to go over their heads, brush them aside. They're not even important anymore. We're going to go to the people. The Governor General isn't important.

John Baird: We live in a democracy. They're the ones that rule. They're speaking up loudly. I think there is a lot of concern within the Liberal caucus that this is not what their constituents want, and frankly I have a lot of confidence in the Canadian people. They're speaking up loudly. They'll continue to. There will be rallies across country. E-mail petitions. I've never seen anything like this.

Don Newman: So this is Kiev a couple of years ago. Are you all going to have different coloured scarfs?[12]

The government had essentially returned to arguments used by the

Reform Party in 1994 when it suggested that the Bloc Québécois should be denied the role of Official Opposition despite having the second-largest number of seats in the House and two more than the Reform Party. Popular opinion may have supported that position but the Speaker of the House followed parliamentary tradition and accorded the office to the leader of the second-largest party regardless of what that party stood for and where it came from.

Lessons Learned

The prorogation, the change in Liberal leadership the next week, the report that Prime Minister Harper 'will no longer threaten elections to force opposition compliance on secondary policy matters,'[13] and the adoption of the budget introduced on 27 January appear to have ended this parliamentary crisis. But events of the last few months and years should be a wake-up call to those who want to preserve a Westminster-style parliamentary system.

The first lesson we should draw is that, if we are going to have more minority governments, it is incumbent on our leaders to find ways of dealing with implications arising from the parliamentary combinations the people elect. Failure to do so could result not in another King-Byng crisis of 1926 but something more like the political stalemate of the 1850s when successive elections produced deadlock because political leaders of the day failed to work together. Only after years of chaos and with help from the British and from Nova Scotia and New Brunswick did a new entity emerge with different political institutions. Today, few men and women go into politics because they are interested in parliamentary institutions, so perhaps it is time to embrace Professor David Smith's recommendation for the creation of an independent body or royal commission 'to study the law, conventions, usages, and customary understandings that guide parliamentary government in Canada.'[14]

Second, we should either repeal or change the fixed-date election law. It has done no good and much harm. Other parliamentary democracies have considered ways to limit the prime minister's unfettered right to dissolve Parliament.[15] Perhaps that is another question that could be considered by the proposed royal commission.

Third, we need better procedural ways to deal with non-confidence motions instead of piggybacking them onto supply days where they can be delayed by the government. This essentially new procedure has not served the public interest on at least two occasions in the last four years.

A change to the standing orders on this matter would invite changes to other rules. Unfortunately, procedural reform has not been a high priority for many years. We have been entrusting this task to House leaders who are really concerned with short-term political strategy rather than with the long-term health of Parliament. We need a better process to review the standing orders, preferably one that involves the presiding officers, as was the case in the 1960s when Prime Minister Lester Pearson specifically asked Speaker Alan Macnaughton to take the lead in dragging the House into the twentieth century. Over the next six years, Speaker Macnaughton and his successor, Lucien Lamoureux, coordinated the work of several subcommittees on different aspects of reform. They also cajoled, challenged, and probably threatened members into rethinking their House of Commons. The Speakers lent credibility and wisdom to the reform process. Our Speakership (the four officers who preside) is a vastly underutilized cog in our parliamentary system. The Speakers are the only ones whose job encourages them to think seriously about how to improve the House of Commons for the long-term good of the institution and the country and not merely for short-term political advantage.

The fourth and final lesson has been expressed in one way or another by just about every student of Parliament except those directly associated with the current government. As Michael Prince of the University of Victoria puts it: 'These extraordinary events suggest that our prevailing constitutional principles and values are poorly understood by the public, and easily manipulated by politicians through wild claims and rhetorical statements that generate plenty of heat but little light for the citizenry.'[16]

Peter Russell and others suggest elsewhere in this volume that the legitimacy of our institutions is based ultimately on the informed consent of the governed. We all have a long way to go if we are to have both a political class and a population capable of sustaining responsible government for another 160 years.

NOTES

1 See Adrienne Clarkson, *Heart Matters* (Toronto: Viking Canada, 2006), 192.
2 For a discussion of the issue of confidence, see Graham Eglinton and

Eugene Forsey, *The Question of Confidence in Responsible Government*, report prepared for the Special Committee on Reform of the House of Commons, 1985.

3 Andrew Heard, 'The Curious Case of May 10, 2005,' *Canadian Journal of Political Science*, 40, no. 2 (2007): 412.

4 Three provinces (British Columbia, Ontario, and Newfoundland) have held elections in accordance with fixed dates. All of them have single chambers and all had majority governments.

5 Edward McWhinney, 'Fixed Election Dates and the Governor General's Power to Grant Dissolution,' *Canadian Parliamentary Review*, 31, no. 1 (2008): 15–16.

6 Canada, Senate, Standing Committee on Legal and Constitutional Affairs, 14 February 2007.

7 The most famous case was the Senate's handling of the Canada-U.S. Free Trade Agreement which led to the 1988 election.

8 Canada, House of Commons, *Debates*, 11 February 2008.

9 *Globe and Mail*, 4 January 2008.

10 See Guy Tremblay, 'The 2008 Election and the Law on Fixed Election Dates,' *Canadian Parliamentary Review*, 31, no. 4 (2008–9): 24–5.

11 See Andrew Heard's chapter in this volume and also his article 'The Governor General's Decision to Prorogue Parliament: Parliamentary Democracy Defended or Endangered?' Centre for Constitutional Studies, Discussion Paper no. 7, January 2009.

12 CBC Newsworld, Transcript of Interview with John Baird, 4 December 2008, 10:00 a.m.

13 See *Globe and Mail*, 8 January 2009.

14 See David Smith, *The People's House of Commons: Theories of Democracy in Contention* (Toronto: University of Toronto Press, 2007), 140.

15 See Peter Aucoin and Lori Turnbull, 'Removing the Virtual Right of First Ministers to Demand Dissolution,' *Canadian Parliamentary Review*, 27, no. 2 (2004): 36–9.

16 Victoria *Times-Colonist*, 8 December 2008.

PART TWO

The Governor General's Decision to Prorogue

3 To Prorogue or Not to Prorogue: Did the Governor General Make the Right Decision?

C.E.S. (NED) FRANKS

The precedents are clear: no governor general has ever refused a prime minister's request for prorogation. The governor general should have followed this well-established and unambiguous list of precedents and granted the request for prorogation without hesitation. Or the precedents indicate the opposite: what applies to a prime minister's request for a dissolution of a Parliament so a general election can be held should apply to a request for prorogation. It is well established that the governor general should not allow a prime minister to use dissolution of a Parliament to escape facing a vote of confidence in the House, especially when the session is new (and Parliament had sat for only thirteen days in the first session of the 40th Parliament when Prime Minister Stephen Harper requested prorogation of the governor general to avoid a vote of confidence the following Monday). The dissolution precedent dictates that the governor general should reject a prime minister's advice to prorogue a session when a viable alternative government exists. The Liberal Party, New Democratic Party (NDP), and the Bloc Québécois had made a public commitment to support a Liberal-NDP coalition government for at least a year and a half. Following this precedent, the governor general should have refused Harper's advice to prorogue. Needless to say, these two views on precedents do not agree, and also needless to say that scholars and others do not and will not agree as well on whether the governor general made the right decision on 4 December 2008.

The power of the governor general to grant or refuse a request from the prime minister in this sort of issue is not a matter of law but of convention. Conventions give guidance but are not absolute clarion calls for one specific course of action. Nor are conventions legally binding like laws. Conventions are flexible and adapt and change over time as circumstances change. The confidence convention itself is relatively new in the long history of parliamentary democracy, having become firmly entrenched only in the second part of the nineteenth century. Though some conventions, like the confidence convention, are fundamental to our constitution, conventions are not normally enforceable in the courts of law. A basic convention of our system of parliamentary government is that, unless there are compelling arguments to the contrary, a governor general should act on the advice of the prime minister. This is the key to our system of responsible parliamentary government. The prime minister and his cabinet have the responsibility for governing and are accountable in Parliament and ultimately to the people in a general election. The governor general is not.·

In December 2008 Governor General Michaëlle Jean's judgment was that the arguments against accepting the prime minister's advice were not as compelling as those in favour. Since governors general do not reveal the grounds for their decisions, those on the outside must engage in an effort of post hoc haruspication into the entrails of the circumstances surrounding the decision to divine the factors and arguments that formed the grounds for the decision. In this particular instance, the governor general had to act in real time, and a very short time at that. She did not have the leisure to reflect, consult, delay, research, and discuss that historians and other scholars have when they assess the wisdom of past events and actions. She had to act, and either reject or accept Harper's advice. To accept it would mean that the parliamentary session would end and a new one would begin seven weeks later, in January 2009. To reject it would mean that Prime Minister Harper would face and almost certainly lose a vote of confidence in the House of Commons four days later, and the coalition of Liberals and NDP, supported by the Bloc Québécois, would take over government under the leadership of the then head of the Liberal Party, Stéphane Dion.

Her judgment call could have been based on a narrow set of criteria, including only precedents on the granting and refusal of advice to prorogue. This would have led quickly to a decision to accept the prime minister's advice and prorogue the session. Or her decision could have relied on the quite different criteria of precedents on dissolution, and follow the principle that the governor general should not accept advice from a prime minister to dissolve a Parliament when, early in a session, doing so would allow the prime minister to avoid a vote of confidence. Or the governor general could have taken into account factors well beyond precedents and conventions, and include consideration of questions such as: What sort of certainty could be expected that the coalition would be able to enjoy the confidence of the House for the promised length of time? What support would the proposed coalition have, not just in Parliament but in the country? Would the coalition be stable and able to govern the country in a way that met the essential criterion of a parliamentary democracy that a government must enjoy not only the confidence of the House but also, ultimately, the confidence of the people? Would rejecting the prime minister's advice to prorogue the session increase or reduce the likelihood of another early and unwanted general election? Would rejecting the prime minister's advice prevent or only delay the impending vote of confidence? In short, should and did the governor general take into account factors beyond the small world of Parliament and the conventions and rules of parliamentary government as interpreted by scholars and other observers of the parliamentary scene?

It is clear that the governor general took into account, and acted on, a broader range of factors than precedents. In a surprising but probably necessary divergence from custom, details of the encounter between the prime minister and the governor general that could have been known only by someone in attendance at the meeting were revealed two days later, on 6 December, in an article in the *Globe and Mail* by the well-respected journalist Michael Valpy. That the meeting had lasted two and a half hours was known because Harper did not emerge from Rideau Hall until two and a half hours after he had entered it. However, it had not been known before Valpy's revelations that the governor general and the prime minister had discussed 'Canada's economic situation, the viability of an alternative coalition government and the mood of Parliament,' or that those present were 'Ms. Jean, Mr. Harper, Clerk of the Privy Council Kevin Lynch, and the Governor-General's secretary, Sheila-Marie Cook,' or that 'Ms. Jean made clear to the Prime Minister that she was not a rubber stamp for his request to shut down Parliament until late January; that it was within her constitutional discretionary power to turn him down.' Nor had it been publicly known that, 'halfway through the meeting, Mr. Harper and Mr. Lynch, Ottawa's top civil servant, were left alone in the room while the Governor-General and Ms. Cook went to confer with special adviser Peter Hogg, former Osgoode Hall law dean and author of the definitive scholarly work on constitutional law in Canada,' and that 'when Ms. Jean returned, there was more discussion, and then she granted the Prime Minister's request to prorogue.'

The identification of the persons present, the fact that the governor general broke off the meeting at one point to confer with her special adviser, or that she did not feel that she was obliged to rubber stamp the prime minister's request show clearly that she regarded the decision as one in which she could exercise her reserve powers and refuse the prime minister's request if she had felt that desirable. In other words, if any precedent was set in this decision, it was a precedent that the governor general is free to refuse to accede to this sort of request from a prime minister. That she did not refuse does not prove that she was obliged to accede to the request, but in this particular set of circumstances she chose to do so. A different set of circumstances might have produced a different answer.

'Canada's economic situation, the viability of an alternative coalition government and the mood of Parliament' are the particular factors and circumstances identified by Valpy as relevant to the decision of the governor general to accede to the prime minister's request for prorogation. These were clearly not the topics of casual discussion, or as icebreakers and warm-up before Mr Harper said to the governor general: 'Oh, by the way, I would like you to prorogue the session of Parliament today and have Parliament reconvene for a new session on January 26 next year,' to which the governor general replied: 'Of course, Mr. Harper, I'll do it immediately.' They were important and substantive factors that Harper brought up in order to justify his unprecedented request for a prorogation before the session had hardly begun, a prorogation intended to allow him to avoid being defeated on the vote of confidence the following Monday. They were publicly identified by an informed source as important to the governor general's decision to accede to the prime minister's request for prorogation. The following sections will examine these three areas of discussion, and suggest the sort of arguments that Harper might have presented to the governor general in that long meeting at Rideau Hall on 4 December 2008.

Canada's Economic Situation

The government's fiscal update that instigated the uproar, prospective vote of confidence, and coalition was optimistic enough about the economy and prospects for Canada over the next few years as to border on wishful thinking if not fantasy. Harper might well have told the governor general that, although that forecast was likely to be correct for 2008, the situation was deteriorating rapidly and the Canadian economy would for some years be subjected to unforeseen stresses and risks. He would have added that his government had committed itself to introducing a new budget on 27 January 2009, and that this budget would bring in many measures, both tax and expenditure, to help Canadians and Canada to weather the worldwide economic storm. Further, now was not the time to bring in a new, untested government that clearly did not enjoy the support of a majority of the people of Canada. He and his party had been the choice of the electorate, and they deserved the opportunity to present a full budget and comprehensive fiscal plan to Parliament and the people.

The Viability of the Alternative Coalition Government

Harper would likely have waxed eloquent on the question of the viability of the proposed coalition. In the general election of 14 October 2008, Harper's Conservative Party gained 37.6 per cent of the popular vote, Dion's Liberals 26.2 per cent, Jack Layton's NDP 18.2 per cent, Gilles Duceppe's Bloc 10.0 per cent, and Elizabeth May's Greens 6.8 per cent. The Conservative Party was governing with the support of less than 40 per cent of the electorate, while more than 60 per cent had voted against him and, in theory, might have supported the coalition government. Nevertheless, Harper and the Conservative Party mounted an astonishingly speedy and successful anti-coalition public-relations campaign. They had only seven days to do this between his government's disastrous fiscal update of 27 November and his meeting with the governor general on 4 December. The opposition began to consider a possible coalition the day of the fiscal update. On 1 December the Liberals and NDP announced their intention to form a coalition supported by the Bloc. While the Conservative anti-coalition campaign was filled with misrepresentations and half-truths, it worked brilliantly. Public opinion turned formidably against the proposed coalition.

Harper's attack on the coalition had two main thrusts: first, that it had not been democratically elected and had not been and would not be supported by the people; second, that it was a coalition of separatists and socialists that not only did not represent the voting wishes of Canadians but would destroy the country. On 1 December, a few days before Harper met with the governor general, the Conservative Party issued a statement which claimed:

Voters offered no mandate to Stéphane Dion and the Liberals to govern

the country. They offered no mandate to Jack Layton and the NDP to influence the economy.

Voters offered no mandate for the Liberals and NDP to form a coalition
government – and in fact, the Liberals ran against such an arrangement.
And voters certainly offered no mandate for the Liberals and NDP to form
a formal coalition with the separatist Bloc Québécois – a movement dedicated to the destruction of the country.

Yet that is what the opposition are promising.

A government led by Prime Minister Stéphane Dion.

The socialist NDP running the economy.

And Bloc Québécois having a veto over all policies while they continue
to destroy Canada.

Neither the Conservative Party nor Harper, of course, mentioned here
or anywhere else that more than 60 per cent of Canadians had voted
against his party in the recent election and presumably did not support
his government. Among the other half-truths and outright misrepresentations in Harper's and his party's statements were the claim that
the opposition coalition would be an 'illegitimate' government while
his government was 'legitimate.' Nor was much of the rest of their position any more accurate. While Harper's promise to the nation on 3 December that 'Canada's Government cannot enter into a power-sharing
coalition with a separatist party' may be noble-sounding rhetoric, it was
absolutely and viciously incorrect in its claim that the Bloc would have
formed part of the coalition. The three opposition parties had made it
clear that the governing coalition would include only the Liberals and
the NDP. The Bloc had committed itself only to supporting the coalition
for at least eighteen months. The governor general might have pointed
out that Harper's Conservatives proposed a similar alliance with the
Bloc and NDP in the 2004 minority Parliament.

Regardless of the truth or accuracy of Prime Minister Harper's statements and those of his party, they were effective. The notion of a coalition government headed by Dion proved so unpopular to the electorate
that, by 4 December when the prime minister met the governor general,
only a week after his government's disastrous fiscal update and the
first murmurings about a coalition, the electorate's support for Harper
had risen dramatically, to 45 per cent or more, enough to convert his
minority in Parliament into a majority. The Conservative's lead over the
Liberals had increased to over 20 per cent from 11 per cent in the election. More than 50 per cent of those polled said they would rather go to

another election than let the coalition govern. Public opinion in Quebec supported the coalition; opinion in the rest of Canada was even more opposed than the aggregate figures above suggest.

Perhaps Harper made certain that the governor general was aware that in the 2008 election the Liberals had received the lowest percentage of popular vote in their history. Outside Quebec, where the Liberals had actually gained a small amount, they had lost 952,952 votes compared with their support in the 2006 election. These votes had not gone to another party, because the votes had gone down for all other parties except the Greens. The Conservatives had, outside Quebec, lost only 56,098 votes, the NDP 246,374, while the Greens had gained 271,500. Since the beginning of the November imbroglio, support for the Liberals had declined further. Dion was even less popular than his party. He lagged far behind Harper as the person Canadians wanted as their prime minister. While it is not unusual for prime ministers to drop in popularity at the end of their reign – consider Pierre Trudeau and Brian Mulroney – this sort of chute even before a prime minister takes office is unprecedented, and suggests that Dion would likely have had a short and difficult tenure as prime minister. Worse, Dion had committed himself to retiring as party leader in May, so a lame-duck prime minister with sagging popularity would lead the country as head of a weak coalition in a time of great economic stress and turmoil. Who had the country voted for, who did it still by a wide margin prefer as leader? Harper might have argued.

In strictly constitutional terms, Harper's claim that he, not the Liberals, had received a mandate to govern was nonsense. The people of Canada had voted for individual members of Parliament, not for Harper. The only persons who had actually voted for Harper were the 38,548 persons in his riding of Calgary Southwest who had put an 'x' beside his name on the ballot. On the other hand, studies of the behaviour of the electorate have found that only about 5 per cent of Canadians vote on the basis of the local candidate. The overwhelming majority of the electorate votes on the basis of party, party leader, and perceptions such as the state of the economy. In a subjective sense and their own minds, therefore, most persons who voted Conservative had not voted because of a desire to see their local candidate in Parliament but because they wanted Harper as prime minister, because of the Conservative Party's brand, and because of their sense of who they wanted to govern. And many voters who would normally have supported the Liberal Party had not voted at all because they could not support Dion as prime minister, or they objected to his policies, or they did not feel confident of his leadership in difficult economic times. Canadians vote for local candidates as a proxy for national leaders, parties, and concerns.

In the days the coalition was being formed, an opinion arose outside Quebec that, if it came down to being led by Harper or Dion, the electorate strongly preferred Harper. This impressive achievement in public-opinion formation was orchestrated by the Conservative Party. But it could be successful only because there was fertile ground to build on. Dion was not seen as a good leader. There was a profound disconnect between the majority opinion within Parliament – that Harper should go – and that of the country – that a coalition led by Dion should not be allowed to govern. How people had voted in the last election was not an accurate proxy for their opinion on who they wanted to lead them. These points, too, might have been raised by Harper.

Not least of the governor general's concerns might have been the disconnect between Quebec and the rest of Canada in these polls. Normally Canadian prime ministers work towards encouraging national unity and a common sense of purpose among Canada's French and English populations. Not so Harper in this political dogfight. His and his party's rhetoric was the most anti-Quebec, and by inference anti-French, of any major party, let alone a government, of at least the post–Second World War period. Perhaps Harper, after having failed to gain increased support in Quebec in the 2008 election, felt it expedient to abandon Quebec and appeal to the latent hostility towards bilingualism and Quebec in his political heartland of the west. Perhaps his party's polling had indicated that this line of attack was a winner outside Quebec.

Regardless, there was no doubt that Harper's inflammatory and tendentious rhetoric was stunningly effective in mobilizing public opinion against the proposed coalition. The opposition parties and their leaders seemed unable to counteract it. Harper and the Conservative Party had set the agenda and the terms of the discussion. The other parties seemed unable to respond. They were like a deer paralysed by the headlights of a speeding automobile, doomed to a quick and unpleasant fate. A final blow to the Liberal-led coalition came on the evening of 3 December when, after Prime Minister Harper made his address to the nation, Dion, as leader of the opposition, flubbed his opportunity to respond. Not only was his address an hour late in reaching the national television networks (a major no-no for the media, which must adhere to a rigorous schedule), so late that one major network, CTV, did not broadcast it, the video address itself was so amateurish, out of focus, grainy, and ill-prepared that its sloppy production values received media attention to the exclusion of its contents. In this single mess-up, Dion lost whatever remaining confidence the media and his party had in his leadership. Quite likely he lost the nation's confidence as well. Perhaps Harper was able to use this as ammunition in his meeting with the governor general. Dion lasted only a few more days as leader of the Liberal Party before the Liberal caucus replaced him with Michael Ignatieff.

These political realities suggest that the proposed coalition probably would not have proved to be robust and long-lived. It would have taken only a few defections or absentees for the coalition to lose a vote of confidence, and sure knowledge that they are going to be on the losing side in an election is a powerful persuader to MPs to move across the floor of the House. How much of an influence this argument was in persuading the governor general to agree to prorogation will likely never be known, but it certainly was one of the topics of the discussion between Harper and Madame Jean. Rideau Hall itself had been deluged with anti-coalition e-mails, far more than had been received on any other issue, and enough to make its e-mail system crash under the volume of incoming messages.

The Mood of Parliament

The 39th Parliament, from 2006 to 2008, had not been a happy one. Though it had lasted longer than any other minority Parliament but one (the 14th Parliament survived from 1921 to 1925), there had been little common ground in it between the new Harper Conservative government and the three opposition parties. The 39th Parliament would have had a much shorter life if the main opposition party, the Liberals under Stéphane Dion, had not absented themselves from many votes of confidence. As Eugene Forsey observed: 'Minority government can be not a "problem" but an opportunity, not a threat but a promise.' Some have been resoundingly successful, including, for example, Lester Pearson's two minority governments between 1963 and 1968, in which the government proposed, and Parliament agreed to, such fundamental reforms as medicare, the Canada Pension Plan, and the influential royal commission on bilingualism and biculturalism. Harper's first minority Parliament did not enjoy this sort of success. It was not only fractious but unpleasant, and both sides of the House indulged in name-calling, taunting, and schoolyard bullying at the expense of serious discussion.

The processes of accommodation and compromise needed to lead to productivity in any Parliament, but especially in a minority one, broke down.

In September 2008, while Parliament was adjourned, Harper asked for and was granted a dissolution a year before the fixed election date set by his government's own legislation. His professed reason was that Parliament was dysfunctional. Perhaps it was, but dysfunction, like beauty, is in the eye of the beholder, and the Liberals had shown no signs of wanting to defeat Harper's government on a vote of confidence. The ensuing election of October 2008 did not give Harper his hoped-for majority. The first session of the 40th Parliament began with a commitment from the government that business would be conducted with more civility and accommodation than before. However, even before the economic update of 27 November, rumours were rampant that the government intended to end the financial support to political parties of $1.95 per year for each vote received in the last election. While the Conservatives stood to lose the most by this measure, they also stood to gain the most because their fund-raising has been much more effective than that of the opposition parties. The proposal would have bankrupted the Liberals and the Bloc; the NDP would not have fared much better.

This $30-million reduction was the only specific cut proposed in the fiscal update. It was an insignificant drop in the bucket in the government's budget, and intended solely to attack and harm the opposition parties. It exhibited a mean-spirited nastiness rather than an intention to work towards compromise and accommodation. Other provisions in the fiscal update to suspend public servants' right to strike and weaken the push towards pay equity were also seen by the opposition as gratuitous political attacks instead of a serious effort to come to terms with the looming economic crisis.

The mood of Parliament, then, at the time Harper met with the governor general on 4 December, was one of blazing anger in the three opposition parties because they felt betrayed. Harper had violated his promise of a new civility with a vindictive political manoeuvre whose sole intention was to harm his opponents. Even though the government promised to drop the offending provisions, the opposition refused to be mollified. If the vote of confidence had taken place, the anger and determination of the opposition would have led to a defeat of the government. In all likelihood, the governor general would have refused a request by Harper for dissolution and a general election. Less than two months had passed since the previous election, and the coalition, at least on paper, appeared to be a viable alternative that would enjoy the confidence of the House. The coalition would have taken power.

Harper might have told Governor General Jean that he accepted that she would not grant a dissolution under the circumstances. But, he might have argued, prorogation is another matter. It would not have allowed the government to avoid a vote of confidence. Instead, it would have provided a time out, a cooling-off period. His government had already won a vote of confidence on the Speech from the Throne. Prorogation would allow the next vote of confidence to take place in a less heated atmosphere after everybody had had seven weeks to reconsider and cool down. The opposition parties would still have an opportunity to defeat the government when Parliament met again in January.

Harper might even have gone so far as to tell the governor general that he regretted having introduced the offending fiscal update, and that his government would make every possible effort to introduce a budget that met the needs of Canadians, that would deal responsibly with the looming economic crisis, and that the opposition could support with a clear conscience. While some might regard this as unlikely because so out of character for Harper, it is not an impossible scenario. After all, ability to learn from mistakes is an essential component of maturity.

A week is a long time in politics; seven weeks is an eternity. The governor general had given Harper a reprieve that allowed his government to survive. Though for how long is not certain.

The Governor General's Decision

Only those who were present know what was said at the meeting between Governor General Jean and Prime Minister Harper. I have tried to explore the factors and information available at the time on the three subject areas identified as having been discussed at the meeting. In no way do my words and thoughts rely on inside information, nor am I attempting to propose how the discussions actually went. I have simply tried to describe what might have had a bearing on the decision of the governor general to accede to the request of the prime minister at a time when, if the request had not been granted, the prime minister would almost certainly have lost an imminent vote of confidence in the House of Commons.

I have not dealt in any detail with what the governor general might have said to the prime minister. The powers of the governor general – apart from the exercise of reserve powers of the sort that Governor General Jean would have exercised if she had refused Prime Minister Harper's request – are, following Bagehot, described as the rights to be consulted, to advise, and to warn. The governor general might have warned Harper that the path he had taken in lumping all Quebec nationalists and supporters of the Bloc together as separatists was dangerous, that his tactics were harmful to national unity, that his gross misinterpretations of the rules of the parliamentary system were debasing rather than strengthening public understanding and discussion, that he was lucky to escape by the hair of his chinny chin chin this time but it wouldn't happen again in her tenure as governor general.

She might have reminded Harper that he was prime minister to the whole country, not just the 37.6 per cent of Canadians who voted for him, and that his duty was towards the whole country, not just his supporters. She might have added something to the effect that this decision of hers was not to be regarded as setting a precedent that a governor general must always accede to a prime minister's request for prorogation, but she was satisfied this time that, on balance, though only by a very thin margin, the arguments against granting the prorogation were not persuasive enough to reject his request. She might have added that the only precedent set was that in these sorts of circumstances the governor general should think long and hard, and that a governor general's right to reject such a request remained a real and viable option. A discussion that goes on for two and a half hours, even with a break in the middle, can cover an enormous amount of ground, and the governor general, with her concern for the country, must have taken the opportunity to advise and to warn, as well as to be consulted.

Her decision, regardless of whether it is argued to be right or wrong by the standards of pure constitutional law and custom, was hers to make. It is clear that she and Harper considered many more aspects of the decision than simply what was going on in Parliament, and what the precedents suggested. It is worth repeating that conventions are not laws, and have adapted and will continue to adapt to changing circumstances. Was the decision the right one? Consider what the consequences were of the one she made. The Liberal Party has a new leader, Michael Ignatieff, and the opinion polls indicate that he has much more support across the country than his predecessor. The Harper government appeared to be taking their near-death experience and the economic crisis seriously, and produced a budget and policies that better respond to the needs and concerns of a country under a great deal of stress. The Liberals have supported the Harper budget, but at the cost of requiring the government to give a quarterly account of the impact of the budget on jobs and the economy. The coalition has broken up, and a defeat of the Harper government on a vote of confidence would lead to an election. The governor general's decision took her out of the battle and tossed the government's fate back into the hands of the politicians, where it properly belonged.

Consider what is likely to have happened if the governor general had refused Harper's request for prorogation. Some experts believe that, if the governor general had refused Harper' request, constitutional convention dictates that he would have had to resign. Neither law nor precedent support this belief. The only precedent, that of Prime Minister Mackenzie King's resignation in 1926, is a bad one. At the time, King, facing a vote of censure in the House, asked Governor General Lord Byng for a dissolution so he could avoid the vote. King resigned when Byng refused the request, leaving Byng with no choice but to ask the leader of the opposition, Arthur Meighen, to form a government. Meighen accepted, but his government soon lost a vote of confidence. Mackenzie King made Lord Byng's action and the false allegation that the British government had interfered in Canadian affairs a main part of the ensuing election campaign. King won the election, and the office of governor general suffered. King's resignation was roundly criticized by many, including Eugene Forsey.

Regardless of what might or might not have been said at the meeting, I believe that if Governor General Jean had refused the request for prorogation, it is unlikely that Harper would have resigned. Instead, he would have continued his battle by whatever means he found at his disposal. He would have continued making the claims of illegitimacy and anti-democratic behaviour that had been so successful in mobilizing public opinion against the opposition coalition in the preceding week. Only now the governor general would have been identified, along with the coalition, as one of the enemies of democracy. Likely, Harper, after the governor general's refusal, would have gone to his podium outside Rideau Hall and made the claim that an unelected official appointed by the Liberals from Quebec had denied a legitimate request from the government chosen by the Canadian people. He would have added that he intended to face the House and, if defeated, would ask that same unelected official for a dissolution of Parliament that would allow the people of Canada to make it clear who they wanted as prime minister.

He might well have been defeated in the ensuing vote of confidence, and the governor general would have been faced with the prospect of rejecting Harper's request for a dissolution and a general election, at a time when public opinion was already running heavily against the cobbled-together coalition.

If the governor general had refused this request for a dissolution, as she would have had every right and precedent to do, I believe that Harper would then have continued his inflammatory and constitutionally incorrect but popularly supported (outside Quebec) rhetoric. He would have advanced the claim that an unconstitutional act by the unelected Liberal-appointed governor general from Quebec had allowed an illegitimate coalition of socialists, Quebec separatists, and Liberals under the disliked Dion to take over the government without ever having to face the electorate. Despite the constitutional and parliamentary legitimacy and correctness of the governor general's decision to refuse prorogation and allow the installation of the coalition government that enjoyed the confidence of the House, the rhetoric of illegitimacy and anti-democratic behaviour would have prevailed. The King-Byng dispute of 1926 would have been replayed all over again, only worse. The fight between Conservatives and the rest would have split the country on east-west, linguistic, and perhaps other lines (for example, socio-economic class). Canada would have been governed by a coalition built through a marriage of convenience headed by a prime minister who was supported by far fewer Canadians than the prime minister who had been deposed. The coalition would almost certainly, as its demise shows, have proven to be a weak, unpopular, and not very durable government.

The governor general made the right decision.

4 The Governor General's Suspension of Parliament: Duty Done or a Perilous Precedent?

ANDREW HEARD

It might appear to the casual observer that the 2008 constitutional crisis was really nothing more than a storm in a teacup, with the usual partisan jockeying for power spilling into the governor general's saucer for a change of scenery. With Michael Ignatieff's announcement on 28 January 2009 that the Liberals would support the Conservative government's budget after all, the political turmoil of late 2008 seemed to evaporate in the face of a collective sigh of relief from many Canadians. But the events of late 2008 were much more than a storm in a teacup and quite worthy of being called a real crisis. At the heart of this controversy lay profound disagreements on some fundamental issues that cut to the core of our political life. A particular question to emerge from this crisis is whether Governor General Michaëlle Jean made the right decision to prorogue Parliament. Should she have acted on Prime Minister Stephen Harper's advice, or should she have refused and insisted that Parliament be allowed to continue? We need to know the answer because the repercussions of her decision will likely be felt for many years to come.[1]

The Governor General's Role in Parliamentary Democracy

In order to judge the propriety of this decision, we need to understand the basic role of the governor general to determine whether she, as an appointed official, had any business even contemplating refusing the prime minister's request. Then we can examine the personal powers of the governor general and the constitutional principles that determine how and when they should be used. There are differing perspectives on her powers and these constitutional principles, but some clear answers about the decision to suspend Parliament can be determined once these issues are worked through.

The governor general exists as an integral fail-safe mechanism for our parliamentary system of government. Every major parliamentary system around the world continues to include a separate position of head of state, because an independent official is needed on rare occasions to protect the proper functioning of Parliament and cabinet. The powers of the governor general have been likened to a fire extinguisher to put out constitutional fires.[2] The governor general can also be seen as a kind of referee who ensures that the major players are on the field and that the most basic rules of the game are obeyed. When the governor general is called upon to play a personal role in the political system, she exercises what are known as reserve or prerogative powers. These powers are generally limited to being able to hire and fire the prime minister, to summon and dissolve Parliament, and, in very rare circumstances, to refuse to follow the advice of the prime minister and cabinet. Some examples of the possible scenarios in which the governor general might exercise these reserve powers can illustrate the need for these powers in the first place:

- The governor general can prevent a government from clinging to office despite having clearly lost a general election. The governor general can simply dismiss the prime minister and cabinet and appoint as new prime minister the leader of the party that had won the majority of seats in that election. As well, the basic principle of parliamentary government is that the government must win and maintain the confidence of the elected members of Parliament. If the prime minister loses a clear vote of confidence, then the prime minister must either resign or advise the governor general to call an election. However, a desperate prime minister might react by ignoring the defeat and simply carrying on and telling the governor general to suspend Parliament for up to a year. This would be a clear abuse of power and the prime minister's democratic right to continue governing would expire with the loss of confidence of our elected MPs. In those circumstances, the governor general would be justified in firing the prime minister and inviting the leader of the opposition to form a government.
- In certain situations, the governor general can insist that Par-

liament be summoned to meet and conduct business. A prime minister leading a minority government might decide to avoid meeting Parliament if he or she believed that a defeat on a confidence motion was likely. Since Parliament is required by law to meet just once every twelve months, there is the potential for a very long period of avoidance by the prime minister. This evasion would be all the more problematic if the prime minister refused to meet Parliament after an election in which he or she was reduced to a small minority position, and a combination of other parties with a majority was prepared to form a new government.

- The governor general can also dissolve Parliament and call a general election in some situations. For example, the governor general might decide to break an interminable deadlock in Parliament by calling an election to resolve matters.
- The final reserve power is the ability to refuse to follow the advice given by the prime minister and cabinet. An important example of the power to refuse advice is the widely accepted ability of the governor general to refuse to call an election when asked by a prime minister in the early months following an election if an alternative government might function in the current Parliament. Indeed, former Governor General Adrienne Clarkson has written that she was prepared to refuse an election for the first six months following the 2004 election.[3]

The reserve powers are all the more needed in Canada, where the formal constitution is an incomplete and archaic document which has never contained the details of some fundamental aspects of our system of government. There was no mention in the constitution of the prime minister until 1982, and there still is no mention of how that office is filled or what powers the prime minister has. Virtually the entire workings of parliamentary government are left out of the constitution as well. The only relevant reference is a vague statement in the preamble to the Constitution Act, 1867, which said that the colonies uniting to form the Dominion of Canada 'have expressed their Desire to be federally united into One Dominion under the Crown of the United Kingdom of Great Britain and Ireland, with a Constitution similar in Principle to that of the United Kingdom.'[4] It was simply assumed at the time that Canadians understood what British parliamentary government involved and would continue to respect its rules.

Constitutional Conventions

The prerogative powers of the governor general remain constitutional conventions, which are informal rules that bind political actors to behave in a certain way and which are not normally enforceable in the courts. These conventions impose obligations because they protect basic constitutional principles that would be seriously harmed if the rule were ignored. Because constitutional conventions are informal rules and most are not authoritatively written down somewhere, there is room for some disagreement over just what is and is not required or permitted of a political actor in particular circumstances. Although widespread consensus does exist on some fundamental conventions, there can be disagreement about the exact details of a rule or what someone should do when there are several rules in play that result in conflicting duties. Both of these problems are at the root of the controversy about what the governor general should or should not have done when Prime Minister Harper advised her to prorogue Parliament. They were also compounded when media coverage of many experts' views failed to canvass properly the full range of principles, or differing applications of those principles, that were related to the governor general's decision to suspend Parliament. Therefore, it is essential to review the constitutional principles involved and how they might be applied to the governor general's decision.

One school of thought, most clearly championed by Quebec legal scholar Henri Brun in the French press, argues that the governor general actually had no personal decision to make about whether to prorogue Parliament.[5] That decision was Stephen Harper's alone, and the governor general was obliged simply to ratify and proclaim it into law. The prime minister and his government must accept sole responsibility for the decision to suspend Parliament, and it is up to the Canadian electorate to pass judgment on this choice. In this view, the governor general was bound by the principles that she should intervene as little as possible in the political process and that she must act upon the advice of a prime minister who has the confidence of the House of Commons. Furthermore, the principle of democracy requires that important decisions, such as proroguing Parliament, be taken by elected politicians who are directly accountable to the electorate. It therefore would have been unconstitutional for the governor general to have done anything other than act on the prime minister's advice.

While this perspective is very appealing in its simplicity and clarity, it accounts neither for all the constitutional principles in play nor for alternative perspectives on the principles the argument is founded upon. Indeed, all of the three principles mentioned also lend themselves to the argument that the governor general had not only a right to make a personal decision but also a duty to refuse the prime minister's request to suspend Parliament. With an examination of each of the full range of relevant principles, a clearer view emerges of the complex position that the governor general faces in discharging her duties.

Perhaps the prime duty of the governor general is similar to that of any physician: first, do no harm. In the context of a modern democracy, this duty manifests itself as an obligation to intervene as little as possible in the political process. The appointed governor general should allow the elected politicians considerable leeway to resolve political disputes among themselves, and leave the electorate to pass judgment at the next election. However, Michaëlle Jean's decision to prorogue Parliament on 4 December can be looked at in two very different lights under this principle. The first perspective is that described above; the governor general should avoid interposing herself in the political process and simply ratify the decision made by Prime Minister Harper to suspend Parliament. However, the prorogation of Parliament can also be viewed in a very different light. By agreeing to the prime minister's request, the governor general actually prevented our elected politicians from resolving the problems and a cascade of other political events resulted. A vote was due to be held in four days' time, and a majority of the newly elected members of the House of Commons had signed a document stating their intention to vote non-confidence in the Conservative government and to support a Liberal-New Democratic Party (NDP) coalition government. In this perspective, the governor general should not have agreed to prorogation because she in effect shut down a newly elected Parliament and put a stop to the normal political processes that were unfolding. Prorogation was a serious and substantial intervention into the political process. Key to this second perspective is whether the governor general did in fact have a personal decision to make or was bound to act upon the prime minister's request. An answer to this question is crucial and depends on the application of several other constitutional principles.

The most immediate principle that applies to whether the governor general had a personal decision to make is one already mentioned: that the governor general must act on the advice of a prime minister who enjoys the confidence of the House of Commons. However, neither the terms of this principle nor its application to the events in late 2008 are as clear as might first appear. First of all, the broadest consensus among constitutional experts supports the view that the governor general has a duty to act on any *constitutionally valid* advice, not any and all advice a prime minister might offer. This particular formulation of the rule is built upon a consensus that there are at least two contexts in which the governor general can properly refuse the prime minister's advice: when a new election is requested following within months of an election that produced a Parliament in which another party (or parties) can form an alternative government; and when a range of major decisions, including Senate and judicial appointments, are to be made once the prime minister has announced that his or her government will resign in favour of another party.

A few constitutional authorities continue to argue that the governor general must not make personal judgments on the constitutionality of her prime minister's advice. Patrick Monahan, for example, believes that the courts are the proper avenue to address actions that contravene constitutional law and the judgment of the ballot box can deal with other alleged transgressions.[6] Furthermore, governors general are not trained as judges are to make decisions about something's constitutionality. However, this argument is not convincing on a number of grounds. First of all, it often does not take an expert to recognize unconstitutional behaviour, just as we in the public need not be lawyers to identify many illegal actions such as rape, murder, or theft. Second, many prime ministers are not personally qualified as lawyers either, but that does not excuse them from making judgments about the constitutionality of a proposed course of action. Both prime ministers and governors general rely on the support of experts to help form an opinion. Third, a great many unconstitutional actions involve breaches of constitutional convention that are not subject to formal judicial review. The basic rules of parliamentary democracy are not detailed in constitutional law and are not subject to judicial enforcement in any ongoing or meaningful way. Fourth, the electoral system provides a very incomplete check on the powers of government, with many parties forming majority governments despite the fact that the majority of voters had voted against them; only two of the last nine governments since 1958 with a majority of seats in the House actually also won a majority of the votes cast. Essentially, a recalcitrant government need convince only about 40 per cent of the electorate of the wisdom of its ways to be re-elected with a majority in the next election. Finally, some harms cannot be undone after the fact, either by the courts or by an election. Some injuries to property, to lives, or even to the political system have to be prevented before they occur, since no remedy can undo the damage. Certainly, the governor general should leave most constitutional problems to either the courts or the electoral system to sort out. Yet there are still some matters that are perhaps best dealt with by the governor general refusing to act on unconstitutional advice.

Was the Prime Minister's Advice Constitutional?

The next important question, therefore, is whether Stephen Harper's advice to suspend Parliament was constitutional. Even among those constitutional authorities who supported the governor general's prorogation of Parliament, many question the propriety of the prime minister's decision to prorogue Parliament rather than face the vote of confidence on 8 December. The problem is that his actions undermine the most fundamental principle of our parliamentary system of government: that the government of the day must win and maintain the confidence of a majority of the elected members of Parliament. This principle is known as responsible government, and it ensures that the executive branch of government is accountable to those directly elected by the citizens.

The accountability of the government to Parliament is essential because of a basic fact of parliamentary systems: people elect legislatures not governments. When the national election was held on 14 October 2008, there were in fact 308 simultaneous local elections. In those elections, Canadians could vote only for or against the candidates running in their own local electoral district. There is no nation-wide election for prime minister or for a political party. Ultimately, the only person with a democratic right to rule after that election is the leader of the party (or parties) who can win the confidence of those 308 elected representatives of the people. Not only must a government win the confidence of our MPs right after an election, but it must continue to do so in a variety of confidence votes throughout the period to the next election. One of the major advantages of the parliamentary system is that the government of the day is held continuously responsible for its actions between elections, and it could lose the right to govern any time that a majority of the people's elected representatives vote non-confidence in it.

When an election returns a Parliament in which no party has won a majority of votes, the incumbent government has a right to remain in office and to meet Parliament in order to win its confidence. Winning that first test of confidence, however, does not provide the government with an enduring right to continue governing. It must continue to win each and every confidence vote that occurs until the next election. The Conservative Party was in office at the time of the 2008 election, and it did win the most seats, 143 out of 308. However, it did not 'win' the election in any meaningful way. With only 38 per cent of the vote and 46 per cent of the seats, it failed on every measure to secure a majority, which is the absolute bedrock of democracy. In order for the democratic principle of majority rule to be given life, the Conservative government has to win and maintain the support of a majority of the elected MPs.

When Stephen Harper met with the governor general, he had already won the first confidence vote of the new Parliament, when the House of Commons approved the Speech from the Throne on 27 November. If nothing significant had transpired since the Speech from the Throne had been approved, then the governor general would have been un-equivocally obliged to act on the prime minister's advice to suspend Parliament. However, the reality was quite different. The same day that the Speech from the Throne was approved, the finance minister delivered an economic statement which caused an uproar. The opposi-tion parties all denounced the statement and indicated that they would vote against it in the confidence votes that were originally scheduled to be held four days later, on 1 December. Over the intervening week-end, the government announced that it would postpone the confidence votes for one week. The opposition party leaders met and signed an agreement for the Liberals and NDP to form a coalition government. Thus, Stephen Harper's authority to advise the governor general was severely undermined by the time he met with her on 4 December. On the same day that Harper met with the governor general, a petition was delivered to her that had been signed by 161 opposition MPs in which they stated their intention to vote non-confidence in the Conservative government and to support an alternative government.

The prime minister's decision to suspend Parliament was unconsti-tutional on several levels. First of all, he intended to prevent Parliament from expressing its non-confidence in his government and its support for an alternative government. This is an unprecedented manoeuvre among modern established democracies. It is a tactic that is normally condemned by Western governments when employed by a struggling Third World regime threatened with a legislative revolt, such as oc-curred in Sri Lanka in 2001. This defiance of Parliament was all the more dramatic since it occurred only seven weeks after a general election and less than three weeks into the life of the newly elected Parliament. Second, Harper had already postponed the confidence vote by a full week and the suspension of Parliament meant that it would be at least two months before another confidence vote was held. This delay contravenes an accepted constitutional convention that serious doubts about whether a government has lost the confidence of the House must be resolved in relatively short order; previous discussions of this rule had established a seven- to ten-day window within which the government must resolve the issue. This period is believed to give the political actors ample opportunity to reflect on the gravity of voting non-confidence in the government.[7] Harper had already delayed the vote by this acceptable margin, and yet he proposed an even further delay of undetermined length that amounted to at least two months after the original vote was to have been held. Again, this type of manoeuvre is simply unheard of among modern established democracies. It is a fundamental abuse of power to shut down a newly elected Parliament at the moment when it is poised to vote non-confidence in the incumbent government.

In summary, then, it appears that the governor general was not bound by her normal duty to act on the prime minister's advice. That advice was unconstitutional and the prime minister's authority to offer binding advice was substantially undermined by the stated intentions of a clear majority of MPs to vote non-confidence in the Conservative government and to support an alternative. However, the question whether the governor general made the right decision to prorogue Parliament requires further analysis.

Did the Governor General Make the Right Decision?

While a range of considerations come into play in trying to assess whether Michaëlle Jean properly prorogued Parliament, the view that it is improper for the prime minister to advise prorogation in the circumstances, but acceptable for the governor general to use her own discretion to do so, seems illogical. Nevertheless, it is important to canvass the alternatives open to Jean once freed from her duty to act on the prime minister's advice.

One important issue is whether the governor general should, or even could, take note of the positions taken by the opposition members of the House. Some might suggest that she must ignore any unsolicited advice, whether it comes from opposition parties, academics, or the media. Instead, she must resolutely follow the advice of her prime minister. The prime minister is certainly the only minister who can offer binding advice to the governor general. But the prime minister and cabinet are not the governor general's only acceptable sources of either information or advice. Indeed, the governor general has a duty to remain fully informed of political events and competing perspectives, particularly when there are doubts about whether the House of Commons has confidence in the government of the day. In any exercise of the prerogative powers, governors general have at their disposal a range of people from whom they can draw advice; information and advice may be properly offered by her secretary, by the clerk of the Privy Council, and by any academic authorities she may wish to engage privately.[8] In all cases these individuals can offer only advice in the normal sense of the word; they provide their professional opinion on events and of the wisdom of the alternative courses of action. The governor general must then make up her own mind about what to do.

The governor general has a duty to receive information from other political party leaders as well. This duty is particularly clear when the opposition parties control a majority of seats in the Commons. It is even more so when the governor general may be placed in a position of even considering whether to refuse the advice to be offered by the prime minister. It is a fundamental convention of the constitution that the governor general can take no action that will not be publicly defended by the prime minister. If she insists on a course of action that the current prime minister would rather resign than accept, then the governor general must be absolutely certain that she can appoint another prime minister who does support her actions. Many critics of the reserve powers of the crown forget that this convention exists and the reasons for it. The convention provides democratic accountability for all of the personal decisions made by the governor general. Personal decisions by the governor general are thus acceptable in a modern democracy because they are agreed to and defended by the prime minister, whether incumbent or new. The certainty of appointing a new prime minister cannot be a subject explored after the fact by a governor general who has already exercised her reserve powers. She must be in full possession of the facts before deciding upon her course of action.

In the context of Stephen Harper's meeting with Michaëlle Jean on 4 December, the governor general would also have been well aware that there is an expectation that a prime minister will resign immediately upon the governor general's refusal to accept his advice. The rationale is that the governor general would not refuse advice unless she had lost confidence in the prime minister's judgment. Thus, a prime minister cannot remain in office in the face of this loss of confidence. However, C.E.S. Franks has cast doubt upon the necessity for a prime minister to resign, and there are indeed good reasons why there need not be an automatic resignation.[9] Even so, there is little a governor general could do if a prime minister were determined to resign in protest. And in 2008 there were very clear indications that Stephen Harper would not remain in office simply to be defeated in the House. In facing the possibility of appointing a new prime minister, the governor general cannot be contented with any person willing to take office. Any alternative prime minister must be capable of winning the confidence of a majority in the House. She cannot know this unless she is made aware of the positions of different parties represented in the Commons. So the letters sent by the three opposition leaders to the governor general, as well as the petitions signed by the opposition MPs, were indeed constitutionally appropriate and important to consider.

One related argument that has been advanced by several defenders of the governor general's decision to prorogue Parliament relates to whether the governor general should take any notice of impending confidence votes in the House of Commons. In this view, a prime minister retains full authority until formally defeated on a definitive vote in the chamber. The petition signed by opposition MPs and sent to the governor general does not have any constitutional weight. Harper had won a vote of confidence a week before meeting with the governor general and nothing had changed since then. The argument continues that the perceived likelihood of defeat remains only a probability until a vote actually occurs. And surprises can unfold in the interim that result in victory being snatched from probable defeat; a prime example of such a surprise would be the Paul Martin government's survival of the final confidence vote in May 2005 owing to the defection of Conservative Belinda Stronach to the Liberal cabinet. While this is an attractive argument, it does not sufficiently account for the very novel facts of the case in December 2008.

Never before in federal politics had all opposition parties combined to sign formal agreements to create and support a coalition cabinet. These agreements were signed by the three party leaders and approved by their caucuses; the agreements were publicly released.[10] Furthermore, the petition sent to the governor general on 4 December stated the intention of the undersigned to vote in favour of the motion moved by Liberal leader Stéphane Dion.[11] This motion was also unprecedented in Canadian politics because it stated not only that the House had lost confidence in the government but also that it would support an alternative government. The fact that 161 out of the 308 members of the House had signed this document must surely be taken note of by the governor general. The governor general has a duty to weigh the chances of survival of an alternative government against those of the incumbent government in light of the facts known at the time. Given the opposition MPs' petition, the incumbent government's viability would have been nil had Parliament not been prorogued. In only four days time, that majority of the House who had signed the petition would have voted against the government. The alternative government also would have been viable for some substantial period, even if we can never know if it would have lasted the full period of time in the signed agreements.

Certainly, the petition could never have the status of an actual vote of non-confidence formally passed in the House of Commons by those very same signatories. As such, the signing of the agreements and the petition did not create the same constitutional obligation for the prime minister to resign that would have flowed from a formal vote. Neither could it form the basis for the governor general to dismiss outright the prime minister and replace him with Stéphane Dion. However, those agreements and the petition do serve as valid evidence that the authority of the prime minister was in serious doubt, and that the intentions of a clear majority in the House of Commons were indisputably clear. That information was vital to another duty expected of the governor general.

The governor general has a responsibility to ensure that Parliament is allowed to function. This is why she has a right to summon Parliament if a prime minister takes too long to do so, particularly following an election. If a Parliament ceases to function, the governor general has the prerogative power to dissolve it and order fresh elections in the hopes that the new Parliament will be able to function. These actions would not be undue interventions in the political system, since the governor general would be acting purely to ensure that Parliament is able to do its vital work. In the early weeks and months following an election in which no party wins a majority, there is no more important task for the House of Commons than to decide which party (or parties) has its confidence to govern. The prime minister's request to suspend Parliament came less than three weeks into the life of the new Parliament, seven weeks after the election, and only because the opposition parties had announced that they would vote non-confidence in his government and signed an agreement to support an alternative government for a minimum of eighteen months. Clearly, his intent was to prevent Parliament from functioning normally. Thus, the governor general had a choice either to prevent Parliament from functioning or to insist that it be allowed to pass judgment on the government. Faced with such a choice, she had a duty to ensure that Parliament continued sitting. In the parliamentary system there is no more crucial function for Parliament than voting confidence in the government in a timely fashion; without the ability to do so, responsible government is dangerously threatened.

It has been suggested that the governor general might also consider public opinion or whether she would face an antagonistic public-relations campaign if she were to act one way rather than another. Certainly, any governor general must normally avoid bringing the office into fundamental disrepute, but this does not mean that any exercise of her prerogative powers must have public support. To concede that would allow unconstitutional abuses of power by a governor general that are popular. Neither has Jean been proven right to suspend Parliament because opinion polls have since shown that a majority of Canadians supported that decision. An Ekos poll conducted the day of the decision found 45 per cent in favour and 43 per cent opposed.[12] An Angus Reid poll conducted over the next four days found 51 per cent in favour and 41 per cent against.[13] Two important points need to be made about these polls. First, the suspension of Parliament was not the clear choice of a strong majority of Canadians. Second, the level of support recorded for prorogation is largely due to the support of Conservative voters. In the Ekos poll, 80 per cent of Conservative supporters agreed with the governor general's decision, compared to less than a quarter of those supporting the three main opposition parties. Such a clear partisan split hardly represents a national consensus. The governor general also should not have been concerned about an impending public-relations backlash by the Conservative government if she had refused prorogation.[14] Whenever a governor general might refuse to act on a prime minister's advice, it is to be expected that the government will react harshly with public attacks, as was the case in 1926. But the governor general has a duty to resist such considerations, because she would otherwise have to cave into any government intent on abusing its powers of office. Her duty to defend the principles of parliamentary

government should outweigh the desire to avoid any ensuing controversy that would be generated.

There is a final issue that any governor general must consider very
seriously when contemplating the exercise of the reserve powers, and
this consideration should have sealed the matter for Michaëlle Jean.
The question is what precedent would a particular course of action set
for the future. In this instance, the events of December 2008 now provide a clear precedent for any future prime minister to demand that
Parliament be suspended whenever he or she feels threatened with
defeat. There could be no greater certainty that a government would
have been be defeated without prorogation than the circumstances in
December 2008. And yet the governor general suspended Parliament.
Now a prime minister can demand that Parliament be suspended
whenever he or she believes that such a course might break the resolve
of the opposition; the length of that suspension is also indeterminate.[15]

Conclusion

The governor general did indeed have a personal decision to make
when advised by the prime minister to prorogue Parliament. Her normal duty simply to act on the prime minister's advice was suspended
by the impropriety of that advice and by the signed commitment of
a majority of MPs to vote non-confidence in the government. In fact,
the governor general had another duty in the circumstances – to ensure that Parliament was allowed to function. Her decision to suspend
Parliament instead amounted to a serious intervention in the political
process that stymied our elected representatives' ability to resolve the
crisis. Far from justifying the wisdom of her decision by illustrating
the fragility of the proposed coalition, the subsequent resignation of
Stéphane Dion and the hurried election of a new Liberal leader are part
of a substantially new chain of events caused by her intervention.

The relief that some have expressed in the wake of the governor
general's decision may prove to be very short-sighted in the years to
come. Without any substantial challenge to this precedent, future prime
ministers can claim that they are entitled to suspend Parliament at any
time, for any reason. By this single action, the governor general has
risked gutting Parliament's ability to exercise its most important duty
in a timely fashion. The only meaningful hold that our elected representatives have over the government of the day is the threat to vote
non-confidence. The members of the House of Commons are the only

people who are directly elected by the citizens of Canada. Now, the ability of our elected MPs to vote non-confidence in the government is subject to the whim of that government.

NOTES

1 The governor general's decision to prorogue Parliament is analysed in greater depth by the author of this chapter elsewhere; see Andrew Heard, 'The Governor General's Decision to Prorogue Parliament: Parliamentary Democracy Defended or Endangered?' Centre for Constitutional Study, *Points of View*, no. 7 (January 2009), http://www.law.ualberta.ca/centres/ccs/uploads/PointsofView7.pdf.

2 Frank MacKinnon, *The Crown in Canada* (Calgary: McClelland and Stewart West, 1976), 123.

3 See Adrienne Clarkson, *Heart Matters* (Toronto: Viking Canada, 2006), 192.

4 30 & 31 Victoria, c.3 (U.K.).

5 For example, Henri Brun, 'Michaëlle Jean n'a pas le choix,' Cyberpresse.ca, 4 December 2009, http://www.cyberpresse.ca/opinions/forums/la-presse/200812/04/01-807213-michaelle-jean-na-pas-le-choix.php. See also B. Thomas Hall, 'The Governor General, the Prime Minister, and Prorogation: Why the Governor General Made the Right Decision,' *Hill Times*, 12 January 2009, 14.

6 Patrick Monahan, *Constitutional Law*, 3rd. ed. (Toronto: Irwin Law, 2002), 76–9.

7 Lester B. Pearson faced a defeat on a tax bill in 1968 when he and many other Liberal MPs were out of Ottawa; he held a definitive confidence vote the next week, and Parliament did no substantive business in the interim. Paul Martin held a definitive confidence vote the week after the opposition passed a motion that it believed to have been a test of confidence. In all discussions about these prior events, there was firm agreement that any serious doubts about whether the government had lost the confidence of the House must be resolved quickly, within the week to ten-day window.

8 Indeed, media reports revealed that the clerk of the Privy Council, Kevin Lynch, accompanied the prime minister to his meeting with the governor general on 4 December, and that a constitutional authority, Peter Hogg, was also present in another room for the governor general to consult with privately. Michael Valpy, 'G-G Made Harper Work for Prorogue,' *Globe and Mail*, 6 December 2008, A4.

9 C.E.S. Franks, 'Would Prime Minister Harper Have Had to Resign if the

Governor General Had Refused His Request for Prorogation?' 15 December 2008, manuscript.

10 For details of the agreements, see the Liberal-NDP coalition agreement, 'An Accord on a Cooperative Government to Address the Present Economic Crisis,' http://www.liberal.ca/pdf/docs/081201_Accord_en_signed. pdf, and the Liberal, NDP, and Bloc Québécois Agreement, 'A Policy Accord to Address the Present Economic Crisis,' http://www.liberal.ca/pdf/docs/081201_Policy_Frame_en_signed.pdf (accessed 3 December 2008).

11 All three opposition petitions are available at Liberal Party of Canada, 'Opposition Parties Deliver Petitions to Governor General,' http://www. liberal.ca/story_15520_e.aspx (accessed 5 January 2009). Each of the petitions read:

> We the majority of the members of Canada's House of Commons, humbly inform you that we would vote in favour of the motion proposed by the Official Opposition and that reads as follows:
>
> That, in light of the Conservatives' failure to recognize the seriousness of Canada's economic situation, and its failure in particular to present any credible plan to stimulate the Canadian economy and to help workers and businesses in hard-pressed sectors such as manufacturing, the automotive industry and forestry, this House has lost confidence in this government, and is of the opinion that a viable alternative government can be formed within the present House of Commons.

12 Ekos, 'Poll Results: A Deeply Divided Public Ponders Prorogation,' http://www.ekoselection.com/wp-content/uploads/poll-results-dec-5-final.pdf (accessed 5 February 2009).

13 Angus Reid, 'Half of Canadians Think Governor General Made the Right Decision,' http://www.angusreidstrategies.com/uploads/pages/pdfs/2008.12.08_Jean.pdf (accessed 5 February 2009).

14 The government's intention to mount a strong public-relations campaign against the governor general was clearly implied by John Baird in an interview with CBC Newsworld on 4 December while the Harper-Jean meeting was under way at Rideau Hall.

15 The only legal obstacle facing the prime minister is the requirement in section 5 of the Constitution Act, 1982 that a session of Parliament be held every twelve months. In the past, there was a practical problem that the government might run out of money if Parliament did not meet periodically to authorize money for the government to spend. However, modern financial arrangements ensure that the government can continue to spend for a very considerable period of time without Parliament's approval.

5 Prime Minister Harper's Parliamentary 'Time Out': A Constitutional Revolution in the Making?

LORRAINE E. WEINRIB

When Governor General Michaëlle Jean prorogued Parliament in December 2008, she complied with the request of a prime minister determined to avoid an impending vote of non-confidence in the House of Commons. His request and her acquiescence were unprecedented. Some commentators considered the situation so exceptional as to call for conditions restricting Prime Minister Stephen Harper's powers to routine matters for the duration of the prorogation of Parliament. No conditions were imposed. The prime minister went on to appoint one Supreme Court justice and eighteen senators during the period of prorogation – hardly routine matters – when the question of his support in the House was under a cloud.

The events that led to the prorogation of Parliament demonstrate the fragility of one of the basic principles of British parliamentary government, the principle of responsible government. This principle stipulates that a particular government continues in office only as long as it enjoys the confidence of the elected members of the House of Commons. For this reason, minority governments are by definition less stable than majority governments. They are particularly unstable when a prime minister's preference is to denigrate the opposition parties and their leaders, rather than to build upon common ground.

Delaying a vote of confidence is a serious matter because it creates the possibility of the democratically illegitimate exercise of public power. Prorogation itself does not raise this spectre of illegitimacy. It is a useful option, for example, when a government needs a pause at the end of a policy cycle before going forward with a new phase of state business.

Harper sought prorogation to protect his new minority government from the reaction of the House to his remarkably ill-advised and politically aggressive economic update. This statement announced policies that were known to be anathema to the opposition parties: restrictions on labour rights and women's equality. In addition, it repudiated public financing of political parties according to the measure of their success in the last election. This change in financing would not have made much difference to the ruling Conservatives, given their mode of fund-raising. It would have had a devastating effect on the opposition parties, however.

Why did Harper throw down this partisan gauntlet? Presumably, he wanted to take the first opportunity to establish his dominant authority over the new minority Parliament. This tactic had worked in the previous Parliament. The Liberals, the Official Opposition, had to support the government more than they would have preferred because of Harper's tactics and also because they had in Stéphane Dion a comparatively ineffective leader and lacked the resources to contemplate bringing down the government and running an election campaign.

Prorogation enabled Harper's government to weather the crisis that his ill-conceived economic update precipitated. Having experienced the near death of his government, he has retreated from his economic policy statement. The embarrassment of that retreat is intensified by the fact that his actions precipitated the political renewal of the Liberal Party. Michael Ignatieff became interim leader of the Liberal opposition, displacing Stéphane Dion months before the scheduled leadership convention. Ignatieff has asserted the leverage that the Official Opposition usually enjoys in a minority government. He has introduced a substantive focus and positive tone in parliamentary debate. He has enunciated standards that Harper's government must meet to sustain the confidence of the House of Commons. The polls show higher numbers for Ignatieff and for the Liberal Party.

Harper's position has been weakened in another way. Commentators widely criticized the Conservative government's January 2009 budget as a repudiation of every economic principle the government has espoused and rebuked him for his appointment of eighteen senators to fill seats he had pledged to leave empty pending reform of the Senate.

The near collapse of a minority government is not a significant event. The circumstances that surround this near collapse, however, signal that there may be further serious repercussions arising from the events of December 2008 to January 2009. Such would be the case if, as I argue in this chapter, these events reflect a pattern of disregard by Harper of a number of deeply embedded constitutional principles and practices. Each individual element poses cause for concern. The accumulation suggests that Harper is capable of precipitating a serious constitutional crisis to avert responsibility for his own mistakes and miscalculations and to stay in power.

Harper and the Canadian Constitution

The Recent Crisis

The prime minister claimed that he sought prorogation, in December 2008, to give Canadians the opportunity to assess his government's January 2009 budget. This budget, he pledged, would respond to the unfolding global economic crisis, which he had ignored and then trivialized much longer than was politically astute. Harper might have addressed the nation with an abject apology for his failure to meet his responsibilities on the economic and fiscal front. He might have acknowledged that he had misread the House of Commons when he issued his highly partisan economic update statement.

Harper took a different approach. He appealed to the democratic legitimacy of his actions and accused his opponents of betraying Canadian democracy and national unity. He and his supporters invoked the recent election results as proof of public support for his new government and its course of action, as well as faxes and e-mails received and projected rallies. They also invoked the vote in the House of Commons supporting the Speech from the Throne.

Harper and his supporters deduced from the election success of the Conservative Party that the Canadian public had both chosen him as their preferred prime minister, and repudiated Dion, then the leader of the Liberal Party. It followed that the opposition parties' call for a non-confidence vote was illegitimate. Also illegitimate was the opposition parties' creation of a coalition ready to govern.

The prime minister's game plan was to convince the Canadian public that he was animated by democratic values, playing by the existing rules and serving its best interests. To this end, he progressively veered further away from the framework that Canada's parliamentary mode of government provides for minority governance.

Within this constitutional framework, seeking prorogation to avoid a non-confidence vote was a highly controversial initiative. This is not to say that the governor general acted improperly. She likely took into

account the seriousness of the economic downturn, which made prorogation a prudent choice that would enable the Ministry of Finance to
finalize its budget. She likely considered it wise to give time for the new
coalition to demonstrate its character. She might also have considered
that prorogation during the holiday season would not seriously undermine governance. The governor general, by tradition, does not indicate
her concerns or give reasons for her decisions, but informed commentators have all agreed that these would have been relevant questions.

Many elements of Harper's stance were questionable. The prime
minister claimed, for example, that the House of Commons' endorse-
ment of his government's Throne Speech settled the question of confidence for some unspecified period of time. That speech had acknowledged the minority status of his government as well as the exigencies of
the principle of responsible government noted above and, on that basis,
had expressed the government's intention to work together with the
opposition. Harper's later economic update statement repudiated this
conciliatory stance to such an extent that it prompted the opposition
parties to rethink their support of the government. Harper's desire was
to make himself the arbiter of confidence in the House, rather than the
opposition parties themselves.

The prime minister and his supporters took liberties with their account of the events as they took place. While it was the case that the
electorate had elected more Conservative members to the House of
Commons, when compared to members of the other parties, it was not
the case that Harper was the electorate's designated prime minister. In
total there were more members who did not necessarily support Harper as prime minister. Accordingly, if the non-Conservative members
joined together in a coalition that had more members than Harper's
Conservative caucus, they could quite legitimately precipitate events
so as to replace the government.

The prime minister and his supporters denounced the coalition as
opportunistic and politically unsavoury. One minister went so far as
to suggest that the coalition constituted a coup d'état. These claims
were disingenuous. Coalitions are common in parliamentary systems
that have multiple political parties. Moreover, Harper had engaged in
a similar coalition-building plan to oust the Liberal minority government of Paul Martin, a plan that included a signed agreement with the
leaders of the NDP and the Bloc Québécois. The taint of support from
a separatist party didn't seem to bother Harper when that support
worked in his favour.

Harper's strong condemnation of the arrangement reached with the Bloc Québécois was misleading as well. He and his supporters suggested that the Bloc would have a veto over the coalition's legislative agenda, for example. In fact, the Bloc was not a member of the coalition and would not have a veto. Rather, it agreed to give stability to the coalition by supporting it for a period of time.

Harper played on the ignorance of the Canadian public as to the constitutional framework within which our parliamentary system of government operates. Polling at the time confirmed the public's lack of familiarity with the working of a minority government, in particular the governor general's role in the changing of governments. It is a matter of concern that a prime minister would feel comfortable exploiting, indeed encouraging, views that were inconsistent with some of the most basic features of our system of government.

John Baird, minister of transport, infrastructure and communities, further delineated the government's stand. Like Harper, he insisted that the government was following the rules in seeking a 'time out' from the governor general through prorogation. He did not mention the many ways in which the government's position departed from the only relevant rules – the unwritten principles of parliamentary governance. He too identified the Conservative government's stance as serving the best interest of Canada, in contrast to the coalition, which he described as having delivered a great victory to leaders of the separatist movement in Quebec. He admonished the Liberals for doing what Pierre Trudeau, their revered former leader, would never have done. He repeated the statements that the Bloc was part of the coalition and refused to respond to the fact that Harper had himself tried to build a similar coalition in 2004, as noted.

Baird's most significant addition to our understanding of the Conservatives' intentions was embodied in these words:

What we want to do is basically take a timeout and *go over the heads of the members of parliament, go over the heads frankly of the Governor General, go right to the Canadian people.* They're speaking up loudly right across this country in a way I've never seen ...

I think in a democracy, I think – I speak for myself and I will let you summarize other issues. But you know what I'm saying is *we're going over the heads of the politicians and the Governor General directly to the Canadian People.* We live in a democracy. They're the ones that rule. They're speaking up loudly.[1]

Harper controls his government's message very tightly. Conservative members of Parliament, even cabinet members, do not speak freely with the press. During election periods, candidates' interaction with the press is tightly controlled. For Baird to make the point, twice, that the government was bypassing both Parliament and the governor general, just before the prime minister sought prorogation of the House of Commons in unprecedented circumstances, gives us insight into Harper's game plan.

These statements reveal that the government well understood that its appeal to the people was not to the people as democratically represented in Parliament. Just as Harper tried to create political facts that would enable him to govern as if he presided over a majority government, he was also willing to dispense with Parliament altogether if necessary to hold onto power or at least to prevent the coalition from taking power if he lost the confidence of the House.

These statements also suggest that the government was ready to precipitate a confrontation with the governor general. Let's say that the governor general had refused prorogation. Would Harper have attempted to replace her with a more compliant individual rather than facing a non-confidence vote? Harper had said that he would use all legal means at his disposal. Did he regard the dismissal of the governor general as one option? Such a move would have created a very serious constitutional impasse, drawing in the queen, as Canada's head of state, and upsetting the traditional status accorded to the governor general as her representative.

In assessing the long-term implications of the recent political crisis, it is important to determine whether Harper accepts the governor general's traditional authority to decide what happens when a young minority government receives a vote of non-confidence, that is, to call an election (as the prime minister would presumably want) or invite another party or parties to form a government.

Canadians deserve an answer to this question. Yet Harper is unlikely to be forthcoming on it, if asked. The best indicators lie in his past statements and actions. He often tries to legitimize his positions with reference to democracy and democratic functioning. But our system of government has many other related principles and practices, which in effect legitimize the majoritarian democratic function. In Harper's case, even cursory investigation reveals an extended track record of disdain for many of the principles and practices that lie at the foundation of the Canadian constitutional order.

Harper's Record on Basic Constitutional Principles and Practices

There are many examples of Harper's predilection to concentrate public authority in his own hands, ostensibly in the name of democracy
but actually at the expense of our complex system of parliamentary
democracy. His actions reveal an understanding of democratic engagement that barely tolerates the dispersal of power, extensive public engagement, and respect for equal citizenship that modern parliamentary
democracies cherish.

So, for example, Harper championed the recent passage of the fixed-
date election law[2] but did not honour its purpose. He precipitated the
October 2008 election to suit his political advantage, presumably fear-
ing a loss at the polls at a later date as the economic situation deterio-
rated. He asserted that Parliament had become dysfunctional, but there
was no vote of non-confidence to support this claim. Indeed, the obvious examples of dysfunction seemed to lie at his door, not at the door
of the opposition parties. It is not clear that precipitating this election
supported democratic engagement more than a different course would
have, namely, honouring widely supported legislation designed to cur-
tail the advantage that prime ministers have traditionally held to call
elections at the time best suited to their prospects of re-election.

Harper has undertaken the project of Senate reform, also in the name
of democracy. Such reform is properly taken through the mechanism of
constitutional amendment, which reflects wide and deep national consensus. Failure to achieve this consensus has not deflected the prime
minister. He has decided to create advisory elections and eight-year
terms. These proposals may undermine the service that the Senate now
contributes to Canadian governance. They may increase the authority
of the Senate at the expense of the House of Commons. The overlay of
an eight-year term on an appointment that is, under the constitution,
designated to last until age seventy-five may invalidate the appointment. The transformation of the Senate along these lines by a minority government has been called 'an end run around the Constitution.'[3]
Meanwhile, Harper's concern for the quality of Canadian democracy
does not extend to ensuring that House of Commons ridings reflect the
best efforts at representation by population.

Harper also denigrates our Charter of Rights and Freedoms, which
has the constitutional status of supreme law. He disdains most of its
substantive guarantees, especially the right to equality, as well as the
judicial protection afforded those guarantees. Instead, he regards legis-

latures as the sole source of social policy, despite the fact that the Charter stands as a popular amendment to our written constitution and that Charter-driven judgments stipulating conformity of social policy to its guarantees enjoy strong public approval. Harper even castigated Prime Minister Martin for being soft on child pornography because he defended the Supreme Court of Canada's ruling protecting those private types of personal expression which were determined to pose no danger to children. More generally, he berates judges for excessive activism when they decide cases that conflict with his own political preferences.

While Harper insists that legislatures alone should make social policy according to popular will, he does not articulate or defend his disregard for formal constitutional amendment, which stipulates otherwise. Moreover, he does not articulate or defend his conservative approach to social policy during elections nor does he allow his candidates to speak openly on these questions. Again, his asserted respect for democratic ordering raises questions.

Consider this example. During the long public debate on same-sex marriage, Harper insisted that Parliament could maintain heterosexual marriage by simply legislating to that effect – and that the courts would defer. In his view, the appellate court rulings across the country extending civil marriage to gays and lesbians stood as precedents only in regard to judge-made common law, that is, they were not applicable to legislation.

The whole point of the Charter, however, is to protect certain fundamental rights in order to put them beyond the reach of politics, electoral platforms, and ordinary legislation. Equality is one of those rights. If a government wants to operate free of the obligation to respect equality, it must legislate to that effect, invoking the Charter's politically costly notwithstanding clause. This Harper was not willing to do.

While Harper criticizes the courts frequently, he is not reluctant to use the courts to serve his own political purposes. He was the named complainant in a leading Charter case seeking invalidation of restrictions on third-party spending under the Canada Elections Act – to vindicate freedom of the electoral purse. Presumably, he would have been delighted if the court had declared the provisions he challenged invalid, owing to their incompatibility with the Charter. It is not clear why what he terms 'judicial activism' is anti-democratic when his political preferences lose out but permissible if his preferences prevail.

This case provides insight into Harper's rather thin understanding of civil society. In his view, the political marketplace needs no regulation of third-party spending during elections because the influx of money does not distort the electorate's preferences. Similarly, his government cancelled the Court Challenges Program, which provided funding to litigate cases raising equality rights and minority-language rights. He considers it inappropriate for the government to fund Charter cases to assist those who feel that Charter rights to equality and use of minority languages have been infringed. Harper apparently believes that Charter challenges should be the exclusive preserve of those who can fund their own litigation, on the one hand, and publicly funded government lawyers, on the other. This stance undermines the fundamental character of the Charter's transformative guarantees by rejecting their stipulated priority over ordinary policy preferences.

This approach also flies in the face of the political purpose of the Charter. The Canadian public supported the Charter to impose standards on the work of legislatures in the form of guarantees of individual autonomy, equality, and fair process. These standards were designed to improve the operation of electoral systems and legislative institutions that had long displayed strong defects both in their ability to provide representation and accountability to all members of the electorate and even in their commitment to these goals.

Harper seems to believe that important elements of constitutional entitlement depend on the resources one has at one's disposal. On this basis, he cancelled funding for women's equality advocacy. So too, as noted above, he attempted to withdraw the funding hitherto available to all political parties in Canada, based on their electoral support, in order to secure a dominant position in his second minority government.

Harper's distinctive views on minority government and the Charter's legitimacy are connected to his views on the administration of government. He has staged confrontations with those who hold high positions in government and are charged with expert and non-partisan responsibilities. For example, in 2007 Harper took the position that Parliament had passed legislation requiring visual identification of voters. On this basis, he sharply criticized Marc Mayrand, the chief electoral officer, for 'making law' when he pointed out that the clear wording of the Elections Act permitted modes of identification other than visual. Mayrand had even brought that point to the attention of a Senate committee as well as to the major political parties when the statute was drafted. No action was taken to expressly require visual identification in the statute's text.

Many questions arise in the aftermath of this deplorable incident. Why hadn't Parliament paid more attention to ensuring that the legislation required visual identification, if it considered this stricture of paramount importance? Why did the controversy arise in the specific case of Muslim women, who in no instance had refused to remove their veils to vote? Whatever political impulse animated this altercation, the prime minister engaged in a public altercation with a government official who was doing his job properly.

This incident is helpful in illuminating Harper's critique of the judiciary. The prime minister contended that Mayrand's sensible reading of the clear text of the statute, which was consistent with the most basic canons of statutory interpretation, was tantamount to 'making law.' This is the same complaint that the prime minister makes against 'activist judges' – that they 'make' rather than interpret and apply law. Harper's long-standing critique of judicial activism, noted earlier, takes on new meaning in the light of his condemnation of Mayrand's reading of the election statute. It would appear that what Harper condemns is not, as one might think, a reading of a statute that is contrary to its text. Rather, it is a reading that stands contrary to his view of the 'correct' policy result when a particular application of the statute arises for determination, *despite* the statutory text.

By extension, it would appear that Harper's injunction that courts defer to legislatures, as the sole expositors of public policy based on democratic legitimacy, entails judicial deference to what politicians, or perhaps prime ministers, want the text to mean but didn't bother to make sure it did mean.

Harper again asserted the authority to stipulate the meaning of legislation in regard to the operation of the Canadian Nuclear Safety Commission, which oversees the safety of nuclear energy production in Canada. The head of the commission, Linda Keen, had ordered the shutdown of the medical-isotope-producing nuclear reactor at Chalk River, Ontario, in December 2007, on the ground that it had infringed international safety standards. The Harper government was concerned that the shutdown stopped the production of radioisotopes used for medical purposes around the world and moved quickly to reopen the facility.

It later fired Keen abruptly to prevent her from making a scheduled appearance before a Commons committee to explain her actions. When she did testify two weeks later, she indicated, on the one hand, that the safety risks were high and, on the other, that the international health repercussions related to the shortage of radioisotopes were not matters that she was authorized to consider.

Natural Resources Minister Gary Lunn and Prime Minister Harper attempted to discredit Keen, the former as to her judgment and the latter as to her alleged political allegiance to the Liberal Party because it was a Liberal government that had appointed her. Absent in this incident was any acknowledgment by the Conservative government of the independence and expertise of the commission or attention to its specific legislated mandate.[4]

Finally, there are the appointments made by Harper during the prorogation of Parliament during December 2008 and January 2009. The prime minister had proposed Thomas Cromwell for appointment to the Supreme Court just days before he approached the governor general to call the October 2008 election. In so doing, he pre-empted a process leading to the creation of a short list upon which the prime minister was to base his selection. The prime minister made negative comments about the process, which prompted expressions of surprise from those involved. This nomination left the appointee in an awkward position for months. If there had been a change in government either at the election or thereafter owing to a vote of non-confidence, the new prime minister would also have found himself in an awkward position, perhaps feeling his authority to appoint a new justice constrained by Harper's action.

Harper then acted precipitously during the prorogation of Parliament, when his government operated under the cloud of an impending non-confidence motion, to make important long-term appointments. In this instance, he confirmed the appointment of Cromwell to the Supreme Court. Because of the prorogation, it was not possible for the candidate to go through the interview process by members of Parliament established for the previous appointee, Justice Marshall Rothstein. Harper also appointed eighteen new senators during the prorogation period, whose tenure will likely extend to age seventy-five.

Harper made these appointments despite the fact that his government might fall on the delayed non-confidence vote as soon Parliament resumed. He thus seized the opportunity to make some of the most important, longest-lasting appointments within the authority of a prime minister when the support of the House of Commons was in question.

These examples demonstrate that Harper places little importance on the complex mesh of powers and restraints that make up the framework of parliamentary governance – including the rule of law, the separation of powers between the main institutions of governance, and the fundamental rights and freedoms entrenched in our Charter of Rights and Freedoms.

Conclusion

Prime Minister Harper might read this account of his departures from the orthodoxies of parliamentary governance as confirmation of his distinctive views on Canadian governance. The response to such an assertion must be that the prime minister of Canada cannot construct his own constitutional framework. Just as he derives his power from our particular constitutional arrangements, so too must he operate within them.

While Harper touts the democratic principle as his ideal, his actions align with another principle – an all-powerful executive authority that makes its own rules on a play-by-play basis. His democratic model lacks the stable commitment to representation and accountability that legitimizes democratic ordering. Even with effective representation and accountability, however, democratic ordering no longer meets the standards of modern governance. The model of the modern constitutional state includes a strong commitment to individual autonomy, equality, and fair process. It also includes separation of politics from law and respect for the institutional roles and arrangements that sustain that separation.

Harper's actions have demonstrated the weaknesses of our constitutional framework. This framework is informal, resting on principles and practices inherited from the United Kingdom. It depends on the sense of responsibility and the self-restraint of those who exercise political power. Harper does not subscribe to these principles and practices. Indeed, he has repeatedly refused to admit and stand accountable for his own mistakes. He has acted in disregard of the cooperation that minority governance mandates and the respect for the opposition parties and their leaders entailed. He has emphasized partisan politics at the expense of the rule of law. He has denied the bureaucracy and public administration the respect due their independence, expertise, and delegated authority. While he has been a strong critic of the courts, he has no compunction in turning to them when they can be useful to shield him from the consequences of his actions or to forward his political agenda. When all else fails, he accuses his opponents of the partisanship that is much more evident in his own actions than in theirs. Unfortunately, the informal but nonetheless foundational components of our constitutional order that Harper flaunts lack effective enforcement mechanisms.

There are no obvious ways to prevent recurrence of the type of crisis as occurred in December 2008 to January 2009. Every element of this crisis makes clear the importance of a citizenry that is deeply versed in the basic principles of parliamentary governance. Each element suggests the need for Canada to embark on a project of solidifying the fundamental principles of Canadian governance and incorporating them into our written constitution. These responses would not stop a prime minister bent on his own political agenda, but they would make things much more difficult. Time will tell whether the regular political processes have checked Harper's arrogant inclinations. It may be that, as time passes, this critical period will be remembered as demonstrating that there is a high political price to be paid by politicians who entertain an inflated view of their temporary electoral mandate at the expense of the received rules of parliamentary governance.

NOTES

1 CBC Newsworld, 4 December 2008, 9:30. Filename: CBCNMORNING-0412DOC1. Emphasis added.
2 See, in this volume, the chapters by Peter Russell and Jennifer Smith.
3 Senate reform: 'Et tu, Stephen? An Elected Senate, without Proper Safeguards, Will Not Be More Representative, Says Parliamentary Expert Ned Franks,' *Globe and Mail*, 8 September 2006, A23.
4 *Literary Review of Canada*, 16 (2008): 3–5.

PART THREE

Constitutional Conventions

6 Why the Governor General Matters

BRIAN SLATTERY

Is the governor general nothing more than a living relic of British imperial rule, who serves symbolic and decorative functions but otherwise acts as the pawn of the prime minister? Or does she continue to exercise important constitutional powers and responsibilities in her own right? To answer this question, we need to shine a light on some neglected corners of the Canadian constitution and consider the delicate interplay between written and unwritten law, constitutional law and constitutional convention. Only then will we be in a position to say whether the office of the governor general is more vital than vestigial, more active than archaic.

The Role of the Governor General under the Written Constitution

Leafing through the pages of the Constitution Act, 1867 – Canada's founding document – we might be forgiven for thinking that the governor general holds very extensive powers. According to the act, the executive government of the country is vested in the queen, who appoints a governor general to carry on the government of Canada on the queen's behalf. The governor general is aided and advised in this task by the Privy Council, whose members she chooses.[1] The queen, through her representative the governor general, also plays an essential role in the federal legislative process and is one of the three components of Parliament, the other two being the Senate and the House of Commons.[2]

The governor general summons the House of Commons in the queen's name and may also dissolve the House before the end of its normal term. When a bill is passed by the House of Commons and the Senate, it is presented to the governor general for the queen's assent. The governor general has the power to give or withhold assent to the bill or to reserve it for the queen's pleasure.[3] The governor general is also authorized to appoint the judges of the Superior Courts in the provinces, who hold office during good behaviour but are removable by the governor general on address of the Senate and the House of Commons.[4]

All this contrives to suggest that the governor general plays a central role in Canada's governmental system, with a finger (or fist) in every constitutional pie – be it executive, legislative, or judicial. The Constitution Act, 1867 seems innocent of what every schoolchild knows: the prime minister and his cabinet are the real repository of political power in this country, not the governor general. Yet neither the prime minister nor the cabinet makes even a cameo appearance in the 1867 act.

How can this anomaly be explained? The answer lies in the fact that the constitution of Canada is not found in a single document suitable for framing and hanging on a classroom wall – not the Constitution Act, 1867, which gave birth to the Canadian federation, and not the Constitution Act, 1982, which introduced the Canadian Charter of Rights and Freedoms. In fact, you could paper the walls of an entire schoolhouse with all the relevant constitutional documents and still not reach an end of the matter. For not only does the constitution comprise a large number of written texts, it also contains a host of unwritten principles and rules that fill out and explain the texts. The point was made with great clarity in the *Patriation Reference*, decided by the Supreme Court of Canada in 1981.[5] The court's exposition of the character and sources of the constitution repays careful study.

The Patriation Reference

The Supreme Court observes that the phrase 'Constitution of Canada' carries a broad meaning and embraces the global system of rules and principles that govern the exercise of constitutional authority in the whole and every part of the Canadian state. It goes on to note that the constitution is not composed entirely of written sources, such as statutes and orders. It also includes unwritten rules of the common law, which the courts have developed over the centuries in the course of deciding concrete cases. These rules are 'unwritten' in the sense that they are nowhere written down in a final or definitive form – although, of course, they are often cited and described in judgments and textbooks.

The court explains that many of these common law rules deal with the powers and prerogatives of the crown. Although the Constitution Act, 1867 states that executive authority over Canada is vested in the queen, it says little about what this includes. To find out we have to consult the common law, which informs us that the crown has a wide range of powers, including the power to declare war, conclude treaties, appoint ambassadors, issue passports, exercise the prerogative of mercy, and incorporate companies – among other things.

The parts of the constitution composed of statutory and common law rules make up the *law of the constitution*. In disputed cases, it is the role of the courts to declare what the law is, to determine whether it has been breached, and to apply the appropriate sanction. So, for example, when the courts find that a statutory provision exceeds the constitutional powers of the enacting legislature, they declare the provision null and void and refuse to give effect to it. In that sense, the law of the constitution is administered and enforced by the courts.

But there is more to the constitution than rules of law, be these statutory or common law. In fact, says the court, important parts of the constitution are not *law* at all but *constitutional convention*. For example, it is a fundamental constitutional requirement that, if an opposition party gains a majority of the seats in the House of Commons in a general election, the existing government must tender its resignation. Fundamental though this requirement be, it is not part of the law of the constitution. It is also a rule that the person who is appointed prime minister by the crown must have the support of the House of Commons; normally this person is the leader of the political party that has won a majority of seats. Other ministers are appointed by the crown on the advice of the prime minister. Ministers must continuously have the confidence of the House of Commons. Should they lose it, they must either resign or ask the crown to dissolve the legislature and call a general election. Most of the powers of the crown are exercised only upon the advice of the prime minister, which means that they are effectively exercised by the latter.

Yet, observes the Supreme Court, none of these essential rules of the constitution can be said to be a *law* of the constitution. They are, in the words of the British constitutional scholar A.V. Dicey, 'conventions of the constitution.'[6] Under this rubric, Dicey included the principles and rules of responsible government, just described, which regulate the relations between the crown, the prime minister, the cabinet, and the Houses of Parliament. These rules developed in Great Britain by way of custom and precedent during the nineteenth century and were exported to Canada and other British colonies when they attained self-government.

The main purpose of constitutional conventions, explains the Supreme Court, is to ensure that the legal framework of the constitution is operated in accordance with prevailing constitutional values or principles. The constitutional value that underpins the conventions relating to responsible government is the *democratic principle*: namely, the principle that the powers of the state must be exercised in accordance with the wishes of the electorate. So, for example, if a government refuses to resign after an election in which the opposition gains the majority of seats, it would be guilty of a fundamental breach of convention. In such a case, the remedy would lie with the governor general, who would be justified in dismissing the ministry and calling on the opposition to form the government. But should the governor general be slow to act, says the court, there is nothing the courts can do about it.[7] A regulation passed by a minister under statutory authority cannot be invalidated on the ground that, by convention, the minister should no longer be a minister.

In sum, concludes the court, constitutional conventions are distinguished from constitutional laws by the fact that the job of enforcing them lies, not with the courts, but with other institutions of government, such as the governor general, the Houses of Parliament, or ultimately the electorate. For this reason, constitutional conventions are generally said to be 'political.'

While the court emphasizes that conventions are not laws, it notes that sometimes they are actually more important than laws. Their importance stems from the values or principles they safeguard. As such, conventions form an integral part of the 'constitution,' as that word is used in the preamble of the Constitution Act, 1867: 'Whereas the Provinces of Canada, Nova Scotia, and New Brunswick have expressed their Desire to be federally united ... *with a Constitution similar in Principle to that of the United Kingdom.*'[8] So, in the court's view, it is correct to say that an act that violates a convention is 'unconstitutional,' even though it has no direct legal consequences.[9] In effect, says the court, *constitutional conventions plus constitutional law equal the total constitution of the country.*

This broad view of the Canadian constitution, as set out in the *Patriation Reference,* has been confirmed and elaborated by the Supreme Court in a string of subsequent cases.[10] So doing, the court has increasingly emphasized the extent to which the two major components of the constitution – law and convention – rest on a common bedrock of unwritten principles. This development is best exemplified by the *Secession Reference*[11] of 1998, which we will now consider.

The Secession Reference

The Supreme Court begins by observing that it is impossible to answer the questions posed in the case without taking into account a number of underlying principles, which have not only academic interest but also immense practical utility. These principles and rules, which include constitutional conventions and the workings of Parliament, are a necessary part of the constitution because problems may arise that are not expressly covered by the written text. In order to endure over time, a constitution must contain a comprehensive set of rules and principles providing an exhaustive legal framework for government.

What are those underlying principles? The Canadian constitution, notes the court, is primarily a written one, the product of many years of evolution. However, behind the written word is an historical lineage stretching back through the ages, which helps to identify the underlying constitutional principles. These principles inform and sustain the constitutional text: they are the vital, unstated assumptions upon which it is based. Although they are not explicitly incorporated in the constitution, other than by the oblique reference in the preamble to the Constitution Act, 1867, it would be impossible to conceive of our constitutional structure without them. For these principles dictate major elements of the architecture of the constitution itself. They are its lifeblood. They assist in the interpretation of the text and the delineation of such matters as spheres of jurisdiction, the scope of constitutional rights and obligations, and the role of our political institutions. Equally important, they are a major force driving the evolution of our constitution as a 'living tree.'

Given the existence of these underlying constitutional principles, what use may a court make of them? On the one hand, observes the Supreme Court, the principles should not be taken as an invitation to dispense with the written text of the constitution. To the contrary, there are compelling reasons to insist on the primacy of the written constitution, which promotes legal certainty and predictability and provides a touchstone for the exercise of judicial review. However, it is also true that, when the preamble to the Constitution Act, 1867 incorporates certain constitutional principles by reference, it invites the courts to turn those principles into the premises of a constitutional argument that plugs gaps in the constitutional text.

Indeed, in certain circumstances, underlying constitutional principles may give rise to substantive legal obligations that pose limitations upon government action – that have real legal force. These obligations may be very abstract, says the court, or more specific and precise. In either case, the principles are not merely descriptive but are invested with a powerful normative force and are binding upon both courts and governments. In other words, in the process of constitutional adjudication, the courts may have regard to unwritten postulates that form the very foundation of the constitution of Canada.

The court identifies four fundamental principles that are relevant to the case under consideration, while noting that these are not exhaustive. They are the principles of federalism, democracy, constitutionalism and the rule of law, and, finally, respect for minorities. Of these, the principle of democracy has the most interest for us here.

The court states that democracy is a fundamental value in Canadian constitutional law and political culture and has always informed the design of our constitutional structure. It continues to act as an essential interpretive consideration and functions as a baseline against which the framers of the constitution and elected representatives have always operated. Although the democracy principle was not explicitly identified in the text of the 1867 act, the constitution evidently contemplates that Canada shall be a constitutional democracy. The silence of the text on this point only serves to demonstrate the importance of unwritten constitutional principles. The representative and democratic nature of our political institutions is simply assumed.

Historically, democracy has been interpreted to mean the process of representative and responsible government and the right of citizens to participate in the political process as voters and as candidates. Thus, the right to vote in elections to the House of Commons and the provincial legislatures, and to be candidates in those elections, is guaranteed to every citizen of Canada by section 3 of the Canadian Charter of Rights and Freedoms. In addition, section 4 of the Charter obliges the House of Commons and the provincial legislatures to hold regular elections and to permit citizens to elect representatives to their political institutions.

Although the constitution of Canada includes both constitutional laws and constitutional conventions, these different sorts of rules are enforced in distinctive ways. As laid down in the *Patriation Reference*, the law of the constitution is generally enforced by the courts, while other constitutional rules, such as the conventions of the constitution, carry only political sanctions. Even in relation to the law of the constitution, judicial intervention is subject to the court's appreciation of its proper role in the constitutional scheme.

What These Cases Mean

If we step back from the *Patriation* and *Secession* decisions, several important themes attract the eye. Prime among these is the thesis that the Canadian constitution comprises three elements: written rules, rules of common law, and constitutional conventions. All three fall within the meaning of the term 'constitution' as used in the constitution acts of 1867 and 1982. The first two elements – written rules and common law rules – make up the law of the constitution, which the courts play a special role in enforcing. The third element – constitutional conventions – normally cannot be enforced directly in the courts. Rather, the task of enforcing conventions lies with other constitutional actors and institutions, among which the governor general figures prominently. This task may be more 'political' than strictly 'legal,' but it is clearly *constitutional*.

The *Patriation* and *Secession* cases also testify to the existence of another component of the constitution – underlying principles. Despite their importance, these elude easy classification as either laws or conventions. In truth, they seem to make up a sui generis category – one possessing its own distinctive character. Constitutional principles are norms of a fundamental character that underpin both constitutional laws and constitutional conventions and provide the foundation for the constitution as a whole. Not only do they serve as a basis for interpreting the terms of the written text, but in some instances they also give rise to substantive legal obligations that place limits upon the powers of governments. To that extent, they are enforceable in the courts. In other contexts they help explain the existence of constitutional conventions and shape their character and scope. Here the principles are enforced, not by the courts, but by other constitutional actors including, once again, the governor general.

In laying out this scheme, the Supreme Court rejects what might be called a 'judicial theory' of the constitution.[12] Such a theory draws support from certain strands of legal positivism, as represented most strikingly by the Oxford legal philosopher H.L.A. Hart. In his influential work *The Concept of Law*,[13] Hart suggests in effect that modern Anglo-American constitutions can be understood without reference to the notion of constitutional duty, which is relegated to a peripheral and unessential role. According to this view, the constitution does not impose *duties* on the executive and legislative branches of government so much as it creates *disabilities*. In other words, the constitution does not generally oblige governmental bodies to act in any particular way; it simply states the conditions under which the acts of these bodies will or will not be *valid*. The constitution's strictures are enforced by the courts, which are authorized to strike down governmental acts that exceed the limits placed upon the powers of their authors. In effect, the courts have an exclusive and final say on the interpretation of the constitution and its application to governmental acts.

The judicial theory is opposed by another viewpoint. This holds that the constitution represents a complex scheme of both powers and duties that are distributed among the three branches of government – executive, legislative, and judicial. These branches are all mandated to pursue the constitution's goals, which ultimately represent aspects of the common good of the community as a whole. Like physicians tending to the health of a community, they work from a shared body of rules, principles, and traditions and are committed to a common set of objectives. Yet they differ in their particular aptitudes, experience, and expertise, and sometimes also in their assessment of what ails the community and its members, and the proper course of treatment. Citizens dissatisfied with treatment received from one body may seek a second opinion, and the body rendering that opinion may take into account the credentials of the first. Although the various bodies may at times be at odds with one another, they more usually work in a coordinated way, for only thus are they able to achieve the broader goals they all share. Each body recognizes that it would be unable to minister to the needs of the entire community on its own and that the pool of wisdom present in the group as a whole is far greater than that held by any single member. This theory of the constitution, which stresses the reciprocal powers and responsibilities of the three branches of government, may be called the 'coordinate theory.'

Returning to the *Patriation* and *Secession* decisions, we readily observe how far they carry us along the road that leads from a 'judicial' to a 'coordinate' theory of the constitution. In their stimulating chapter in this collection, Jean Leclair and Jean-François Gaudreault-DesBiens go somewhat farther. They argue that the *Secession* case suggests that the fundamental principles of the constitution are *legally* binding upon all constitutional actors, including the prime minister and the governor general. They emphasize that, even though such principles may not always be enforceable in the courts, justiciability is not essential for characterizing a norm as law. However, we do not have to agree that fundamental principles are 'law' in the strict sense in order to appreciate their significance as basic building blocks of the constitution. In either case, it is clearly right to say that constitutional actors such as the prime minister and the governor general are legitimate interpreters of the constitution in their respective institutional capacities. As such, they have to cultivate an understanding of their own constitutional roles, powers, and obligations. 'They may be right or wrong in their interpretation,' comment our two authors, 'and they risk suffering political or legal consequences if they are wrong, but having an institutional role implies in our view the possibility of developing a vision of that role.'

One underlying norm that the Supreme Court singles out for particular attention is the *democratic principle*, which holds that the powers of the state must be exercised in accordance with the wishes of the electorate, as expressed in free and democratic elections. Closely related to this is the *principle of responsible government*, which dictates that the executive branch of government – the crown as represented by the governor general – may govern only with the support of the elected representatives of the House of Commons. The latter principle gives rise to some important constitutional conventions. In particular, the governor general must select as her prime minister the individual who is capable of commanding and maintaining the confidence of the House of Commons. If the prime minister loses the confidence of the House, he must tender his resignation to the governor general or request her to call a general election.

It is evident that the principle of responsible government poses significant constraints on the powers of the governor general. These constraints are thought to be largely conventional in nature, in the sense that they cannot be directly enforced in the courts. However this may be, it is clear that the principle of responsible government does not dispense altogether with the powers of the governor general. For the principle of responsible government is not self-administering. It requires the active participation – indeed intervention – of the governor general. She has the responsibility of identifying the person who will occupy the office of the prime minister. And this in turn requires her to determine who commands the support of the majority of the House of Commons. Where a single political party enjoys an absolute majority, the governor general's job is an easy one: she is bound to appoint as prime minister the individual who leads the majority party. Where no single political party commands an absolute majority, the governor general must seek to appoint the individual who has the best chance of being able to form a minority or coalition government capable of securing the confidence of the House. This choice may entail the exercise of a certain discretion, whose scope depends on the factual configuration of the House and any alliances, formal or informal, among the various parties. Where no individual can be found who commands the support of the House, the governor general must dissolve the House and call an election.

What is important to understand is that the self-same constitutional principle that limits the powers of the governor general also requires that she retain a certain discretion – what is often called her 'reserve power.' This reserve is not just a vestigial pool that has *not yet* been drained away by the principle of responsible government (but might be some day). Rather, it is *essential* for the proper operation of the principle of responsible government. For the governor general has the constitutional responsibility to ensure that the prime minister possesses and continues to hold the confidence of the House of Commons and does not attempt to govern in the absence of such confidence.

The Supreme Court is so explicit on this matter in the *Patriation Reference* that it is worth drawing attention to its precise words: 'If after a general election where the opposition obtained the majority at the polls the government refused to resign and clung to office, it would thereby commit a fundamental breach of convention, one so serious indeed that it could be regarded as tantamount to a *coup d'état*. The remedy in this case would lie with the Governor General ... who would be justified in dismissing the ministry and in calling on the opposition to form the government. But should the Crown be slow in taking this course, there is nothing the courts could do about it except at the risk of creating a state of legal discontinuity, that is, a form of revolution.'[14]

In other words, the governor general has a grave constitutional responsibility. It is her role to ensure that the principle of responsible government is observed and not flouted. If she fails to exercise this responsibility, or fails to exercise it properly, the courts may not be able to take up the slack. In the final analysis, it is the governor general who stands in the breach against unprincipled political action that threatens to bring about a virtual coup d'état. She is the ultimate protector of the constitutional order.

What can we say, then, about a situation where the prime minister requests the governor general to prorogue the House in order to avoid

a confidence vote that he seems likely to lose – as in the recent constitutional crisis? Is the governor general bound by constitutional convention to accede to the prime minister's request, or does she have the
power to take her own advice on the matter? Insofar as the governor
general has the constitutional duty to uphold the principle of responsible government, it follows that she has the power to determine whether
a prorogation would violate this basic principle in the circumstances,
and to grant or refuse the request accordingly. In making this decision,
the governor general acts as a trustee of the Canadian constitution.

NOTES

1 Constitution Act, 1867, ss.9–11. The royal letters patent issued by the queen
  to the governor general authorize the latter to exercise all the powers and
  authorities lawfully held by the queen in relation to Canada; see Letters
  Patent Constituting the Office of the Governor General of Canada, effective 1 October 1947, reproduced in Maurice Ollivier, ed., *British North
  America Acts and Selected Statutes* (Ottawa: Queen's Printer, 1962), 653–7.
2 Constitution Act, 1867, s.17.
3 Ibid., ss.38, 50, 55–7.
4 Ibid., ss.96–9.
5 *Reference re Resolution to Amend the Constitution*, [1981] 1 S.C.R. 753 (*Patriation Reference*). My discussion here follows the majority opinion of Mart-
  land, Ritchie, Dickson, Beetz, Chouinard, and Larmer JJ, at 874–84.
6 A.V. Dicey, *Introduction to the Study of the Law of the Constitution*, 10th ed.
  (London: Macmillan, 1959), 24ff. For discussion of constitutional conventions, see: Andrew Heard, *Canadian Constitutional Conventions: The Marriage
  of Law and Politics* (Toronto: Oxford University Press, 1991); Peter W. Hogg,
  Constitutional Law of Canada, 2008 Student Edition (Scarborough, Ont.:
  Thomson Canada, 2008), 22–31; Patrick J. Monahan, *Constitutional Law*, 3rd
  ed. (Toronto: Irwin Law, 2006), 7–8, 53–79.
7 But see *Air Canada v. B.C. (A.G.)*, [1986] 2 S.C.R. 539 at paras. 12–14, where
  the Supreme Court made the interesting point that all executive powers, whether derived from statute, common law, or prerogative, must be
  adapted to conform with constitutional imperatives.
8 Emphasis added.
9 Nevertheless, the court also notes that the term 'unconstitutional' is sometimes used in a narrower legal sense.
10 See especially: *Ontario (Attorney General) v. OPSEU*, [1987] 2 S.C.R. 2; *Os-*

borne v. Canada (Treasury Board), [1991] 2 S.C.R. 69; *New Brunswick Broadcasting Co. v. Nova Scotia (Speaker of the House of Assembly)*, [1993] 1 S.C.R. 319; *Cooper v. Canada (Human Rights Commission)*, [1996] 3 S.C.R. 854; *Reference re Remuneration of Judges of the Provincial Court (P.E.I.)*, [1997] 3 S.C.R. 3; *Reference re Secession of Quebec*, [1998] 2 S.C.R. 217; *Ontario English Catholic Teachers' Assn. v. Ontario (Attorney General)*, [2001] 1 S.C.R. 470.

11 *Reference re Secession of Quebec*, [1998] 2 S.C.R. 217.

12 The following draws on my article 'A Theory of the Charter' (1987) 25 Osgoode Hall Law Journal 701 at 704–7.

13 (Oxford: Clarendon Press, 1961), esp. 26–41, 64–9.

14 *Patriation Reference* at 882.

7 When Silence Isn't Golden: Constitutional Conventions, Constitutional Culture, and the Governor General

LORNE SOSSIN AND ADAM DODEK

As is now well known, the prime minister met with the governor general for more than two hours on 4 December 2008 before he exited Rideau Hall and informed the gaggle of waiting press that she had agreed to his prorogation request. The prime minister would not say what they discussed nor did the governor general issue any statement. As Michael Valpy notes in his contribution to this book, 'by convention,' what transpires between a prime minister and the governor general is not made public, and again 'by convention,' no reasons were disclosed for the governor's general's decision on 4 December. In this article, we refer to these practices collectively as the 'Practice of Non-Disclosure.'

We examine whether the Practice of Non-Disclosure should be considered a constitutional convention, and if so, what the implication of such a convention would be given the evolution of Canada's constitutional culture. We question the existence of this convention, and, to the extent it does exist, we argue that that our constitution has evolved to the point where the veil of secrecy should be lifted from such crucial settings of democratic accountability. Consequently, in the case of the events of December 2008, we conclude that the public has a right to know the basis for the prime minister's request as well as the reason or reasons for the governor general's decision granting that request. Absent a compelling public purpose to be served by silence, public officials ought to be expected to justify their actions, particularly when the legitimacy of Canada's democratic institutions itself hangs in the balance.

This chapter is divided into three parts. The first part explores the nature of constitutional conventions and the distinction between conventions and mere customs or usages. Next, we outline the inconsistency between a Practice of Non-Disclosure and Canada's evolving constitutional culture. Third and finally, we suggest how a regime of transparency and accountability could have and should have operated in the context of the parliamentary crisis of 2008–9.

Conventions and Non-Conventions

There is a tendency to refer to any existing constitutional practice as a 'convention.' This is not only inaccurate but misleading as well. When we are speaking of 'conventions' in the context of the parliamentary crisis of 2008, this is short form for 'conventions of the constitution.' Constitutional conventions are very specific and important constitutional creatures.

Conventions are rules that define significant rights, powers, and obligations of officeholders in the three branches of government, as well as the relations between governments or organs of government.[1] 'Convention' and 'law' are often distinguished from one another. We believe that this distinction may obscure more than it reveals. While conventions may develop in the political arena and may ultimately be enforced through that same arena, conventions form part of constitutional law and it falls to the courts to interpret the scope and meaning of constitutional conventions.[2] While courts cannot enforce conventions, they are nonetheless justiciable questions which form part of Canada's constitutional structure.[3] In this sense, they are related to the unwritten constitutional principles recognized by the Supreme Court in the *Secession Reference* (which dealt with whether Quebec has the constitutional authority to secede unilaterally from Canada).[4]

As Andrew Heard explains in his landmark book on Canadian constitutional conventions, there has been a clear consensus since A.V. Dicey's time that the main function of conventions is to allow legal powers to be exercised in some manner other than that prescribed by the letter of the law.[5] In this respect, conventions are meant to put the flesh on the 'dry bones' of the law.[6] Some conventions set out that the powers of a particular office can be exercised only under certain circumstances.[7] Thus, in 2008–9, the whole crisis was a debate over the meaning and scope of the convention regarding the governor general's reserve powers, which are prescribed only by convention. Other conventions ensure that the legal powers held in law by one body are in practice exercised by some other actor. Examples include the prerogative powers of the monarch, which are exercised by cabinet.[8] Other conventions negate formal powers such as the convention that the federal government will no longer disallow provincial laws. In short, conventions are about defining or restricting the exercise of formal powers that exist in law but are circumscribed in practice.

Importantly, there is a vital normative component to conventions. As Geoffrey Marshall puts it, conventions are 'a body of constitutional morality'[9] whose main aim is 'the effective working of the machinery of political accountability.'[10] In the *Patriation Reference* the Supreme Court stated that the main purpose of constitutional conventions is 'to ensure that the legal framework of the Constitution will be operated in accordance with the prevailing constitutional values or principles of the period.'[11] Conventions must play 'a necessary constitutional role ... [allowing] the political process to function in a way acceptable to the community.'[12] As recognized by the Supreme Court and by many commentators, conventions often conflict with the letter of the law – which is why they cannot be enforced by the courts. In other words, a practice should not be considered a convention simply because it is a practice. An example might be the practice of successive Canadian governments in appointing men of either the Catholic or Protestant faith to the Supreme Court of Canada. This had become so entrenched by the 1960s that further nuances to the practice developed whereby one of the three judges appointed from Quebec would be a Protestant and one of the remaining six judges appointed from the rest of Canada would be a Catholic.[13] The appointment of the Jewish judge Bora Laskin in 1970, however, fundamentally altered this practice in relation to the religious make-up of the Supreme Court, just as the appointment of Bertha Wilson in 1982 accomplished a similar change in relation to gender. These practices, while they may have become customary, clearly did not accord with the 'constitutional values' of the day, which included freedom from discrimination on, among other grounds, those of religion and gender, both in the Bill of Rights and later in the Charter of Rights and Freedoms. They were discontinued with little comment or protest.

In contrast to conventions, therefore, there are practices in relation to legislative, executive, and judicial authority that are understood as usages, customs, or traditions. These practices fall short of qualifying as conventions and therefore should not be construed as part of Canada's constitutional structure. We think that Andrew Heard is correct to criticize the penchant for treating all practices relating to the constitution as 'conventions' rather than distinguishing between conventions and mere usages and distinguishing among conventions based on different levels of importance.[14] These non-conventions, as it were, lack the defining characteristics of a convention discussed above. They cannot be considered integral parts of our constitutional system.[15]

Usages may have no particular reason for existence beyond ceremony, habit, or convenience, while conventions generally advance principles that define the essential characteristics of our constitution.[16] For example, it was widely noted that the governor general eschewed constitutional traditions in the January 2009 Speech from the Throne by, among other things, not reviewing an honour guard.[17] Such constitutional traditions cannot conceivably be considered constitutional conventions because they fail to go to the heart of the necessary operation of our constitutional system. It is to this litmus test that we now turn.

Properly understood, it is hard to see any way in which the Practice of Non-Disclosure could be considered a convention of the Canadian constitution. When closely scrutinized, the Practice of Non-Disclosure simply lacks any of the qualifying features. Whether or not the prime minister explains the basis for his request or the governor general discloses the basis of her decisions does not speak to how or under what circumstances a particular power is exercised. These questions do not relate to one person exercising power that is formally held by another. They neither confer nor negate a specific power. On the contrary, the Practice of Non-Disclosure undermines public understanding of and confidence in the functioning of democracy. As discussed below, this practice is inconsistent with the 'culture of justification' that has emerged as a key constitutional value in Canada. Thus, the Practice of Non-Disclosure is not really a convention at all in the constitutional sense (and thus is not part of the constitution in the conventional sense). In our opinion, we should view the Practice of Non-Disclosure as a vestige of an historical period that should be justifiably left behind as Canada's constitution continues to evolve.

Another way to examine whether the Practice of Non-Disclosure qualifies as a convention is to apply the tripartite test set out by the Supreme Court in the *Patriation Reference*. Under this test, in order for a convention to exist, there must be: (1) a practice or agreement developed by political actors; (2) a recognition by political actors that they are bound to follow the conventions; and (3) the existence of a normative reason – a purpose – for the convention. While the commitment of political actors to the practice of non-disclosure regarding discussions between the prime minister and the governor general is a questionable proposition,[18] we will focus on the critical third prong, the purpose for the purported conventions.

Normative reasons for the Practice of Non-Disclosure are by necessity speculative, since none have been offered. It might be said that non-disclosure encourages candour and ensures the smooth functioning of government. It might be said that an advisory function necessarily includes a measure of confidentiality in the advice sought and provided. It might be said that silence is necessary to ensure that the governor general is seen to be above the partisan fray. The Practice of Non-Disclosure could be said to prevent direct challenges to the authority of the governor general,[19] or to accord best with the historical roles of the monarch in a constitutional monarchy: 'the right to be consulted, the right to encourage and the right to warn.'[20] All of these arguments could be made, but it is difficult to imagine arguments such as these being persuasive in a twenty-first-century constitutional democracy. Trust in a democracy is founded on what we know about vital democratic institutions and key democratic actors, not what is kept from view. To accept that the Practice of Non-Disclosure enhances public confidence in the governor general is to accept that citizens will respect institutions more the less they know about them and the less they see them in action. This would be a depressing conclusion were it true. Recent history, at least in Canada, suggests the contrary logic.

One final way to determine whether the Practice of Non-Disclosure qualifies as a convention is to examine the consequences if the practice had not been followed in December 2008. First, if the prime minister had disclosed what he said to the governor general and the governor general had provided an account of the basis for her decision, would it have conflicted with any written rules of the constitution? The answer is decidedly no. Second, as the Supreme Court has stated, it is appropriate to say that to violate a convention is to do something which is unconstitutional although it entails no direct legal consequence. Would it have been 'unconstitutional' for the prime minister to have posted on his website, the night before he went to visit the governor general, his brief detailing his reasons for his request to her for a prorogation? Surely it would have been unusual, but hardly unconstitutional. Similarly, if the governor general had provided reasons of any length or depth, at the time of the decision or subsequently, in oral or written form, through her own office or via a delegated intermediary, it is hard to see how such actions could be considered unconstitutional. Indeed, no one has suggested that it was improper of Michael Valpy to investigate and impart the tidbits of the meeting at Rideau Hall which were reported in the days that followed.[21] Thus, the case for recognizing the existing Practice of Non-Disclosure as a convention of the constitution is decidedly weak. If we are wrong, and the Practice of Non-Disclosure can be considered a constitutional convention, we address below why it should be abandoned.

The Governor General and the Culture of Justification

If our analysis above is indeed flawed, and the Practice of Non-Disclosure does qualify for recognition as a constitutional convention, we argue that the time has come to abandon this convention. We wish to clarify in this analysis that we are here referring only to those settings where the governor general exercises a meaningful discretion (such as in the cases of dissolution or prorogation of Parliament). In many other settings (such as signing laws into effect), the governor general performs a function but does not exercise any meaningful discretion. There are some obvious parallels between the demand for transparency in Rideau Hall and the growing requirements of transparency throughout Canada's legal and political system. A raft of federal and provincial access-to-information legislation now entitles citizens to see and scrutinize many aspects of public life and government decision making that were once conducted behind closed doors. While cabinet discussions and advice to cabinet ministers are still protected from disclosure to ensure that the debates leading to government decisions are full and candid, those decisions must still be justified once they are made. Indeed, the Supreme Court recognized that even the exercise of the crown's prerogative powers must be justified.[22] Traditionally, neither judges nor administrative decision makers were under a duty to provide reasons for their decisions. Now, the Supreme Court of Canada has recognized that both judges[23] and administrative decision makers[24] are under such a duty. The statutory and common law evolve. They evolve, moreover, in a particular direction for a particular reason.

In this case, this evolution mirrors, and has been shaped by, the evolution of constitutional law. In the *Secession Reference*,[25] the Supreme Court observed that 'our constitutional history demonstrates that our governing institutions have adapted and changed to reflect changing social and political values.'[26] The court further recognized that Canada's tradition is one of evolutionary democracy.[27]

Canada's constitutional law since the entrenchment of the Charter of Rights and Freedoms has embraced what the chief justice of Canada has referred to as a 'culture of justification.' She observes that this culture views arbitrary state action as impermissible; the exercise of power must both be justifiable and justified. She adds: 'Societies governed by the Rule of Law are marked by a certain *ethos of justification*. In a democratic society, this may well be the general characteristic of the Rule of Law within which the more specific ideals ... are subsumed. Where a society is marked by a culture of justification, an exercise of public power is only appropriate where it can be justified to citizens in terms of *rationality and fairness*.'[28]

Lorraine Weinrib, in her article, 'Canada's Constitutional Revolution: From Legislative to Constitutional State,'[29] explains the link between Canada's constitutional development and the culture of justification: 'This structure creates a constitutional culture of justification that affects every exercise of official power, whether legislative, executive or judicial. As exemplars of this culture, courts have the duty of defining the scope of an enumerated right in the context of specific government action and of determining whether the right was breached ... The legislature and the executive must measure their actions so as not to encroach on the enumerated rights or, if they do, to be capable of showing the justification for their actions according to the constitutional standards. Within this culture of justification, respect for rights is the public norm.'[30]

Beyond a concern for rights as a public norm, justification is critical for at least three reasons. First, justification allays the concern that a decision has been motivated by improper, ulterior motives, such as currying the favour of the government of the day. Second, justification ensures that the decision is reasonable and based on legitimate and valid factors. Third, justification promotes transparency and accountability and, in so doing, enhances public confidence in the country's democratic institutions.[31]

In the case of the governor general's decision to prorogue Parliament and allow Prime Minister Harper's government to avoid a vote of confidence which there was every reason to believe it would lose, the absence of justification creates doubt and uncertainty. What reasons did the prime minister present to the governor general to justify his request? We do not know. Was the governor general aware of the letter signed by the MPs in the coalition parties indicating that they intended to bring down the government? We do not know. Did she consider the viability of the coalition? We do not know. Did she consider the scope of conditions which could legitimately be placed on the government if prorogation was granted? We do not know.

Much has been made of the fact that the meeting took over two hours, and that the prime minister was kept waiting while the governor general conferred privately with her advisers.[32] In our view, the attempt to read meaning into silence is untenable. The truth is that we do not know if the governor general's decision was proper. We do not know if it was improper. Not knowing whether such an important decision was proper is unacceptable in a constitutional democracy.

The last time a Commonwealth governor general was faced with a decision affecting the legitimacy of Parliament was in Australia in 1975. The opposition Liberal-National Country Party coalition had a majority in the Senate and used its leverage to defer voting on annual supply bills from the House of Representatives. The Australian government was faced with being unable to meet its financial obligations.

On 11 November 1975 the governor general, John Kerr, dismissed Prime Minister Gough Whitlam and appointed the leader of the opposition, Malcolm Fraser, as the caretaker prime minister. Following this move, the Senate approved the supply bills. On the advice of Fraser, the governor general next dissolved both the Senate and the House of Representatives (the 'double dissolution') and called an election. In that election, the opposition coalition won a majority and formed a new government. At the time of the dismissal of Prime Minister Whitlam, the governor general issued a one-page set of reasons, which began as follows:

> I HAVE GIVEN careful consideration to the constitutional crisis and have made some decisions which I wish to explain.

> **Summary**

> It has been necessary for me to find a democratic and constitutional solution to the current crisis which will permit the people of Australia to decide as soon as possible what should be the outcome of the deadlock which developed over supply between the two Houses of Parliament and between the Government and Opposition parties. The only solution consistent with the constitution and with my oath of office and my responsibilities, authority and duty as Governor-General is to terminate the commission as Prime Minister of Mr Whitlam and to arrange for a caretaker government able to secure supply and willing to let the issue go to the people.

> I shall summarise the elements of the problem and the reasons for my decision which places the matter before the people of Australia for prompt determination.

Why was Canada's governor general, Michaëlle Jean, unable or unwilling to offer a similar explanation to the Canadian people for her decision? Arguably, there was insufficient time to pen a set of reasons, even if only one page in length. But the requirement of justification does not require written reasons. It requires, rather, conveying the basis or bases for the decision. This may be accomplished orally, in writing, directly or through intermediaries. In this case, the only official indication of the decision was a terse two-sentence announcement from Prime Minister Harper that he had asked the governor general to prorogue Parliament and she had agreed.

The prime minister's statement also sheds little light on his motivation for the prorogation. The 'ethos of justification' applies to the prime minister as well as the governor general. Had the prime minister provided a fuller account of his request for the prorogation, or a fuller account of her response, the concern about transparency in the wake of her decision would have been lessened. To the extent the prime minister felt bound by the Practice of Non-Disclosure from revealing details regarding his interaction with the governor general, this is yet another reason for clarifying that the practice does not bind either player.

In summary, if a constitutional Practice of Non-Disclosure does apply to the governor general's decision making generally, or in relation to prorogations in particular, it should be discarded. Discarding conventions for political expediency or personal whim, in our view, would do irreparable damage to Canada's constitution. But, similarly, allowing conventions to remain in force when they contradict core constitutional principles also may damage the constitution.[33] One might ask what utility conventions have if they can be abandoned so easily. We suggest that the utility of conventions is precisely their flexibility and adaptability to changing circumstances.

Canada's parliamentary traditions have evolved over time to adapt to the fundamental constitutional principles of modern governance. For example, the British North America Act (now called the Constitution Act, 1867) authorized the queen and her representatives to invalidate legislation passed by the federal Parliament and also authorized her representative, the governor general, to invalidate legislation passed by the provincial legislatures. Eventually, these powers fell into disuse because they were inconsistent with the principles of self-government, democratic legitimacy, and federal arrangements. The Practice of Non-Disclosure, if it is recognized, is similarly out of alignment with Canada's constitutional culture and should be consigned to the annals of Canada's constitutional history.

Constitutional Evolution

The defining metaphor for the Canadian constitution has been the 'living tree.' Its ability to adapt, to evolve, and to mediate conflict through a principled and pragmatic structure is particularly important in times of crisis.[34] The parliamentary crisis of 2008–9 demonstrates that the time has arrived for the governor general's role to adapt to Canada's modern constitutional principles. These principles dictate that public authorities must respect the rule of law and exercise their discretion with the appropriate degree of accountability. As Lorne Sossin and Lorraine Weinrib note, 'there is no room for constitutional "black boxes" in 21st Century Canada. The Governor-General's exercise of her reserve powers to prorogue Parliament must be based on good-faith arguments consistent with Canada's constitutional principles.'[35]

We agree with Jean Leclair and Jean-François Gaudreault-DesBiens that the governor general should be a constitutional 'actor' and not a constitutional 'object.' Giving voice to her perspective, the considerations she must balance, and the basis for her actions would go a long way in accomplishing this goal. Similarly, this duty of justification falls on the prime minister, requiring him to explain the rationale for requests to the governor general. This requirement is especially important in settings such as this parliamentary crisis, where no other form of accountability was possible. Parliament could not hold the prime minister accountable since granting the request would mean that Parliament would not sit, and the decision to prorogue also could not easily be challenged in court. The governor general's review of this request, therefore, serves as a key accountability forum for moments of crisis in Canadian democracy.

To recognize a requirement of justification operating on both the governor general and the prime minister raises as many questions as it resolves. What form should this requirement take, and does it apply with equal force in all circumstances, or with greater and/or lesser force in some circumstances? To take just one example, one could imagine a requirement to provide reasons of the kind that Governor General Kerr did in the Australian context where a request from the prime minister was being *denied*, but not where it was granted. In circumstances of a request being granted, the rationale provided by the prime minister would be presumed to constitute the governor general's basis for the decision. Consider the example of September 2008, when Prime Minister Harper described Parliament as 'dysfunctional' and asked the governor general to dissolve Parliament and call an election. By grant-ing this request, we would conclude, the governor general undertook an independent assessment of the situation (including, presumably, the implications of the fixed-date election legislation) and agreed that Parliament was sufficiently dysfunctional to justify the calling of an election.

To insist on justification presupposes that the governor general must weigh requests from the prime minister with an open and independent mind. This aspect of the requirement, too, raises important questions. What standard should the governor general be applying to requests from the prime minister? Should she grant requests only if she 'agrees' they are correct and desirable, or deny them only if they appear arbi-trary or illegitimate? Surely, it would be inappropriate for an appointed and largely ceremonial figure to have as active a role in a constitutional democracy as would be the case if she could deny a prime minister's re-quest simply because she disagreed with it. What are the alternatives?

While delineating such a standard lies beyond the scope of this anal-ysis, there are some possible analogies in other areas of constitution-al law. For example, in the *Anti-Inflation Act Reference*,[36] the Supreme Court had to consider whether the government's characterization of the economic crisis of the early 1970s permitted it to legislate in ar-eas under the 'emergency' power contained in the Peace, Order and Good Government (POGG) clause of section 91 of the Constitution Act, 1867. The court indicated that it would not second-guess the govern-ment's statement as to the seriousness of the crisis or determine if it was 'correct' based on evidence. Rather, the court adopted a 'simple ration-ality' test under which it would interfere only if a claim by the govern-ment lacked a rational basis.[37] By analogy to this 'simple rationality' approach, the governor general could deny a request from the prime minister to prorogue Parliament only (1) if the prime minister failed to articulate a legitimate reason for a request, (2) if those reasons were not based on a reasonable factual foundation, or (3) if, viewed globally, the best interests of Parliament and Canadian democracy had not been re-spected. If this test were applied, for example, to the request mentioned above to call an election in the fall of 2008 because of a 'dysfunctional' Parliament, the governor general would have had to consider whether this characterization was based on a reasonable factual foundation. Given the fact that Parliament was not sitting at the time of the prime minister's characterization, this test might have been difficult to meet.

Over time, the body of decisions by the governor general will come to form a key source of knowledge, judgment, and intuition as to the scope and limits of constitutional conventions and democratic legitimacy. This resource, in turn, will lead to greater predictability and coherence in the decisions of future governors general. By analogy, decisions by the Speaker of the House of Commons and provincial legislatures together constitute an invaluable resource on parliamentary conventions. By issuing such rulings in an independent and impartial fashion, Speakers may demonstrate that they are above the fray of parliamentary politics.

Whatever the precise approach adopted in the matter under review here, it would have to be similarly deferential to the prime minister but nonetheless able to accomplish the accountability function inherent in the fact that the prime minister must seek the governor general's approval and the fact that the governor general has the discretion to grant or refuse this request. In short, only in rare and egregious circumstances would democracy be served by the governor general standing in the way of the prime minister's preferred course of action for Parliament. If such circumstances do arise, however, Canada's constitution requires that the governor general do so – and, we would add, that she indicate why.

NOTES

1 Geoffrey Marshall, *Constitutional Conventions: The Rules and Forms of Political Accountability* (Oxford: Clarendon Press, 1984), 210.
2 On the relationship between constitutional convention and constitutional law, see A.V. Dicey, *Introduction to the Law of the Constitution*, 10th ed. (edited by E.C.S. Wade) (London: Macmillan, 1959), 24.
3 See Lorne Sossin, *Boundaries of Judicial Review: The Law of Justiciability in Canada* (Toronto: Carswell, 1999), chapter 1.
4 *Reference re Secession of Quebec*, [1998] 2 S.C.R. 2 [*Quebec Secession Reference*].
5 Andrew Heard, *Canadian Constitutional Conventions: The Marriage of Law and Politics* (Toronto: Oxford University Press, 1991).
6 This quote is attributed to Sir Ivor Jennings in Heard, ibid., 5n.23.
7 Ibid., 5.
8 Ibid.
9 Marshall, *Constitutional Conventions*, 7.
10 Ibid., 210.
11 *Patriation Reference*, [1981] 1 S.C.R. 753 at 880.

12 Ibid. at 857, 858.
13 For a description of these customs, see Paul C. Weiler, *In the Law Resort: A Critical Study of the Supreme Court of Canada* (Toronto: Carswell, 1974), 18.
14 Heard, *Canadian Constitutional Conventions*, 141–9.
15 See *Patriation Reference* at 883.
16 Heard, *Canadian Constitutional Conventions*, 142.
17 See Jane Taber and Josh Wingrove, 'Time to Face Cold Reality? Not with This Honour Guard,' *Globe and Mail*, 27 January 2009, A1; Tonya Mac-Charles, 'Throne Speech Sends Chilly Tone,' Toronto *Star*, 27 January 2009, http://www.thestar.com/Canada/article/577785.
18 Reports from the 4 December 2008 meeting, discussed by Michael Valpy in this volume and in the *Globe and Mail*, had to come from sources close to those in attendance. This would not be the first time that there were leaks from such discussions. Writing within a year of the events in question, Jeffrey Simpson revealed some of the contents of the conversation between Governor General Edward Schreyer and Prime Minister Joe Clark in December 1979 when Clark asked the governor general for a dissolution. See Jeffrey Simpson, *Discipline of Power* (Toronto: Personal Library, Publishers, 1980), 38 (reporting that Clark was taken aback when Schreyer inquired if Clark might consider forming a caretaker government for a few months so that an election would not have to be held in winter).
19 Perhaps akin to what Bagehot described as the 'mystery' of the monarchy. See Walter Bagehot, *The English Constitution*, ed. by Miles Taylor (Oxford: Oxford University Press, 2001), 54 (asserting that the mystery of the monarchy 'is its life. We must not let in daylight upon magic. We must not bring the Queen into the combat of politics or she will cease to be reverenced by all combatants; she will become one combatant among many').
20 Ibid., 67.
21 Michael Valpy, 'There's No Hint Whether Prorogation Came with Strings Attached,' *Globe and Mail*, 5 December 2008.
22 See *Operation Dismantle v. The Queen*, [1985] 1 S.C.R. 441.
23 See *R. v. Walker*, 2008 SCC 34.
24 See *Baker v. Canada (Minister of Citizenship and Immigration)*, [1999] 2 S.C.R. 819.
25 *Quebec Secession Reference*.
26 Ibid. at para. 33
27 Ibid. at para. 63.
28 See the Honourable Madam Justice B. McLachlin, 'The Roles of Administrative Tribunals and Courts in Maintaining the Rule of Law' (1998–9), 12 C.J.A.L.P. 171, at 174, cited by Lebel J., in his concurring reasons in *CUPE*,

Local 79 v. Toronto (City) 2003 SCC 63 at para. 130. See also D. Dyzenhaus, 'Law as Justification: Etienne Mureinik's Conception of Legal Culture' (1998) 14 S.A.J.H.R. 11. Emphasis in original.

29 (1999) 33 Israel L. Rev. 13.

30 Ibid. at 48. Footnotes omitted.

31 The role of accountability as a norm in Canada's constitutional culture has been emphasized by Shalin Sugunasiri in 'Public Accountability and Legal Pedagogy: Studies in Constitutional Law' (2008) 2 J.P.P.L. 93. Professor Sugunasiri is also working on a forthcoming article on 'The Unwritten Constitutional Principles of Public Accountability.'

32 See the account provided by Valpy, 'There's No Hint Whether Prorogation Came with Strings Attached.'

33 This argument is developed further by Jean Leclair and Jean-François Gaudreault-DesBiens in this volume.

34 See Fabien Gélinas, 'Chronicle of a Death Foretold? Conventions of Constitutional Change,' Saskatchewan Institute of Public Policy, 23 May 2007, http://www.uregina.ca/sipp/conference_2007/english/abstracts/F_Gelinas.pdf.

35 'Canada's Constitutional Black Box,' *National Post*, 10 December 2008.

36 *Reference re Anti-Inflation Act*, [1976] 2 S.C.R. 373.

37 Ibid. at paras. 183–4. For discussion of this standard of review, see *Bodner v. Alberta*, 2005 SCC 44, at paras. 29–31.

8 Of Representation, Democracy, and Legal Principles: Thinking about the *Impensé*

JEAN LECLAIR AND JEAN-FRANÇOIS
GAUDREAULT-DESBIENS

The ambiguous nature of the governor general's role in our modern Canadian democracy has been brought to the fore by the recent political 'crisis.' We do not intend to discuss the different precedents that might or might not dictate a particular attitude to the unelected monarchical representative of Canada's head of state. We do not think either that there is a particular Quebec spin on this issue. We rather wish to underline that there might be a danger in addressing this crisis solely through a discussion of the governor general's role. Focusing exclusively on the queen's representative might obscure the more profound causes of the 2008 debate, causes that may actually point to a real, but yet unaddressed, systemic crisis.

In fact, we are of the opinion that the recent political crisis is a direct result of the explosive mixture of Parliament's democratic deficit combined with the erosion of the principle of political representation entailed by equality's inexorable logic. Here, we are talking about equality not as a fundamental right but rather as an idea that broadly shapes the citizenry's political culture, irrespective of its actual implications from a positive-law angle. Moreover, beyond the search for precedents, an inquiry into the role of the governor general requires, according to us, an investigation into the constitutional principles infusing Canada's constitutional order. For instance, a deeper, but also a more contemporary, understanding of the democratic principle might help to prevent the instrumentalization of the office of the governor general, such instrumentalization too often being justified on the basis of a skimpy definition of democracy. In a nutshell, our thesis is: (1) that, in Canada at least, there is an increasing disconnect between Westminster-style parliamentary democracy and the citizens' understanding of democracy; (2) that, for better or for worse, elected politicians are forced to live with that disconnect; and (3) that the current constitutional framework *and* frame of mind are simply insufficient and too outdated to address adequately the deeper problems evinced by the late 2008 parliamentary crisis. In this respect, the mere fact that the said crisis was somehow resolved by the implosion of the coalition as a result of the Liberal Party's support of the Conservative government's budget should in no way be taken as a sign that, to borrow from Voltaire's *Candide*, 'all is for the best in the best of all possible worlds.'

The Logic of Equality and the Crisis of Representation

Ours is a representative democracy and not a direct democracy. The prime minister is not directly elected by the people. The governor general will call upon the leader of the party having won the greatest number of seats to lead government. Such a leader will be able to put on the garb of prime minister if his or her party can establish its ability to garner the confidence of the House. In such a system, the results of an election do not represent the end of the democratic process, although they clearly play an essential role. But whether one likes it or not, the government is chosen not by the people but rather by its representatives, under an elective mandate that is not imperative. This means that, once elected, the people's representatives may change their minds momentarily or permanently disregard their electorate's apparent will (i.e., on the shaky basis of opinion polls), change party, and support or overturn the government. In all those cases, the sanction that they will face will be political.

In some ways, this is more democratic than it might seem at first glance. Whereas the president of the United States can, once elected, be impeached only with the greatest difficulty, in a parliamentary democracy, in times of minority governments, failure to cultivate the confidence of the House will lead to the governing party's and its leader's demise. A prime minister leading a minority government can therefore never override the sovereign will of the House. Thus, failure to obtain the confidence of the latter does not entail an immediate need to put the electoral process in gear, since it can be equated only with an unwillingness expressed by the House to recognize *that particular* party as capable of governing the country. Another party (or alliance of parties) might be successfully invested with that task with the approval of the House. Furthermore, unlike the president of the United States, a prime minister must choose the members of his cabinet from the pool of elected members of the lower chamber, although a Senate appointment to cabinet can be made in exceptional circumstances. In other words, everything turns on the will of the House to which the government is accountable. This idea stands at the very core of our understanding of responsible government.

This consequence of our particular system of political representation strikes some citizens as well as some experts as undemocratic and antiquated. The electoral vote, according to them, should be determinative. Sovereignty lies with the people, not with its representatives, and democracy should be reducible to the will of the electorate as expressed on the occasion of the election. The problem, however, is that dissension arises as to what counts as the will of the people. We must indeed bear in mind that, in a pluralist society such as ours, it is extremely difficult to isolate what that will is, if anything like a univocal will exists at all. For example, one can imagine Stephen voting for party ABC because he supports its economic platform, and Michaëlle voting for the same party because she agrees with its stance on criminality, while disagreeing with the very policy that led Stephen to support it.[1] In fact, notions such as the 'will of the people' more often than not act as epistemological sponges, in the sense that they provide an appealing metaphor that prevents further, and deeper, questioning.[2] In other words, they absorb critical and creative thought and thereby suffocate it.

That being said, some will argue, on the one hand, that citizens no longer vote for individual members of Parliament but for political parties and party leaders, and that the governor general should pay heed only to the prime minister's will, especially in a political crisis such as the one that took place in 2008. On the other hand, many will argue that political legitimacy lies with the party or alliance of parties that garnered the greatest electoral support. Consequently, the governor general should step in and exercise her power in a way that mirrors the will of this majority. The issue, then, is primarily not what the governor general's decision should be but to which political representatives she should lend her ear so as not to act undemocratically. In both cases, though, the governor general is reduced to the role of a parrot, an automaton.

The question then becomes which majority should prevail. For supporters of the Conservative Party, allowing the coalition to defeat the government and to seize the reins of power would have been tantamount to an 'usurpation.' For supporters of the coalition, allowing the prorogation of Parliament would have been equivalent to the very same thing. In both instances, voters view the political negotiations and the strategic delays inherent in a parliamentary democracy as undemocratic and as violating their own sovereign will: 'Je n'ai pas voté pour ça'; 'I did not vote for that.' Or, more precisely, 'I did not vote for him or her, or for his or her policy.' But, obviously, others did.

Viewed under this lens, the crisis – both the immediate one that occupied the minds of (some) Canadians prior to Christmas 2008 and the deeper, yet unaddressed, systemic one that we alluded to – is one of representation. Voters no longer tolerate members of Parliament having the last say on who should head the government. They more often than not envisage their political environment from a 'presidential system' perspective. Their chosen leader (or leaders) should be given the job of leading the country. This is the direct result of the erosion of the principle of political representation, an erosion entailed by an inexorable logic, that of equality, and exacerbated by Parliament's democratic deficit.

In his famous analysis of the U.S. political system, Alexis de Tocqueville underlined that in societies recognizing an inequality of talents, political representation is not only acceptable but welcomed. Individuals not being endowed with similar aptitudes, it is not unreasonable to think that some individuals are better equipped than others to represent their fellow citizens. In the words of Dominique Schnapper, political representation was also legitimized by the 'transfiguration' of the representative brought about by election.[3] Through the process of being elected by the people, the representative somehow came to embody the public interest. This conception of the elevated nature of political representation went along with an understanding of the political community as one that transcended the concrete aggregation of citizens, a *polis* rather than a *genos*.[4]

However, with remarkable prescience, Tocqueville underlined the difficulty, in an age of equality, of justifying the role of a political representative as mediator of the public opinion:

> The nearer the people are drawn to the common level of an equal and similar condition, the less prone does each man become to place implicit faith in a certain man or a certain class of men. But his readiness to believe the multitude increases, and opinion is more than ever mistress of the world. Not only is common opinion the only guide which private judgment retains among a democratic people, but among such a people it possesses a power infinitely beyond what it has elsewhere. At periods of equality men

have no faith in one another, by reason of their common resemblance; but this very resemblance gives them almost unbounded confidence in the judgment of the public; for it would seem probable that, as they are all endowed with equal means of judging, the greater truth should go with the greater number. [5]

Equality, or at least a certain conception of it, therefore elevates common opinion over any other and reduces the representative's role to that of a mouthpiece. Perhaps ironically given the genealogy of today's Conservative Party, political movements lobbying for legal reforms that would allow for the recall of parliamentarians have strongly contributed to establishing that type of zeitgeist.

By putting into question the very concept of inequality of talents, equality also encourages the notion that representatives should be 'like us.' They should avoid any pretence to some superiority of talents in the art of government. During Quebec's last election, citizens were encouraged to vote not for Madame Marois but for Pauline. As if that were not enough, 'Pauline' had to show to the media that she could live with 'simplicity' in her Charlevoix cabin in order to offset the impression of distance created by the disclosure that her principal residence is actually a manor in Montreal's West Island. This insatiable thirst for leaders who resemble us enhances the weight of local – and often trivial – issues in politics. Again, in the words of Tocqueville:

Observe, too, that as the men who live in democratic societies are not connected with one another by any tie, each of them must be convinced individually ... It is extremely difficult to obtain a hearing from men living in democracies, unless it is to speak to them of themselves. They do not attend to the things said to them, because they are always fully engrossed with the things they are doing.

...

I think that it is extremely difficult to excite the enthusiasm of a democratic people for any theory which has not a palpable, direct, and immediate connection with the daily occupations of life; therefore they will not easily forsake their old opinions, for it is enthusiasm that flings the minds of men out of the beaten track and effects the great revolutions of the intellect as well as the great revolutions of the political world.[6]

In a federal system, equality therefore heavily taxes political parties that wish to cater to a truly national electorate. It is much easier to please local interests than national ones, the latter requiring compromises and deference to the legitimate interests and wishes of others.

The relation between equality and federalism is indeed a most complicated one. In the *Federalist No. 10*,[7] James Madison extols the virtues of federalism because the larger the community, he says, the less danger there is that parochial interests will be invoked to stifle the legitimate demands of minorities: 'Extend the sphere [of the community], and you take in a greater variety of parties and interests; you make it less probable that a majority of the whole will have a common motive to invade the rights of other citizens; or if such a common motive exists, it will be more difficult for all who feel it to discover their own strength, and to act in unison with each other.' Even if the truth of this proposition is admitted, it remains that building local political capital is much easier than building national political capital. And, although Madison is right to say that building national political capital naturally entails the burial of parochial interests, one has to concede that such an exercise is extremely difficult when confidence in our politicians' ability to broker compromises is dwindling. Negotiation among politicians inevitably requires some deference on the part of the electorate, a deference that many voters no longer wish to nurture.

This seems especially the case in Canada, for two reasons. First, the federation's significant degree of internal diversity makes it hard to reach any form of consensus.[8] Second, any procedure that smacks of 'elite accommodation' is perceived as inherently undemocratic,[9] even if this particular way of settling disagreements is arguably inevitable in multinational federations or consociational democracies. In this respect, while the *clientélisme* manifested over the years by federal politicians of all stripes is partly to blame for the dilution of a culture of national interest among the citizenry, equality also played a role because of its 'hardening properties.' Indeed, one should not lose sight of the fact that, in contemporary Canada, the notion of equality has taken on a meaning that was virtually unknown when de Tocqueville was discussing its 'levelling' properties.

That more recent meaning stems from the intellectual association of equality with fundamental rights, irrespective of whether or not this association is circumstantially correct from a strict legal perspective. As Judith Shklar observes, rights allow us to achieve our goals against others.[10] In this perspective, the settlement of social conflicts paradoxically requires public declarations of antagonism. Daniel T. Rodgers further notes that 'rights claims invite sharp distinctions between self and others. It is hardly an accident that a political culture repeatedly flooded by popular claims of rights has no easy time talking directly about common possessions, common interests, or entangled and interdependent destinies.'[11] Declarations of antagonism, it bears mentioning, will become increasingly frequent once citizens have appropriated and internalized the discourse of rights and made use of it in all fora. The end result will be the creation of situations of 'non-compossibility,' that is, situations where two ideas cannot exist together, the presence of one making the other impossible.[12] In postmodern, fragmented societies where dissensus, rather than consensus, is the norm, such a zero-sum approach will inevitably preclude, or render extremely difficult, compromises. Actually, compromises will often tend to be perceived as amounting to a net loss.[13] Thus, the mix of equality's 'levelling' and 'hardening' properties creates a rather potent cocktail that discourages the compromises that are necessary in a federation such as Canada.

Strangely enough, as Jacques Julliard and Dominique Schnapper have accurately underlined, although equality has weakened the legitimacy of 'intermediate' representation, it has nonetheless strengthened what one could dub the 'presidential' dynamics of democracy.[14] Even though France's republican system is the focus of these authors' analyses, their diagnosis remains applicable to our own system. Citizens no longer vote for a particular member of Parliament, they vote for the only members of Parliament whose existence they are aware of: the leaders of the different political parties. Television has made possible a tête-à-tête between the citizen and the head of each party, rendering the local representative's mediation unnecessary or, at best, an incidental concern.

This crisis of political representation as well as this new equilibrium favouring the local over the national and the emergence of a presidential dynamics in our political universe are not simply the consequences of equality's steamrolling effect. While our crisis most certainly stems from the inexorable progress of equality, the latter's effect would not be as divisive as it is if it was not buttressed by the failure of intrastate federalism, that is, Parliament's inability to serve as a forum of discussion for interregional conflicts, and by the growing concentration of power in the hands of the prime minister.

Parliament, one must recognize, no longer allows for the expression of regional concerns *as concerns of interest for all Canadians out of a sense of solidarity for one another*. Many factors serve to explain this situation.

First, as is well known, our first-past-the-post electoral system makes it possible for candidates to win their seat with a simple plurality of votes. Many a voice is therefore silenced and finds no avenue to be heard. Second, individual members of the House, whether part of the governing or of the opposition party (or parties), are silenced by party discipline. Only the views that are consonant with those of the party's executive will be allowed. The House of Commons is therefore no longer the place where regional issues will be debated. This very same party discipline, coupled with the powers officially recognized as belonging to the prime minister either by law or by convention, makes him or her an enormously powerful figure. As for the Senate, although useful, it in no way fulfils its function as a house of the regions.

All these features of our parliamentary system of government not only legitimately allow people to forget that ours is a representative democracy and not a presidential one, but also explain the emergence in the last few decades of political parties catering to regional constituencies. Often, these political parties have resorted to political discourses emphasizing radical differences: all Quebecers are separatists; all westerners are polluters. Every appeal to a sense of solidarity is interpreted as a sign of cowardice, of caving in. And, when political defeat is felt to lie close over the horizon, cynicism dictates that local prejudices that helped one gain power be bellowed strongly.

And so, as long as we keep a system that is based on representation, the solution to our political crisis does not rest in a single decision of a governor general, whichever way it may go. It might require a serious examination of our system's democratic deficit, and of some of its structural-constitutional features.

There might indeed be some need to reassess the role of the governor general in view of the changes having attended our democratic fabric since the last dissolution crisis in 1926. British and Canadian constitutional history teaches that, when the facts of the matter are in doubt, it is preferable for a governor general to agree to the prime minister's advice and let the people decide the issue during an election, if such election is needed. That history, as far as the governor general's role is concerned, is one of instrumentalization of the institution. From that perspective, not only was it 'safe' for the governor general to accept the Conservative government's request to prorogue the session, but it accurately reflected the Janus-faced phenomenon of instrumentalization, where one protagonist wants to instrumentalize the other and where the latter accepts to be instrumentalized by the former, irrespective of the legitimacy of its motives or of the fit of those motives with the broader constitutional framework.

The Governor General: From Object to Actor?

Admittedly, there can be strong reasons for the governor general to accept such a fate, but are there not situations where constitutional principles rather that historical precedents could justify a governor general's intervention? Our goal here is not to identify which exact situations would give rise to the application of principles rather than precedents and which would not. Rather, it is to signal that there possibly exists a type of norm in Canadian constitutional law which could provide a strong legal foundation for an active role on the part of the governor general, a foundation that, in some cases, would allow constitutional conventions to be superseded.

As alluded to, the norms we are thinking of here are underlying constitutional principles. In *Reference re Secession of Quebec*,[15] the Supreme Court of Canada stated that these principles 'inform and sustain the constitutional text: they are the vital unstated assumptions upon which the text is based.'[16] It added that 'the principles dictate major elements of the architecture of the Constitution itself and are as such its life-blood,'[17] and that they 'assist in the interpretation of the text and the delineation of spheres of jurisdiction, the scope of rights and obligations, and *the role of our political institutions. Equally important, observance of and respect for these principles is essential to the ongoing process of constitutional development and evolution of our Constitution as a "living tree."*'[18] Thus, like constitutional conventions, principles serve an adaptative function. However, unlike conventions, principles cannot be reduced to mere *political* practices, as structurally and historically important as such practices can be in our system of government. Indeed, principles 'are also invested with a powerful normative force, and are binding upon both courts and governments.'[19] We insist: while such principles may not always be justiciable – justiciability not being a determinative criterion for characterizing a norm as 'law'[20] – they are legally binding upon *all* constitutional actors, including the prime minister and the governor general. It bears noting here that all branches of the state, and, dare we say, all those operating within theses branches, can be considered legitimate interpreters of the constitution when they act within their institutional attributions. This, arguably, encompasses developing their own understanding of their constitutional role, powers, and obligations. They may be right or wrong in their interpretation, and they risk suffering political or legal consequences if they are wrong, but having an institutional role implies in our view the possibility of developing a vision of that role. Obviously, the development of that vision does not take place in a vacuum, which means that these actors must inevitably take into consideration the relevant constitutional norms that frame this self-definition process. Underlying constitutional principles are among those norms. In fact, one of the unwritten principles identified by the Supreme Court, the rule of law, makes this self-definition process mandatory.

Of course, the Supreme Court made it quite clear in the *Secession Reference* that resort to these principles cannot be made 'to dispense with the written text of the Constitution,'[21] thereby affirming the primacy of that text and highlighting the principles' primordial gap-filling function as far as the interplay between them and the text is concerned. As well, we are mindful of that court's rather lukewarm position towards constitutional principles in the 2005 case of *British Columbia v. Imperial Tobacco Canada Ltd.*, where these principles were characterized as 'amorphous.'[22] Indeed, such principles are to some extent 'unfathomable,' as one of us once wrote.[23] However, in that case as in the *Secession Reference*, the court's warnings or reservations had to do with the use of principles in relation to formal textual enactments. More precisely, in the *Imperial Tobacco* case, the Supreme Court rejected the argument that the underlying principle of the rule of law could be relied upon to prevent the British Columbia legislature from enacting a statute it otherwise had the constitutional power to enact, simply because some of those targeted by the statute found it 'unjust.' As can be seen, in that case, if the principle relied upon was to some extent 'amorphous,' so was the argument grounded upon it. Furthermore, as the court was quick to mention, the unwritten rule-of-law principle was being invoked in this instance to constrain the action of the legislative branch of government and not, as is usually the case, that of the executive or the judicial branches.[24] A state institution's particular status might play upon the pertinence of resorting or not to constitutional principles.

Now, if we look back at our recent parliamentary shenanigans, what was at stake was the nature and scope of the conventional limitations on the governor general's legal powers. If we bring into the equation the principle of democracy, which is one of the underlying principles recognized by the Supreme Court, what we end up with is a principle that does not contradict or sterilize a written provision but that rather questions the appropriateness of holding on to an extremely narrow interpretation of the governor general's legal powers, as expounded in a constitutional convention arguably resting on an outdated or highly debatable conception of democracy. Which brings us to a few final observations.

First, the interplay between underlying constitutional principles, which are legal in nature even though they may not always be justiciable, and constitutional conventions, which are often informal, inherently political, and thus not susceptible of judicial sanction, has yet to be thought through. By and large, they remain in the realm of the *impensé*.

Second, granting this *impensée* dimension, it is arguable that underlying principles can be relied upon in order to rejuvenate the governor general's role as a constitutional actor, rather than as a constitutional object, which it currently is as a result of the instrumentalization process that we described earlier. At the very least, the constitutional principle of democracy could be invoked to justify a more transparent decision-making process on the part of the governor general when she is interacting with the prime minister and considering his 'advice.'[25] A stronger use of the principle of democracy could lead to a questioning of the blind instrumentalization of the institution of the governor general. Could it indeed be possible to use that principle as a means by which a more contemporary understanding of democracy would be substituted for an older one, even if it paradoxically leads to allowing a broader discretion to an unelected actor, the governor general? It bears remembering here that the contest essentially boils down to a clash between an informal legal principle and an informal political practice. In our view, there are strong reasons to believe that, in appropriate circumstances, the former should prevail over the latter. Granted, both ultimately rely on principle. But with conventions, principles are somehow bound by the historical context of the precedents that gave rise to the conventions, and that particular context ends up determining the very meaning and scope of the principle. Without being acontextual, the 'principle component' in underlying constitutional principles as defined above can emancipate itself from context and provide a much-needed critical standpoint from which to evaluate age-old, principle-based but context-bound, political practices.

Third, the remark above raises the possibility of using an underlying principle to transform the office of governor general from its current status of constitutional object to that of significant constitutional actor.

It is important not to lose sight of the fact that the governor general is confined to this latter status as a result, it is argued, of constitutional conventions precluding her from exercising any discretion when receiving the 'advice' of the prime minister as to what to do with Parliament. Leaving aside the substantive 'what to do' question, the gist of our argument is that constitutional principles may, in appropriate circumstances, justify constitutional actors (and, should we add, constitutional scholars as well) freeing themselves from their traditional subservience to conventional precedents in order to rethink their role in light of crucial societal changes that render these precedents obsolete. If, for instance, we look at the reason generally invoked to support the view that the governor general is obliged to follow the prime minister's advice about the fate of Parliament (irrespective of the compatibility of that advice with constitutional principles) – that is, democracy – can it not be argued that the conception of democracy that provided the soil for the emergence of this convention is not extant anymore? To take one concrete example, in all likelihood, irrespective of the actual facts that may or may not distinguish the 2008 shenanigans from the 1926 King-Byng incident, there was arguably in 1926 a higher conception of representation shared by both elected officials and their electorate than there is today. As well, there might have been an ethics of representation on the part of elected officials that is currently vanishing. Might not this be of some importance in assessing the role of the governor general? Furthermore, if, in the *Secession Reference*, the federalism principle could form the basis of an obligation on the part of Quebec not to sever long-standing ties with Canada without prior negotiations, could it not allow the governor general to assess the potential strain a prime minister's particular demand might put on the country's political and social fabric? In sum, while precedents are undeniably important and sometimes determinative, there might be strong, principle-based reasons to reject them, and if that is the case, then the actors who reject them bear the burden of transparently providing those reasons.

Fourth, we have referred above to a principle-based broadening of the governor general's discretion *in appropriate circumstances* that would allow her to ignore momentarily, or go against, a particular convention. Again, we have no intention to surmise what such circumstances these could be, except to mention that they could very well be *exceptional* in nature. The further question that this raises is whether or not the prime minister's 2008 prorogation request was exceptional enough so as to warrant the active intervention of the governor general. In this respect, we are not yet convinced that such was the case. On the one hand, the argument that the prime minister was 'using' the institution of the governor general to achieve purely partisan ends does not strike us as evincing the presence of any exceptional circumstance. The prime minister's power to use that institution for whatever purpose that he may see fit is precisely what constitutional conventions have sought to preserve. On the other hand, the argument that the prime minister was trying to avoid a confidence vote in the House, thereby undermining a central feature of the Canadian conception of democracy, appears stronger. Still, it is not clear that the prime minister's conduct was exceptional enough to warrant the governor general's intervention, especially since the allowed prorogation was to be of short duration. Yes, this was to some extent a subversion of democracy, but in no way was that subversion irreversible, since a political sanction by the electorate remained eventually available and, in fact, was close at hand in view of the mere two months' delay (requested by the prime minister or imposed by the governor general, one will never know).

Fifth, the argument that the governor general could step in on the basis of the underlying principle of democracy and bypass a constitutional convention ultimately assumes that her role is that of a guardian of the constitution. This is an appealing role, to be sure, but, in the current state of Canada's constitutional monarchy, it is not without problems. Unlike 'guardians of the constitution' elsewhere, such as the French and German presidents, the fact remains that the governor general (and, a fortiori, the queen) has no elective legitimacy. This may not constitute an absolute impediment, but it does render her position shaky. Moreover, if we compare her position to that of other constitutional monarchs, it is impossible not to notice that there has not been any 'constitutional moment' that has allowed for a strengthening of the governor general's legitimacy.[26] For example, in Spain, the constitutional transition to the post-Franco era was one such a moment, and King Juan Carlos's defence of the newly established democratic regime against Colonel Tejero Molina's attempted coup in 1981 was another. Finally, one does not need to be a supporter of the Bloc Québécois or a radical republican to see the colonial pedigree that still taints the monarchical institution in Canada. All this is to say that, while we are rather sympathetic to a broadening of the role of the governor general on the basis of underlying constitutional principles and to alleviate some of the most deleterious consequences of the crisis of representation that plagues Canadian democracy, it is easier said than done.

Conclusion

The strength of our democratic structure will be measured by our personal willingness to make compromises and sacrifices and by our capacity to defer to our representatives' decisions. However, the latter must demonstrate a capacity to lead us along a path of courage rather than mediocrity. Again, in the words of de Tocqueville:

> I confess that I apprehend much less for democratic society from the boldness than from the mediocrity of desires. What appears to me most to be dreaded is that in the midst of the small, incessant occupations of private life, ambition should lose its vigor and its greatness; that the passions of man should abate, but at the same time be lowered; so that the march of society should every day become more tranquil and less aspiring.
>
> I think, then, that the leaders of modern society would be wrong to seek to lull the community by a state of too uniform and too peaceful happiness, and that it is well to expose it from time to time to matters of difficulty and danger in order to raise ambition and to give it a field of action.[27]

Alternatively, if we prove collectively unable to defer to our representatives' decisions, then we should seriously consider changing our democratic system altogether and undertaking a major constitutional overhaul. For, if we agree that formal law cannot solve everything, we also think that informal law or normative political precedents may sometimes prove insufficient or useless, particularly if they become ossified and impervious to crucial societal shifts. That being said, and irrespective of the path that will be chosen, one thing seems sure: by herself, the governor general cannot save us from the abyss. And, all things considered, it may very well be that we enjoy being at the edge of the abyss.

NOTES

1 Jacques Julliard, *La Reine du monde – Essai sur la démocratie d'opinion* (Paris: Flammarion, coll. Café Voltaire, 2008), 102: 'La pratique des enquêtes d'opinion a radicalement aboli la fiction de la volonté générale ... Grâce à [Gallup], la volonté générale a cessé d'être totalitaire.'

2 On 'spongy' concepts as epistemological obstacles, see Gaston Bachelard, *La formation de l'esprit scientifique: Contribution à une psychanalyse de*

la connaissance objective, 12th ed. (Paris: Vrin, 1983), 78–9: 'Pourquoi aller chercher plus loin? pourquoi ne pas penser en suivant ce thème général? pourquoi ne pas généraliser ce qui est clair et simple? Expliquons donc les phénomènes compliqués avec un matériel de phénomènes simples, exactement comme on éclaire une idée complexe en la décomposant en idées simples.'

3 Dominique Schnapper, *La démocratie providentielle – Essai sur l'égalité comtemporaine* (Paris: Gallimard, NRF essais, 2002), 232: 'La représentation était légitimée par la transfiguration de l'élu du fait même de l'élection.'

4 Ibid., 254.

5 Alexis de Tocqueville, *Democracy in America*, vol. 2, part 1, chapter 2, translation by Henry Reeve, revised and corrected 1899, http://www.xroads. virginia.edu/~HYPER/DETOC/ch1_02.htm.

6 Ibid., vol. 2, part 3, chapter 21.

7 http://www.constitution.org/fed/federa10.htm.

8 Alan C. Cairns, 'Why Is It So Difficult to Talk to Each Other?' *McGill Law Journal*, 43 (1997): 63.

9 This has been the case at least since the Meech Lake era.

10 Judith N. Shklar, 'Liberté positive, liberté négative en Amérique,' in *Les usages de la liberté: Textes des conférences et entretiens organisés par les trente-deuxième Rencontres internationales de Genève 1989* (Neuchâtel: Éditions de la Baconnière, 1990), 107–8.

11 Daniel T. Rodgers, 'Rights Consciousness in American History,' in David J. Bodenmayer and James W. Ely, eds., *The Bill of Rights in Modern America: After 200 Years* (Bloomington: Indiana University Press, 1993), 16.

12 Jeremy Waldron, 'Identité culturelle et responsabilité civique,' *Revue de philosophie et de sciences sociales*, 1 (2000): 178.

13 Jean Leclair, 'Forging a True Federal Spirit: Refuting the Myth of Quebec's "Radical Difference,"' in André Pratte, ed., *Reconquering Canada – Quebec Federalists Speak up for Change* (Toronto: Douglas and McIntyre, 2007), 29.

14 Schnapper, *La démocratie providentielle*, 257; Julliard, *La Reine du monde*, 108: 'Pour le moment, la démocratie d'opinion penche résolument vers le régime présidentiel. Ce n'est pas un hasard. Le système présidentiel, c'est le tête-à-tête de l'opinion publique avec le président au-dessus des corps constitués.'

15 [1998] 2 S.C.R. 217.

16 Ibid., para. 49.

17 Ibid., para. 51.

18 Ibid., para 52. Emphasis added.

19 Ibid., para. 54.

20 On this argument in relation to underlying principles, see Jean-François Gaudreault-DesBiens, 'Underlying Principles and the Migration of Reasoning Templates: A Trans-Systemic Reading of the *Quebec Secession Reference*,' in Sujit Choudhry, ed., *The Migration of Constitutional Ideas* (Cambridge: Cambridge University Press, 2006), 178.

21 *Reference re Secession of Quebec*, para. 53.

22 [2005] 2 S.C.R. 473, para. 66.

23 Jean Leclair, 'Canada's Unfathomable Unwritten Constitutional Principles,' *Queen's Law Journal*, 27 (2001–2): 389.

24 *British Columbia v. Imperial Tobacco Canada Ltd.*, para. 60.

25 This is, in essence, the argument made by Lorne Sossin and Lorraine Weinrib in 'Canada's Constitutional "Black Box,"' *National Post*, 11 December 2008.

26 On the notion of 'constitutional moments,' see, inter alia, Bruce Ackerman, *The Future of Liberal Revolution* (New Haven, Conn.: Yale University Press, 1992).

27 de Tocqueville, *Democracy in America*, vol. 2, part 3, chapter 19.

PART FOUR

Coalitions and Parliamentary Government

9 Coalition Government: When It Happens, How It Works

LAWRENCE LEDUC

Politics is about building coalitions: between groups, regions, inter-ests, and all of the other components that make up a modern, complex, democratic society. The exact way that this process of coalition building works will vary from place to place, because institutional forms and formal rules differ by jurisdiction. But the essence of some type of proc-ess of coalition building lies at the very heart of democratic politics.

Sometimes this process of forming coalitions takes place *within* po-litical parties. For example, the Conservative Party of Canada was formed in 2003 by merging the old Reform/Alliance parties with the remnants of the Progressive Conservatives. In 1961 the New Demo-cratic Party (NDP) was created in a similar manner by bringing the old Co-operative Commonwealth Federation (CCF), based largely in the west, together with the interests of organized labour. But, even when it does not involve a formal restructuring of a political party, we can see such a process of coalition building at work in our everyday politi-cal life. It is common, for example, when discussing the Conservative Party, to speak of the old 'Mulroney coalition,' which involved a careful balancing of the interests of western Canada and those of 'soft nation-alists' in Quebec. Mulroney's success in this coalition-building effort led to landslide victories in the 1984 and 1988 federal elections. When it fell apart in 1993, the party had to rebuild its coalition in order to re-gain power – a process that took more than ten years. Reformers from Alberta, however enthusiastic, could never have achieved power by themselves at the national level.

We can also see the process of coalition building at work by observ-ing how it proceeds under quite different types of institutional struc-tures. In the U.S. Congress it is all but impossible to pass any significant legislation without putting together a coalition that reaches across party lines. The McCain-Feingold party-finance reform legislation, for example, was co-sponsored by Senator John McCain (R. Arizona) and Senator Russell Feingold (D. Wisconsin). This is a common practice in the American legislative process, because voting on legislation never proceeds along straight party lines, as it tends to do in Canada. Although his party holds majorities in both Houses of Congress, President Barack Obama will be aware from the beginning of his administration that he cannot count on Democratic Party votes alone to pass important legislation in areas such as health care, Social Security, or regulatory reform. Such legislation, if and when it is passed into law, will invariably involve the construction of cross-party coalitions of one kind or another. The essence of legislative leadership in the American system lies in the ability of the president and congressional leaders to construct such coalitions. Without them, the American legislative system easily bogs down into what has sometimes been called 'gridlock.'

Minority governments in Canada likewise can succeed only by constructing coalitions around particular issues or policies, whether we describe the process that way or not. Pierre Trudeau's minority government (1972–4) survived with NDP support, as more recently did that of Paul Martin (2004–6). In crafting the budget that brought an end to the most recent parliamentary crisis, the Conservatives pursued a path explicitly designed to maximize the likelihood of gaining Liberal support.[1] As Jack Layton pointed out following Michael Ignatieff's announcement that the Liberals would not oppose it, the budget was the product of a Liberal-Conservative coalition in all but name.[2]

Forming a Coalition Government

While coalition building in some form is a near-universal practice of democratic politics, Canadians might be surprised to learn that coalitions in many countries are constructed in much more formal ways.[3] In countries with multi-party systems – most of the democratic world – parliamentary elections cannot be expected to produce conclusive results. (Presidential elections, where there is a single winning candidate, are a different matter.) While one party may win the largest number of seats in a parliament or legislature, it is relatively rare for a single party to control a majority of the seats. Thus, *after* the election, the process of forming a coalition government begins. In some countries, this process can be quite formal, while in others it begins more informally through talks between the party leaders. In the Netherlands, following an election, the queen appoints an *informateur*, whose job it is to consult all of the party leaders in order to ascertain what coalitions may be possible. Typically, the person chosen for the role of *informateur* is a senior statesman – someone with extensive parliamentary experience and who enjoys the respect of all parties. In the Dutch example, the *informateur*'s role may extend to chairing formal coalition talks between several of the parties, or a different person (a *formateur*) may be appointed to manage this part of the process. When an agreement appears within reach, it is common for the prospective prime minister to be appointed as the *formateur*, so that the process becomes essentially that of constructing the cabinet and concluding the coalition agreement.

The objective of a process of this kind is to determine the shape of the government that will be formed and the manner in which it will govern. If a coalition partner is to receive a share of cabinet positions, this must be discussed. A party that agrees to enter a coalition with one or more of its rivals will generally also seek agreement on the direction of public policy, at least in the areas where it has the most concern. Stability is frequently an important consideration, since a coalition agreement is expected to last for a specified period of time – often a full parliamentary term. In Germany, for example, it is not possible to defeat a government in the Bundestag without proposing an alternative to it at the same time. In the Dutch example, the process that took place following the 2006 election led to the formation of a coalition of three parties. The two largest parties in the Tweede Kamer (the lower house of the Dutch parliament) – the Christian Democrats (forty-one seats) and Labour (thirty-three seats) – joined with one smaller party – the Christian Union (six seats) – in an agreement to share power. Together, these three parties controlled a majority of the seats in the 150-seat chamber, thereby assuring parliamentary stability. The leader of the Christian Democrats became prime minister, and the Labour leader was named finance minister. The Christian Union received two ministerial positions. The agreement that they signed was entitled *Living Together, Working Together*. As of this writing, this cabinet is still in power.

While I have described the Dutch process of forming a coalition in some detail, to give a sense of its organization and formality, the process of forming a coalition may proceed rather differently in other countries. In Australia, for example, the Liberal governments of John Howard were coalition governments, in which the dominant Liberals shared power with their cousins in the much smaller National Party.[4] In this case, however, the shape of the coalition would have been known well in advance, since the Liberal and National parties were long-standing partners in government. Therefore, only a few specific matters, such as the assignment of specific cabinet positions, would have to be decided following the election. The details of a coalition agreement do not need to be hammered out between parties that already have the framework of such an agreement in place prior to the election, and no *informateur* is required if the leader of the largest party remains firmly in control.

Just as there are different processes that may be used in forming a coalition, there are also different types of coalitions. Perhaps the most common type is the one in which the largest party takes on one of the smaller parties as a 'junior partner.' This model works well in those countries where there are one or two large parties in the parliament and a few smaller parties. In Germany, for example, the Christian Democratic Union (CDU) held power for a number of years in partnership with the much smaller Free Democratic Party (FDP). In later years, the Social Democratic Party (SPD) forged the same type of partnership with the centrist FDP. But, when Gerhard Schröeder became chancellor following the 1998 election, he instead formed a coalition with the Green Party. This 'Red-Green' coalition government was re-elected in 2002. Later, following the inconclusive 2005 election, Germany turned instead to a 'grand coalition' of the two largest parties led by Angela Merkel. So we can see that the concept of a coalition government does not always mean the same thing, even in those countries where such governments are commonplace.

Coalitions are generally formed *after* an election, not before. In the German example, the grand coalition that was ultimately formed would not have been considered as an alternative prior to the election result being known. There are exceptions to this general practice, however, even within the same country. The SPD and Greens campaigned as a coalition in 2002, although both parties presented their own separate lists of candidates under the German system. Tom Flanagan, not long ago one of Stephen Harper's closest advisers, argues that the proposed Liberal-NDP coalition would have been illegitimate, because these two parties did not campaign as coalition partners in the preceding election.[5] Under our first-past-the-post electoral system, this would have been extremely difficult to do. It would involve presenting a joint 'coalition' candidate in every constituency or, alternatively, withdrawing either the Liberal or the NDP candidate in each riding. In proportional-representation systems, this issue does not generally arise, and parties typically present their own lists of candidates even if they anticipate subsequent coalition talks with other parties.[6] Under the French two-round electoral system, it is possible for parties to compete in the first round and form alliances in the second, which takes place two weeks later. Socialist and Communist candidates did this routinely for a number of years, and Socialists and Greens have done it more recently on a selective basis.[7]

Types of Coalitions

We have already mentioned, by way of examples, most of the major types of coalition governments that can be found in the democratic world. One of the most common types – *the partnership between a large party and a smaller one* – occurs most frequently in those countries whose electoral arrangements are more likely to produce this type of party configuration. The events of the 2007 election in Ireland provide a good example of the process of coalition formation in parliaments where one or two larger parties tend to dominate. Prior to the election, the largest party (Fianna Fáil), which held 81 of the 165 seats in the Dáil, had been in coalition with the much smaller Progressive Democrats, who held eight seats. This coalition had lasted for a full parliamentary term and it was expected that, if the government was re-elected, the coalition agreement would remain in place. However, while Fianna Fáil emerged as the clear winner with seventy-seven seats, its coalition partner lost six of its eight seats in the election. It soon became evident that the continuation of a coalition with the Progressive Democrats was not tenable. Over the next few weeks, the taoiseach (prime minister) reached a new coalition agreement with the Green Party, which had won six seats in the election. While other coalitions might have been possible, the Fianna Fáil–Green coalition appeared the most viable, even though it was not the first choice of the Fianna Fáil leadership.

But not all countries can quite so easily form a coalition of this kind, or replace a coalition partner that loses ground in an election. In Ireland, there was for a time the possibility that Fianna Fáil might have been unable to form a new coalition. In the event that the largest party were replaced in government by an alternative, the process would have become more complicated. The second largest party in the Dáil, Fine Gael, held only fifty seats and would have had considerably greater difficulty forming a coalition in which it could dominate. A similar circumstance existed in Sweden following the 2006 election, in which the minority Social Democratic government of Göran Persson was defeated. As the largest party in the 349-seat Riksdag, the Social Democrats had generally been able to govern alone, or in partnership with a smaller party such as the Greens. But replacing them has required a four-party coalition, since no other single party commands enough seats to form an alternative government. Thus, following the election of September 2006, in which the governing Social Democrats lost fourteen seats (but remained the largest single party), the government was replaced by a coalition of four centre-right parties.[8]

This brings us to an alternative to the 'junior partner' model of coalition. Particularly in systems that have more proportional electoral arrangements, the number of political parties represented in a parliament may be larger, and the ability of any one party to dominate may thus be significantly reduced. Such an example has already been seen in the case of the Netherlands, in which three parties formed a coalition government following the most recent election. We might refer to a coalition of three or more parties, such as the present governments in the Netherlands and Sweden, as a *multi-party coalition*. An arrangement of this kind tends to function more as a collective form of government. The leader of one of the coalition parties typically becomes prime minister, and cabinet positions are shared among its members in relative proportion to their parliamentary strength. Under such an arrangement, the coalition agreement becomes more important than the cabinet positions, because without such an agreement the policy direction of a government involving three or four political parties could be somewhat unclear. Such governments can, of course, involve a greater risk of instability, particularly if the parties have different policy priorities and find it difficult to work together. But multi-party coalitions also have the advantage of representing a fairly broad spectrum of the electorate.[9] The Netherlands had such a government previously, during the 1990s, which was considered quite successful. Known as the 'Purple Coalition' because of the red and blue colours of its component parties, the participating parties campaigned successfully for re-election in 1998 under the slogan 'Purple Works.'[10]

Yet a third type of coalition government is the *grand coalition*, which is the kind of government that Germany has today. In a grand coalition, the largest parties come together to form a government. This might be done for the purpose of reducing or eliminating the influence of the minor parties in the coalition process. Or it might be a strategy pursued for a period of time 'for the good of the country,' permitting parties that have been rivals in the election to set aside their differences and/ or work out compromises on major policy issues. Austria had a grand coalition of right and left parties for a number of years until eventually one of the parties withdrew from the arrangement and formed a coalition with a smaller party that was more ideologically compatible.[11] In Germany, the decision to form a grand coalition of the CDU/CSU and SPD following the 2005 election came about partly in response to the closeness of the election results, as well as the fact that any possible combination of a larger party with one of the smaller parties would not in itself have produced a majority.[12] But grand coalitions can also be multi-party coalitions. In Switzerland, governments have been formed now for some time by coalitions of four parties spanning the centre, right, and left of the political spectrum.[13] The Swiss refer to this arrangement as the 'magic formula.'

Why Not in Canada?

Given the nature of Canadian society and politics, it is perhaps surprising that coalition governments have not been tried more often in the past. We have had multiple political parties for some time, and we have had periods of minority government with some frequency.[14] But the only instance of a coalition government at the federal level was the Borden Union government of 1917, in which both Conservatives and Liberals held positions. However, this was brought about more by the pressures of wartime than by the tides of politics. There have been other instances that could easily have produced coalitions, and periods of minority government in which one of the major parties held power with the tacit support of another party. Mackenzie King formed a minority government in 1921 with the support of the Progressives but did not appoint any Progressives to cabinet positions.[15] Pierre Trudeau reportedly offered cabinet positions to the NDP following the 1980 election in an attempt to produce a more nationally representative government, but Ed Broadbent declined his offer. At the provincial level, the assumption of power in Ontario by David Peterson's Liberals with the support of the NDP following the 1985 election is perhaps the best-known instance.[16] But the NDP, although it signed a formal two-year agreement to support the Peterson government on matters of confidence, did not seek or obtain seats in the cabinet.

Perhaps the reason why coalitions have not been more common in Canadian politics is that the British political traditions that we have inherited cause us to think of Parliament in terms of 'government' and 'opposition' rather than simply being comprised of different parties and interests. This may have been appropriate when there were only two political parties to deal with, and one or the other of them was always in power. But those days are long gone. After the Progressives in 1921, we had significant representation in Parliament of parties such as Social Credit, the CCF, and today the NDP and Bloc Québécois. Part of the reason that minor parties might be reluctant to go into coalition with one of the major parties, even if they were offered the opportunity, is the fear of losing their separate identity. King hoped that he might entice some of the Progressives into becoming Liberals. Broadbent feared that going into coalition with Trudeau might have put his party's support in the west at risk. On the other hand, Joe Clark's minority government might well have survived had he offered a cabinet position or coalition agreement to the leader of the Créditistes.

Instead of considering coalitions, leaders of minority governments in Canada talk bravely about 'governing as if they had a majority' or 'carrying out a mandate to govern.' Such statements are nothing more than a refusal to recognize political reality. Clark's Conservatives obtained 36 per cent of the popular vote in the 1979 election – the same percentage obtained by Stephen Harper's Conservatives in 2006. The largest party in the House of Commons does not obtain a 'mandate to govern' from little more than a third of the voters. Such a mandate can come only from a majority of the members of the House of Commons, a point emphasized by several of the authors in this volume. But Canadian politicians in this situation typically forge ahead, either oblivious to the risks or believing their own bravado. 'No deals,' they proclaim. Clark's government was defeated after only seven months in office, and all six of the Créditiste members from Quebec lost their seats in the 1980 election. Looked at from the point of view of either the minority governing party or the potential junior partner, 'no deals' can be a losing strategy for both.

Another reason that works against the formation of coalitions in Canada is the common belief held by the leaders of minority governments that they will soon be able to convert their minority position into a parliamentary majority. John Diefenbaker formed a minority government following the 1957 election and, less than a year later, seized the opportunity to seek a majority, winning one of the largest landslide election victories in Canadian history. The Clark government was mesmerized by the Diefenbaker example, believing that if it were defeated in Parliament, the voters would punish the opposition parties for denying the government the legitimate opportunity to carry out its electoral mandate. Of course, the government was proven wrong in that perception. But this has not prevented subsequent minority prime ministers from engaging in the same type of wishful thinking. Following the 2006 election, the Harper government embarked on a course of parliamentary brinkmanship, precipitating one parliamentary crisis after another and eventually getting its wish of a new election in which it tried unsuccessfully to win a majority of seats. The outcome of a second minority government was clearly a disappointment for the majority-seeking Conservatives. Following the election, the party leaders vowed to 'make the minority parliament work,' and Canadians might have hoped in vain that this would actually happen. It was not long, however, before the game of brinkmanship resumed, sparking yet another parliamentary crisis, this time resulting in the prorogation.

Considering the Alternatives

Had the Conservatives been defeated in Parliament so soon after the October election, Stephen Harper almost certainly would have advised the governor general to dissolve Parliament and authorize yet another election. Flanagan argues that this would have been her only option.[17] Of course, this is simply not true, legally or politically, as several of the chapters in this volume convincingly document. She might well have refused Harper's request and instead invited the Liberal-NDP coalition to form a new government. Such a decision would have been in line with the practice of coalition formation in nearly all of the countries discussed as examples in this chapter. There is no reason why Canadians should be subjected to repeated elections until the governing party somehow wins a majority of seats. With 37.6 per cent of the vote and 143 seats in the House of Commons, the Conservatives were able to form a viable government. But, with a combined 44 per cent of the vote and 114 seats, so were the Liberals and NDP. A Liberal-NDP coalition would arguably have been more stable, since it was based on a formal agreement and assurances from the Bloc that the government would not be defeated in Parliament for a period of at least eighteen months. Minority governments that stumble either wilfully or accidentally from one parliamentary crisis to another are considerably less stable than a coalition based on a signed agreement.[18]

Flanagan's argument appears to derive from a modern myth that it is the voters who choose the prime minister, or, as Jennifer Smith argues in this volume, the active promotion of a 'populist' conception of democracy rather than a parliamentary one. Much of the reporting in the media during election campaigns encourages this tendency, focusing as it does on the activities and views of the leaders over the course of the campaign. 'Who won the debates?' we are asked. 'Is Harper up or down in the polls?' We become accustomed to thinking of elections as a contest between the leaders, and indeed many voters may have the leaders or their parties in mind as they cast a vote for their local candidate. But Canadian voters are *not* presented with choices between leaders, as Americans are in electing their president. Canadians did not 'reject' Stéphane Dion as prime minister, nor did they elect Stephen Harper to that position. We have only one vote – for our member of Parliament – and both Dion and Harper were duly elected to *that* office, as were Jack Layton and Gilles Duceppe. Under our political system, it is only the members of the House of Commons who decide together who shall form the government and are accountable to the voters for the choices that they make.

Pierre Trudeau once referred to members of Parliament as 'nobodies.'[19] Members of Parliament are not nobodies. They are our elected representatives – the only ones we have. Neither the governor general nor the prime minister can claim a mandate from the voters, because it is only the elected members who hold such a mandate.[20] This applies to the members of *all* parties, whether they are elected as members of the Conservative Party, the Liberal Party, the NDP, or the Bloc. To argue that a coalition government is somehow illegitimate, or that members of certain parties in Parliament should have no voice in its formation or survival, is simply to deny the reality of our current politics, or even to subvert the fundamental principles of parliamentary democracy.

Despite the outcome of our most recent political crisis, Canada will very likely someday have a coalition government of some type. Peter Russell has argued persuasively in this book and elsewhere that we have to learn to make minority government work, because minority governments in one form or another are here to stay.[21] The share of the popular vote won by the two major parties has declined substantially in recent years, and it is likely to continue to decline in the future as long as there are other choices available to the voters.[22] Of course, minority governments *could* be made to work if our political leaders truly decided to put an end to Ottawa's continual game of political brinkmanship and partisan infighting. But a more practical alternative is the formation of a coalition that reflects the collective views of the voters. The more formal such a coalition was, the better it would work and the more stable it would be. A coalition government would be better able to govern in the interest of all Canadians than a minority government that spends most of its time and energies developing electoral strategies in pursuit of a majority in yet another election. A coalition government would certainly be more stable than a minority government that lurches from one parliamentary crisis to another, sometimes precipitating such crises itself in the hope of engineering its own defeat. A coalition government would also represent a wider spectrum of the electorate than any single-party minority government, and even some majorities.[23] And, best of all, it would be more faithful to the principles of representative democracy.

NOTES

1 Chantal Hébert, 'A Liberal-Red Budget in Tory-Blue Clothing Will Likely Ensure Survival for Harper,' Toronto *Star*, 28 January 2009.
2 News conference, 28 January 2009.
3 On the formation of governments in European countries, see Ian Budge and Hans Keman, *Parties and Democracies: Coalition Formation and Government Functioning in Twenty States* (Oxford: Oxford University Press, 1990); Michael Laver and Kenneth Shepsle, eds., *Making and Breaking Governments* (Cambridge: Cambridge University Press, 1994); and Wolfgang Müller and Kaare Strøm, eds., *Coalition Governments in Western Europe* (Oxford: Oxford University Press, 2000).
4 Howard's Liberal-National coalition government was defeated by Labor in the Australian general election of 24 November 2007.
5 Tom Flanagan, 'Only Voters Have the Right to Decide on the Coalition,' *Globe and Mail*, 10 January 2009.
6 As Grace Skogstad points out in this volume, the conditions needed for the formation of coalitions both within and between parties would be substantially improved by the adoption of a more proportional electoral system. On this issue, she cites Alan Cairns, who made this very point more than forty years ago. Alan Cairns, 'The Electoral System and the Party System in Canada: 1921–1965,' *Canadian Journal of Political Science*, 1 (1968): 55–80. On the electoral-reform debate in Canada more generally, see Henry Milner, *Making Every Vote Count* (Toronto: Broadview, 1999).
7 Lawrence LeDuc, Richard G. Niemi, and Pippa Norris, eds., *Comparing*

Democracies 2: New Challenges in the Study of Elections and Voting (London: Sage Publications, 2002).

8 The four parties were the Moderate Party (M), the Liberal People's Party (FP), the Christian Democrats (KD), and the Centre Party (C). The parties each fielded their own lists of candidates in the election but presented a joint election manifesto as the 'Alliance for Sweden.'

9 See Shira Herzog, 'A Lesson on Coalition Rule, Brought to You by Israel,' *Globe and Mail*, 17 December 2008.

10 The participating parties were Labour (PvdA), the Liberals (VVD), and D'66. The coalition parties spanned the ideological spectrum of Dutch politics from centre-left to centre-right.

11 From 1986 to 2000, Austria was governed by a grand coalition of the Socialist (SPÖ) and Austrian People's (ÖVP) parties – the two largest parties. Following the 1999 election, in which the Freedom Party (FPÖ) substantially increased its share of seats in the 183-seat National Council and the two largest parties both lost ground, the ÖVP formed a new coalition with the FPÖ.

12 The CDU/CSU won 226 seats in the election and the SPD 222. No combination of either of these parties with one of the smaller parties (the FDP, Greens, or Left Party) would have commanded a majority in the 614-seat Bundestag. See Geoffrey Roberts, 'The German Bundestag Election of 2005,' *Parliamentary Affairs*, 59 (2006): 668–81.

13 The four parties are the Swiss People's Party (SVP), the Social Democratic Party (SP), the Free Democratic Party (FDP), and the Christian Democratic People's Party (CVP). Together, these four parties held 167 of the 200 seats in the National Council following the October 2007 election.

14 On the changes in the Canadian party system since 1993, see R. Kenneth Carty, William Cross, and Lisa Young, *Rebuilding Canadian Party Politics* (Vancouver: UBC Press, 2000).

15 The Progressives elected 64 members to the 235-seat Parliament in 1921.

16 There is also a good example of a coalition government at the provincial level in Saskatchewan. Following the 1999 election, the Liberals supported the NDP government of Roy Romanow and also held a seat in Romanow's cabinet.

17 Flanagan, 'Only Voters Have the Right to Decide on the Coalition.'

18 This point was made quite compellingly by Bob Hepburn, 'Coalition Government a Missed Opportunity,' Toronto *Star*, 29 January 2009. Hepburn also argues that coalitions are particularly appropriate in times of national crisis.

19 Peter Russell, *Two Cheers for Minority Government* (Toronto: Emond/Mont-gomery, 2008), 33.
20 Although the concept of a 'mandate' from the voters can have multiple meanings. See Harold D. Clarke, Jane Jenson, Lawrence LeDuc, and Jon H. Pammett, *Absent Mandate: Canadian Electoral Politics in an Era of Restructuring* (Toronto: Gage, 1996).
21 Russell, *Two Cheers for Minority Government*. See also William Cross, 'And the Future Is: Coalition,' *Globe and Mail*, 26 January 2009.
22 Together, the Liberals and Conservatives obtained 63 per cent of the vote in the 2008 election, meaning that more than a third of Canadians voted for other parties.
23 The Liberals, for example, formed a majority government following the 1997 election with 155 of the 295 seats in the House of Commons and 38 per cent of the popular vote. The present Labour government in Britain won its third parliamentary majority in the 2005 election (356 of the 646 seats) with just 35 per cent of the popular vote.

10 Learning to Live with Minority Parliaments

PETER H. RUSSELL

On 14 October 2008 Canadians elected a House of Commons in which no political party had a majority. This result is what we have come to call a minority Parliament. It is the thirteenth time in Canadian history that an election has resulted in a minority Parliament.[1] Half of the eighteen elections held since 1957 have produced minority parliaments. The last three elections all produced minority parliaments. If an election is held in the next year or so, I would bet a lot that it would produce yet another minority Parliament.

The reason for elections resulting in minority governments is clear. No political party is very popular with Canadians. Dyed-in-the-wool Liberals and Tories may hate to hear this, but I speak the truth. In the recent election, the Conservatives and Liberals *between* them garnered only 63.8 per cent of the popular vote. The 37.6 per cent that voted for Stephen Harper's Conservatives is just 1.4 per cent higher than the Conservative total in the January 2006 election. Like it or not, since 1921, a significant minority of Canadians in every federal election have voted for parties other than the Liberals or Conservatives. Indeed, were it not for the distorting effect of our first-past-the-post electoral system, only three elections since 1921 would have produced majority governments.

Because minority parliaments have become so frequent and are likely to remain so in the future, it is high time that we Canadians became more savvy about how best to live with them. The parliamentary crisis we entered into after the 14 October election indicates that we – the politicians and the people – have a whole lot of learning to do.

The Golden Rule

The first thing we all have to learn, or remember, or relearn, is that in parliamentary elections as opposed to presidential elections, voters elect a Parliament. More precisely, in our bicameral parliamentary system, voters elect the members of the House of Commons. The golden rule of parliamentary democracy, as opposed to the U.S. presidential/ congressional system, is that the right to govern depends on having the support of a majority in the newly elected House of Commons.

The traditional exposition of the golden rule rests on the constitution's provision that the queen, or her surrogate the governor general, in whom 'Executive Government and Authority of and over Canada ... is vested,' must be advised by ministers who 'enjoy the confidence of Parliament.'[2] Enjoying the confidence of Parliament may sound a little strained as we watch political leaders manoeuvre to survive non-confidence votes. But the golden rule of parliamentary democracy, not only of ours but of the dozens of others around the world, is that a government cannot carry on if the elected chamber of the Parliament indicates that a majority of its members cannot support the government. That is definitely not the case in the United States, where George W. Bush's administration provided a vivid example of an elected president carrying on without the confidence of the separately elected Congress.

When an election gives one party a majority of seats in the House of Commons, it is very clear how the golden rule works. The leader of the majority party forms a government that, so long as the members of the governing party stick together, will govern through the life of the Parliament. But how does the golden rule work when an election produces a minority Parliament?

Regardless of the election outcome, the incumbent prime minister and government remain in office immediately after the election no matter how badly their party may have done. In a minority Parliament situation, the incumbent prime minister has the first opportunity to form a new government and test its strength in the newly elected House of Commons. The incumbent prime minister has this opportunity even if his or her party has not won the most seats in the House.[3] Parliamentary elections are not like hockey games: a party leader does not win the right to govern simply by leading the party that gets the most seats. The licence to govern comes from being able to secure the support of a majority of members in the House of Commons.

If the incumbent prime minister decides that the government's chances of securing majority support in the newly elected House do not look good, the prime minister resigns and asks the governor general to call upon the leader of the opposition to form a government. That is what Prime Minister Paul Martin did following the January 2006 election when he faced a House in which the Conservatives held twenty-three more seats than the Liberals and appeared likely to have the support of the New Democratic Party (NDP) and the Bloc Québécois, both of which had joined the Conservatives in condemning the Liberals for the sponsorship scandal. Stephen Harper then formed a minority government that was able to secure the support at different times for different measures of the Bloc, the Liberals, and the NDP, and survive until Parliament recessed for the summer in June 2008. In September 2008, with Parliament still recessed, Prime Minister Harper declared it to be dysfunctional and asked Governor General Michaëlle Jean to dissolve it and call a snap election. Jean acceded to his request.

Snap Elections and Fixed Election Dates

A snap election is one that is triggered not by the government's losing a confidence vote in the House of Commons but by the snap of the prime minister's fingers. Prime Minister Harper asked for an election because he was fed up with leading a minority government and thought he had a good chance of getting a majority. That was the only reason for the 14 October election. In Canada, until fixed election dates were legislated by Parliament in 2007, calling a snap election – so long as it was not requested in the early months of a new Parliament – was regarded as a prerogative of the prime minister.

There is a good reason for the constitutional convention, recognized both here and in the United Kingdom, that the crown may reject a prime minister's request for a new election in the early months of a new Parliament. The danger is that an unscrupulous, power-seeking prime minister might not like the results of an election and keep calling for elections until the electorate delivers the desired result. Vesting the power to dissolve Parliament in the governor general, as section 50 of our founding constitution does, provides a check against that danger. Like most of the conventional, 'unwritten' principles and practices of our constitution, the convention about the conditions under which the crown may decline a prime minister's request to dissolve a recently elected Parliament is not a precise rule. In 1926, when Governor General Lord Byng denied Prime Minister Mackenzie King a dissolution, it was only eight months since the last election and King's request was aimed at avoiding likely defeat on a confidence vote. Constitutional commentators generally agree that this was a request that came so early and was made for such a dubious reason that the governor gen-.

eral might well have denied it. They disagree on whether the governor general should have foreseen that the Arthur Meighen Conservative government that replaced the King Liberal government would last only a few days before being defeated on a non-confidence vote.

In 1958, when John Diefenbaker, leading his first minority government, smelt the possibility of a majority and asked for a dissolution just eight months after the 1957 election, Eugene Forsey, a leading constitutional authority, attacked him for failing to show respect for Parliament. But Diefenbaker ignored Forsey's criticism, Governor General Vincent Massey granted him a dissolution, and the Diefenbaker Conservatives won a landslide majority in the ensuing election.

Were it not for the fixed-date election legislation, there would be no doubt that Prime Minister Harper was entitled to the snap election he called for in September 2008. The 39th Parliament was nearing the end of its second year, well past the time when requests for dissolution – under the old rules – are problematic. But what about Bill C-16, the legislation passed with all parties' approval in May 2007?[4] That act of Parliament fixed Monday, 19 October 2009 as the date of the next federal election. It has a loophole, however: it acknowledges that nothing in the act affects the powers of the governor general, 'including the power to dissolve Parliament at the Governor General's discretion.' This means that the governor general might accede to a request to dissolve Parliament before the fixed date. And that, of course, is what she did on 7 September 2008. But should she have granted this request? Should Harper have made the request?

The second question should be answered in the negative. The primary purpose of fixing election dates was to stabilize our parliamentary system of government in an era when elections frequently produce minority parliaments. When the implications of the fixed-date election law were being discussed in a parliamentary committee, Robert Nicholson, at the time the Harper government's house leader and minister of democratic reform, explained that the next election would be held on 19 October 2009 'if the government is able to retain the confidence of the House until then.' When asked what would happen if the prime minister asked for a dissolution even though his government had not been defeated, Nicholson said that 'that would require perusal by the Governor General.' Another purpose of the legislation, acknowledged by the government and important to all parties that compete in parliamentary elections, was to remove the unfair advantage the governing party has over the opposition if it can call elections any time it pleases.

By his own government's standards, the prime minister's request contravened the purpose of the new fixed-date election law.

What about governor general's decision to grant the prime minister's request? It is likely that, if she had refused his request, Harper would have resigned as Mackenzie King did when Governor General Byng refused his request in 1926. We do not know whether the prime minister threatened to do this. But we do know that the prime minister's resignation would require his immediate replacement by another leader with a reasonable chance of securing the confidence of the House of Commons. The crown cannot govern without ministers accountable to Parliament. If Prime Minister Harper's resignation was threatened or anticipated as an immediate consequence of denying his request for a dissolution, absent any indication of opposition parties forming a coalition or making any alternative arrangement, Jean would have had no choice but to grant the request.

On 30 September 2008 Democracy Watch, a non-governmental organization concerned with protecting and promoting Canadian democracy, initiated a court action for judicial review of the calling of the 14 October election.[5] Although the request for an expedited hearing before the election was denied, a Federal Court judge has agreed to hear the case later in 2009. At this stage, the most that this legal action can be expected to yield is a declaration by the court that Prime Minister Harper's request contravened the spirit, if not the letter, of the fixed-date election law. My own affidavit submission in this case argues that fixed-date election legislation and the political leaders' discussion of its implications indicate a change in the constitutional convention governing prime ministerial requests to dissolve Parliament. No longer should prime ministers *at any time* request snap elections. Elections should be called only when the government has been defeated in the House on a confidence matter and no alternative government able to command the House's confidence is available.

However, it is 'the political actors' involved in precedents, not professors, who shape constitutional conventions. On 27 January 2009 Senator Lowell Murray introduced legislation to repeal Bill C-16.[6] In Senator Murray's view, Prime Minister Harper, in asking for a dissolution without suffering defeat on a non-confidence vote, did not break the law but 'he broke his word.'[7] It is my hope that Senator Murray's repeal bill does not pass but instead prompts a renewed commitment on the part of all party leaders to the principle of ensuring that premature elections occur only when a government is defeated in the House and there is no alternative government able to command Parliament's confidence.

For what it's worth, under the terms of Bill C-16, the next federal election is scheduled for the third Monday in October 2012. But if Harper's rules are followed rather than the rules of parliamentary democracy or Senator Lowell's bill is passed, we may have an election well before that date.

Harper's New Rules

In November 2008 Harper was threatened with being replaced as prime minister by Stéphane Dion, who would lead a Liberal-NDP coalition government supported in the House by the Bloc Québécois. Under the rules of parliamentary democracy, the change could come about if his government were defeated and the governor general considered that Dion's coalition government had a reasonable chance of securing majority support in the House of Commons. At this point, Harper offered his own rules of government. Perhaps I should call them the Harper/Flanagan rules, because political scientist Tom Flanagan, a long-time adviser of Harper, has written an elaboration of them.[8]

The primary rule in the Harper/Flanagan system of government is that parliamentary elections result in the election of a prime minister. And the second rule, a corollary of the first, is that the prime minister cannot be changed without another election being called. According to Prime Minister Harper, 'Mr. Dion does not have the right to take power without an election.'[9] I doubt that Harper intends this second rule to apply when the party in power changes leaders. I do not think he would object to the change from PM Chrétien to PM Martin or from PM Mulroney to PM Campbell being done without an election. It is replacing a prime minister with the leader of another party that Harper considers is a breach of the principles of Canadian democracy. A third rule, implicit in his vigorous attack on the proposed Liberal/NDP coalition, is that a coalition government cannot be formed unless it is acknowledged as a possibility in the election campaign and (applying his first rule) the leader of the coalition party who is to be prime minister wins the most seats.

As earlier chapters in this volume make clear, Harper's rules are not consistent with well-established practices of our system of parliamentary government. It will be news to many voters in our last election that, when they cast their ballot, they were really participating in a popularity contest among party leaders for the position of prime minister. Israel is the only parliamentary democracy that has experimented with the direct election of the prime minister. The experiment, which was introduced in 1996, lasted only a few years. It was scrapped when a system in which the prime minister could carry on without the confidence of the Knesset was found to produce political gridlock rather than stability. If Harper is interested in having Canada try Israel's aborted experiment, he should go about building support for the appropriate constitutional amendments. In the meantime he should not mislead Canadians into believing that Canada already has a system of directly electing its prime minister. The vigorous propagation of Harper's rules may already have had a major impact on the public's understanding of Canada's constitution. On 15 December 2008 an Ipsos Reid poll reported that 51 per cent of Canadians believe that the prime minister of Canada is directly elected.[10]

Trying to operate our parliamentary system as if it were subject to Harper's rules would severely restrict the options available to Canadians in an era of minority parliaments. No longer could a governor general accept the resignation of a prime minister whose government was facing defeat on a confidence vote and call on the leader of an opposition party willing to form a government – even though that leader had an excellent chance of being supported by a majority in the House of Commons. The only way to get rid of a government that does not have the confidence of the House of Commons is to elect another House of Commons. If the new rules Harper has promulgated prevail, Canadians could be in for a ton of elections. Before changing our parliamentary system of government to Harper's prime ministerial system, Canadians should consider carefully the various ways of living more productively and less chaotically with minority parliaments.

Five Ways of Governing with Minority Parliaments

The simple arithmetic of minority parliaments requires governments to adopt policies that will be supported by more than one party's MPs. Do the math: with 143 Conservative MPs in a 308-member House, the Harper government must win the support of 12 MPs from other parties to have the support of a majority of MPs. This means that the government's policies cannot be tied tightly to the Conservative Party's pet ideas and ideology. Its policies must be more inclusive than that if it is to avoid defeat and satisfy the golden rule of parliamentary democracy.

On 27 November 2008 the economic policy statement delivered by the government's finance minister failed spectacularly to be sufficiently inclusive. In terms of parliamentary life or death, it was a kamikaze statement.

From a democratic perspective, the requirement that government policy embrace more than the views of the governing party is a good thing. For instance, 61.4 per cent of those who participated in the October 2008 election voted for MPs belonging to parties that are ideologically to the left of the Conservatives.[11] When government policy is adjusted to win the support of some of these members, it is brought more closely into line with the views of the majority of voters. That is a key reason for my preference for minority governments over 'false majority' governments that obtain majorities in the House of Commons with much less than 50 per cent of the popular vote.

To survive in a minority Parliament, a government need not accommodate opposition views on all of its policies. Since the 1960s and 1970s, with minority parliaments becoming more frequent, parliamentarians have come to recognize the wisdom of Eugene Forsey's view that one of the 'fairy tales' about parliamentary government is to regard government defeat on every debatable or 'votable' matter as a vote of non-confidence.[12] The Speech from the Throne and the budget are clearly confidence matters. Other matters become confidence votes only when the wording of a motion makes it clear that either the government or the opposition regards the matter at issue as a confidence test.[13] The art of living with minority governments requires that both the government and the opposition exercise constraint in what they regard as confidence matters. Governments should confine confidence votes to matters crucial to their core program, and the opposition to matters on which they would be willing to fight an election. In the final months of the last Parliament, the Harper government instructed its members to obstruct committee work, and sought its own death by making every vote a confidence matter. That amounted to a deliberate plan to make that minority Parliament dysfunctional.

Minority parliaments can be functional and productive under five different arrangements among the parties. Three of these operate under one-party minority governments, the other two are coalitions – minority coalition governments and majority governments based on a coalition. Under our system of parliamentary government, all five of these possible arrangements are entirely constitutional. Let's look briefly at each.

One-party Minority Governments

For its first year and half, the first Harper minority government survived through a pattern of ad hoc alliances with the three opposition
parties. This pattern suited the circumstances in which the Harper Conservatives found themselves. They needed the support of only one party to have a majority but none of the opposition parties was a natural
ideological ally. On their first budget the Conservatives made a number
of changes to secure NDP support. But the NDP joined the Liberals in
voting against the budget when they saw that the Bloc, attracted by
Finance Minister Jim Flaherty's acknowledgment of federal fiscal im-
balance, would support it. On Afghanistan, the Conservatives secured
the requisite amount of Liberal support by allowing a parliamentary
debate on Canada's participation in the war and following the advice of
an advisory committee chaired by a former Liberal deputy prime minister. On climate change and reducing carbon emissions, they worked
for a while with the NDP, which had a softer approach on that issue
than the Liberals. And so on.

By forming ad hoc legislative alliances, the Harper government was
able to accomplish much of its election platform and begin to address
other issues of concern to a majority of Canadians. It also secured all-
party support for a change aimed at stabilizing government in an era
of minority parliaments – fixed-date elections every four years. But it
was clear all along that Harper's heart wasn't in this kind of legislative
inclusiveness. Like many leaders before him, he yearned for a majority.
Once he sensed Dion's weakness, he pulled the plug and proceeded to
make the minority Parliament unworkable.

A second kind of one-party minority government is an informal but
steady alliance of the governing party with an opposition party. The
Liberal Party has had six of these. Mackenzie King's first two governments depended on the support of Progressives who held the balance
of power in the House and his third (following the King-Byng affair)
on a handful of Liberal-Progressives. The only real constraint on the
productivity of the King minority governments was Mackenzie King's
cautious temperament. In the 1960s Lester Pearson was prime minister of back-to-back Liberal minority governments that had the steady
support of the newly formed NDP led by Tommy Douglas. Pearson's
minority governments with the support of the like-minded NDP were
among the most productive and creative governments in Canada's his-

tory. They brought us medicare, the Canada Pension Plan, and the new Canadian flag. The first of Pearson's minority governments lasted just under two years and the second just under three years. Either could have lasted much longer had the Liberals' high command not hungered for a majority. Pierre Trudeau's only minority government relied on an informal alliance with David Lewis's NDP, orchestrated by Trudeau's house leader, Allan MacEachen. It too was a productive government, introducing reforms in social security, election expenses, and foreign investment, and setting up the Mackenzie Valley Pipeline Inquiry. But again, after a year and half, the Liberals, sensing that an election would give them a majority, concocted a budget sufficiently offensive to the NDP to lead to the government's defeat and an election.

The third kind of one-party minority government is simply a more formalized alliance between the governing party and a third party. We have had only one of these in Canadian parliamentary history and this was at the provincial level. In Ontario in 1985, David Peterson, whose Liberals won four seats less than the incumbent Conservatives, led a minority government that had a written agreement with Bob Rae's NDP, which held the balance of power. The agreement set out a legislative program on which both parties agreed and a commitment from the NDP that for two years it would not support a non-confidence motion against the Peterson government so long as it worked on the agreed-upon program. The program included commitments to broaden the role of House committees and public involvement in the legislative process. Though the agreement provided Ontario with two years of stable and productive minority government, soon after its two years ran out the Liberals called a snap election and got a majority.

A formal legislative alliance is well suited for circumstances in which an opposition party that won fewer seats than the government party nonetheless has the best chance of securing majority support in the newly elected Parliament. Putting the agreement in writing provides strong evidence to the crown that the new government available to replace the incumbent government will command the confidence of the elected legislative assembly. As one who favours minority parliaments' potential for reducing executive domination of the legislature, I prefer this kind of minority government to coalition governments because implementation of the agreed-upon program will take place in open legislative committees rather than in the closed confines of the cabinet room. This type of minority government, however, would be ruled out under the new Harper rules both because its leader's party did not win the most seats and because it makes possible a cross-party change of government without an election.

Coalitions

Coalition governments in which two or more parties form the cabinet may be either majority or minority governments. The only coalition government we have had at the federal level certainly had a majority in the House but was a very unusual coalition. It was formed in 1917 when Conservative Prime Minister Robert Borden invited pro-conscription Liberals to join a Unionist government. The Unionist government went on to win a majority in the 1917 election. It is worth remembering that it was the 'Grand Coalition' formed by John A. Macdonald's Conservatives and George Brown's Liberals that stabilized politics in the minority parliaments of mid-nineteenth-century Canada and brought us confederation. It too was a majority coalition, as was the coalition government that Winston Churchill and the Conservative Party formed with the Labour and Liberal parties in May 1940 and that led Britain through the Second World War. The recently proposed Liberal-NDP coalition, on the other hand, would be a minority government that would secure majority support in the House by means of a formal legislative alliance with the Bloc Québécois.

Larry LeDuc's chapter shows why coalition governments are frequently formed in many parliamentary democracies. When voters go the polls in these countries, they are well aware of the possibility of parties forming coalitions. However, none of them follow the Harper rule that a coalition has to be approved by the electorate or that the head of state cannot sanction a cross-party change of government after the election. Parliamentary democracy needs flexibility in the arrangements for combining party strengths in multi-party legislatures. The form that governments based on minority parliaments can take in order to be effective and secure for a reasonable length of time depends very much on the political circumstances of the time, the distribution of seats in the elected chamber, and the presence of parties close enough in policy or ideology to share power.

The Five Ways and Harper's Rules

All five of the optional forms surveyed above are a good fit for a certain set of circumstances. In a parliamentary democracy in which minority parliaments are frequent, it is foolish to rule out any of the five options. Harper's approach would rule out all but the first two, and permit only those two, without an election, if they are led by the incumbent governing party.

Under Harper's rules, elections in parliamentary democracies are popularity contests to determine the party that has a right to govern. His rules are particularly ill-suited for a parliamentary democracy in which no political party is very popular. The highest popular vote any party's candidates have received in the last six federal elections is the 43 per cent that Brian Mulroney's Conservatives garnered in 1988. With such a fragmented electorate, changing from our existing system of parliamentary democracy to one in which the winner of the most seats in an election is supreme would not serve Canadian parliamentary democracy well. It would mean either being ruled by a party that a significant majority has voted against or being bombarded by an unending series of elections until one party secures a majority.

Conclusion

The decision of Michael Ignatieff, the new Liberal leader, to support the Harper government's budget has ended the parliamentary crisis – at least for the time being. From the perspective of public opinion in the country, this seems to be a reasonably popular outcome. While the leaders of the NDP and the Bloc say that they would have preferred to defeat the budget and replace the Conservative government with a Liberal-NDP coalition, I think most Canadians, including many NDP and Bloc voters, did not want a political eruption in Ottawa at a time when Canada, and the world, are facing a serious economic crisis. The budget, to be sure, is far from being the ideal stimulus package, but its flaws did not warrant throwing the country into a political cauldron.

The immediate crisis is over but it has left a legacy that could be the basis of a serious constitutional crisis in the near future: a country dangerously divided over the fundamental principles and the rules of its parliamentary democracy. That is the primary lesson that I believe Canadians must take from the crisis now ended. As the chapters in this book make clear, the crown has a vital role in protecting parliamentary democracy but the rules governing the exercise of the crown's role are not written down in the text of Canada's constitution. These rules and principles take the form of unwritten constitutional conventions whose legitimacy depends on their being in accord with the views of the people and their democratic leaders. At the present time, it appears that there is neither agreement among our political leaders on what these conventions are nor understanding by the majority of politically engaged citizens of what they mean.

A few days before the new session of Parliament began, a group of thirty-five law and political science professors from all across Canada published a collective article in leading newspapers of English and French Canada setting out their views on the conventions governing parliamentary democracy in Canada.[14] This group included three of the contributors to this book, and the position set out in the article accords with positions taken in virtually all of this book's chapters. But the views of this broad-based group of Canadian constitutional scholars do not accord with the ideas expressed during the recent crisis by Prime Minister Harper or his best-known academic adviser, Tom Flanagan. Nor, if public-opinion surveys are to be believed, are these constitutional scholars' views in accord with the beliefs of a great many Canadians.

The lack of political consensus on fundamental principles of our constitution poses a serious threat to the stability of our parliamentary democracy. It means that the principal players in our constitutional politics do not agree on fundamental rules of the game. This puts the governor general, who may still be called upon during this Parliament to settle disputes between key parliamentary players, in the position of refereeing a game without an agreed-upon set of principles. This situation suggests to me that the time has come to bring those spooky unwritten constitutional conventions down from the attic of our collective memory and try to see if we can pin them down in a manner that is politically consensual and popularly accessible. I do not know how or even whether this can be done. But I am convinced that those of us who share my concern should begin to explore the possibilities. If in the future governors general accept the argument advanced by Lorne Sossin and Adam Dodek earlier in this book that governors general should give reasons for their decisions, this would begin to generate a body of principled statements about the proper use of the crown's reserve powers. But we may not be able to afford to wait for that to happen. If the political crisis Canadians experienced in the winter of 2008–9, and this book that it generated, serve as a spur to moving ahead with the clarification of principles vital to the proper functioning of parliamentary democracy, the crisis may have yielded at least one long-term benefit to parliamentary democracy in Canada.

NOTES

1 For more information on Canadian elections and their outcomes, see Peter H. Russell, *Two Cheers for Minority Government: The Evolution of Canadian Parliamentary Democracy* (Toronto: Emond/Montgomery, 2008).
2 Constitution Act, 1867, s.9.
3 For example, after the October 1925 election, Prime Minister Mackenzie King's Liberals remained in office even though they had seventeen fewer seats than Arthur Meighen's Conservatives. The King Liberal government was able to avoid defeat in the House by securing the support of Progressives who held the balance of power. The King government carried on until June 1926 when King, facing a vote of censure that the Progressives seemed likely to support, asked Governor General Byng to dissolve Parliament and call an election. When Byng refused King's request, King resigned and Byng asked Arthur Meighen to form a government.
4 *Statutes of Canada 2007*, ch. 10.
5 *Duff Conacher and Democracy Watch v. The Prime Minister of Canada and the Governor General of Canada, Federal Court*: File No. T–1500–08.
6 Bill S-202.
7 Canada, Senate, *Debates*, 29 January 2009, http://www.parl.gc.ca/common/index.asp?Language=E.
8 Tom Flanagan, 'Only Voters Have the Right to Decide on the Coalition,' *Globe and Mail*, 9 January 2009, A13.
9 Brian Laghi, Steven Chase, Gloria Galloway, and Daniel Leblanc, 'Harper Buys Time, Coalition Firms up,' *Globe and Mail*, 20 November 2008, A1.
10 'In Wake of Constitutional Crisis, New Survey Demonstrates That Canadians Lack Basic Understanding of our Country's Parliamentary System,' http://www.ipsos-na.com/news/.
11 1 per cent voted for independents.
12 Eugene Forsey and Graham Eglington, 'Twenty-five Fairy Tales about Parliamentary Government,' in Paul Fox and Graham White, eds., *Politics: Canada*, 7th ed. (Toronto: McGraw-Hill Ryerson, 1991).
13 See Andrew Heard, 'Just What Is a Vote of Confidence?' (2007).
14 'What Happens Next if PM Loses Vote on Coming Budget?' Toronto *Star*, 23 January 2009, A6; 'Les règles du jeu parlementaire: quelque clarifications,' *Le Devoir*, 23 January 2006.

11 The Coalition That Wasn't:
A Lost Reform Opportunity

GRAHAM WHITE

Liberal leader Michael Ignatieff's announcement of support for the Conservatives' January 27th budget put paid to any lingering hopes for a coalition government in Ottawa.

This is a great pity.

Much of the debate about the possible coalition centred on whether the Harper Conservatives or a Liberal-led coalition would be more inclined or better placed to bring forward policies Canada needs to manage the difficult economic times we face. Another much-discussed issue was the propriety of the governor general's decision to grant the prime minister the prorogation he sought. This chapter is concerned neither with the likely or possible policy outcomes of a Liberal–New Democratic Party (NDP) coalition nor with the prorogation question. Rather, I will argue that the great pity of the failure of the coalition initiative lies in the missed opportunity it represented for leading the way to substantial and much-needed progress towards real parliamentary reform.

I make no claim that coalition governments are inherently superior to single-party governments in policy or political terms. Perhaps they are, but I leave that debate to others. My enthusiasm for the proposed Liberal-NDP coalition had less to do with the policy directions it might have taken or with any general preference for coalitions than with the clear signal it could have sent that, in the parliamentary realm, change – real change, not just tinkering with inessentials – is possible. It could, moreover, have demonstrated that real parliamentary change is possible without abandoning the principles of responsible government that have long served us well.

Perhaps – just perhaps – experiencing a coalition government at the national level might have emboldened the politicians and the people to move beyond the unsatisfactory status quo that has immobilized and neutered Parliament for far too long. This is by no means a 'change for change's sake' argument. The 'if it ain't broke, don't fix it' approach has much to recommend it in the governmental realm. But does anyone seriously think that Parliament ain't broke?

Stephen Harper's rationale for ignoring his own fixed-term election law last September when he sought and received a dissolution from the governor general was that Parliament had become 'dysfunctional.' What he really meant, of course, was that he thought he could win a majority in an election. In a larger sense, though, he was quite correct. While David Smith's recent magisterial, prize-winning study, *The People's House of Commons*,[1] demonstrates that Parliament is functioning well in some respects (in some instances better than was the case a few decades ago), few would dispute that Parliament's shortcomings as our central democratic institution outweigh its successes.

In what follows, comments about 'Parliament' refer exclusively to the House of Commons. The unique mix of problems and prospects relating to the Senate's role in Canadian democracy are outside the scope of this chapter.

What's Wrong with Parliament?

What's wrong with Parliament? Bearing in mind that no set of governmental institutions lacks for weaknesses and problems, consider the following. If it is anything, Parliament is to be a place of debate, where the great issues of the nation are discussed and policy ideas are proposed, criticized, and refined. Parliament has a great responsibility to educate – to educate the public as to problems facing the country and potential solutions and to inform the people about the policy stances adopted by the various parties vying for popular support. Parliament fails dismally on this count. We did witness a major debate on Canada's role in Afghanistan, but what about major debates – real debates, with substance rather than rhetoric and barracking – on Aboriginal-state relations, on poverty, on the future of cities, on any number of crucial issues?

Parliament can excel at fostering accountability, holding the government responsible for its policy decisions and its administration of public services. To be sure, any number of wrong-headed government decisions or policies and cases of improper management of public moneys and inept program delivery have come to light through parliamentary mechanisms. Yet one has to wonder whether genuine accountability isn't more of a fortuitous by-product of the relentless opposition partisan fusillades of Question Period and various inquisitorial committees – ever seeking the apocryphal 'horses on the payroll' – than an objective sought for the sake of good government.

Individual MPs, including most of those on the government side, have virtually no influence on important policy decisions. In cabinet-parliamentary systems such as ours, power, authority, and responsibility are meant to be centralized in the executive, but this needn't imply total exclusion from power on the part of elected MPs and a crushing concentration of power in the Prime Minister's Office. The saving grace here is that if the public understood how powerless their MPs really are – save in the unquestionably important realms of helping individual constituents with their problems and dealing with local constituency issues – they'd truly be up in arms about the ineffectiveness of Parliament.

As it is, the public does recognize that the debilitating effects of excessive party discipline and the extremes to which adversarial politics are carried in the House severely undercut Parliament's ability to perform its functions. Party discipline is indeed a necessary feature of our Westminster system and adversarial debate can be invaluable in illuminating party positions, promoting accountability, and presenting the voters with clear alternatives. Adversarial politics, however, need not entail, as it too often does in the Commons, mindless partisanship, with members loudly proclaiming that everything said or done by those across the aisle is wrong, venal, and possibly corrupt. Party discipline should mean that on major policy issues – especially those espoused by a party at election time – a party's MPs should be expected to speak and vote with one voice. It does not mean that MPs should risk incurring the wrath of the party leadership if they express independence of mind on matters of minor or local import.

It's not that MPs are simply fools or knaves. Were that the case, the solution would be easy: throw all the rascals out. Instead, the tragedy is that the vast majority of MPs are committed, public-spirited, and hard working and are often called upon to make substantial sacrifices in their personal lives to serve in Parliament. To be sure, certain parliamentary committees and many individual MPs do good, usually unheralded, work. Overall, however, it is a colossal waste of MPs' talents and energies to make such poor use of them.

More could be said, but the point is not to identify or belabour the shortcomings of Parliament, which are well known, but to contemplate how they might be addressed.

The Genius of Responsible Government

Populist proponents of direct democracy, who identify – often quite accurately – the serious flaws in Canada's representative parliamentary institutions, see the solution as lying in shifting power directly to the people through measures such as referenda, plebiscites, and recall. Like Tom Flanagan, who writes that 'Canada has inherited the antiquated machinery of responsible government from the pre-democratic age,'[2] they typically reject and seek to replace the essential principles of responsible parliamentary government. Along the way, as Peter Russell and Jennifer Smith demonstrate in their chapters for this volume, they often distort or misrepresent the key principles and procedures of responsible government.

As an unabashed fan of the Westminster system of cabinet-parliamentary government, I firmly believe that it can serve effectively and democratically in a twenty-first-century political environment. To say that it *can* work is not to accept that it is working well at present, but to emphasize that the genius of Westminster responsible government lies in its adaptability to a wide range of political circumstances.

The trick is to recognize and take advantage of its adaptability.

Unfortunately, altogether too many MPs, pundits, academics, and ordinary Canadians mistakenly view responsible government as hidebound, inflexible, and, ultimately, undemocratic and unsatisfactory. This is not surprising, since, as it has been operating in Ottawa for far too long, responsible government is indeed hidebound and inflexible. It need not be this way.

Consider the variety of political arrangements that fit perfectly well with Westminster-style responsible government. It works just fine with virtually any electoral system – single-member plurality ('first-past-the-post'), proportional representation, or single-transferable vote. It is as compatible with two-party systems as it is with multi-party systems. It's even compatible with political regimes operating without political parties such as those in Nunavut, the Northwest Territories, the Isle of Man, and elsewhere. So long as it's clear which is the confidence chamber, bicameralism is no obstacle. Responsible government handles single-party majority governments, single-party minorities, and coalitions equally well. Houses with hundreds of members? Two dozen or fewer members? Constitutional monarchies? Republics? It matters not; the particular ways in which responsible government functions on the ground will vary but the underlying principles still apply.

A good deal of the problem is rooted in widespread misunderstanding, not to say flat-out ignorance, of just how responsible government operates. A recent poll, by way of illustration, reveals that many Canadians, possibly a majority, wrongly think that when we vote we are directly electing a prime minister and a government rather than a Parliament, which determines who shall govern.[3] No doubt such results partially reflect the success of the Conservatives' hard-edged but constitutionally unsupportable public-relations campaign to retain office once the coalition option surfaced in November, claiming that Stephen Harper had 'won' the October election and any attempt to dethrone him without another election was illegitimate. The underlying reality, however, is that large numbers of Canadians – including altogether too many in the media – do not understand the basic operation of responsible government. They overwhelmingly believe, among other things, in what Eugene Forsey dismissed as the 'fairy tale' that any government defeat in the Commons necessarily entails a loss of confidence and therefore leads inexorably to an election.[4]

Clearly, better education on how our government works is badly needed. That education should, however, include not only the principles of responsible government – which, after all, are pretty simple – but also an appreciation of the range of structural and political possibilities that are perfectly compatible with it. Even more pernicious than the misunderstanding abroad in the land about how responsible government works is the widely held assumption, an assumption both stultifying and wrong, that what we have in Ottawa – single-party government, suffocating party discipline, all but powerless MPs, implacable antagonism between parties – is the only option before us if we want to retain responsible government.

Coalitions Are Not the Devil's Work

This is why experiencing a coalition might have been so valuable. Unfamiliar as it might have been, and no doubt uncomfortable for some, it would have demonstrated that there are very different ways of 'doing' responsible government – that Canadians have many options before them for revitalizing their Parliament and for enhancing their democracy.

Since my objective is not to plump for coalitions per se, but to argue for the flexibility possible in structuring relations between Parliament and cabinet, the discussion of coalitions will be brief, particularly given the overview available in Lawrence LeDuc's chapter. The defining feature of a coalition is that MPs from more than one party sit in cabinet.

Politically, this may entail substantially different policy outcomes and internal decision-making processes than are found in the single-party cabinets that have long been the norm in Canada. Constitutionally, however, all the basic precepts of responsible government – not that there are all that many – operate in exactly the same way. Cabinet gains and retains power through maintaining the confidence of the House; ministers are individually and collectively responsible for government decisions; only ministers of the crown may bring forward to Parliament taxing and spending measures; and so on.

Given the massive misinformation – and not a little disinformation – about coalitions that surfaced during the 'crisis,' it is worth recalling that not only are coalitions exceedingly common in continental European democracies, they are perfectly compatible with British-style responsible government, as evidenced in Australia, New Zealand, the Irish Republic, and indeed Britain itself. They are uncommon but not unknown in Canada. Nationally, the country was governed from 1917 to 1921 by a 'Unionist' coalition. Several provinces experienced coalitions from the 1920s to the 1950s and more recently we've seen them in Saskatchewan and Yukon.

Responsible Government beyond the Queensway

Given the current configuration of political forces in this country, it is unwise to discount the possibility of a coalition government at the national level in years to come.[5] For now, we can only speculate as to what changes, in terms of policy outcomes, decision-making processes, and political manoeuvring, might have ensued from the advent of a Liberal-NDP coalition. Had the coalition lasted the two years its proponents envisaged, it likely would have entailed the most far-reaching set of changes for decades to how Ottawa in general and the House of Commons in particular operate. Doubtless some would have been beneficial and others slightly or seriously problematic. But change there would have been. Would such changes have endured if the coalition failed to last beyond two years? Impossible to say, of course, though it is well to recall that the history of responsible government – and the basis of much of its success – has been one of adopting and adapting beneficial changes while abandoning innovations that proved harmful or ineffective.

The point, though, is not that change – positive change, with any luck – could come about only through the coalition route. Rather, the significance of a coalition would have lain as much in the clear message it would have sent that far-reaching parliamentary change is possible and that it can come in many different forms. And within the four corners of responsible government.

Do other substantial, realistic reform possibilities exist? Indeed they do. We do not lack for thoughtful analyses of the workings of Parliament and feasible proposals for reform. Recommendations proposing changes both modest and far-reaching abound. These include changes to the internal workings of Parliament through amendments to the standing orders or through modifications to the structure, membership, and operation of parliamentary committees; changes in the behavioural norms followed by MPs, ministers, and indeed the prime minister; and changes to the fundamental relationship between Parliament and cabinet. Gary Levy's chapter offers a number of specific proposals. Among the more cogent reform agendas in recent years is that put forward in Thomas Axworthy's extensive report 'Everything Old Is New Again: Observations on Parliamentary Reform.'[6] It provides a range of possibilities for change, from parliamentary committees with better staff support and more stable membership to enhanced outreach facilities to foster better public understanding of Parliament.

The Anglo-Celtic Westminster systems on other continents can also provide ideas. The 'community cabinets' that emerged a few years ago in some Australian states represent one example. In this innovation, every few weeks the entire cabinet, along with its senior bureaucratic advisers, ventures out of the state capital for a weekend in a small community to hold formal meetings and informal public consultations. Ministers settle in at simple tables scattered about the local gym or community hall, making themselves and a few senior officials available to speak directly to anyone with a problem, a complaint, or an idea.[7]

We need not look so far afield for innovative ideas for revamping relations between cabinet and Parliament. Just as coalitions have been more common at the provincial and territorial level than nationally, experiments in modifying the operation of responsible government have occurred far more frequently in the provinces and territories than in Ottawa. We will never, of course, see the House of Commons follow the example of Nunavut and the Northwest Territories, whose legislatures follow all the precepts of responsible government, Westminster-style, but without political parties.[8] They bear mention, though, to illustrate the wide range of real-world political arrangements compatible with responsible government.

Less improbable ideas are at hand. Various provinces have developed different models and approaches to responsible government. To be sure, some have been insubstantial, others ineffectual, and yet others at best half-hearted if not little more than public-relations gimmicks (in this category we find such phenomena as British Columbia's 'open cabinet': the monthly televised or webcast cabinet meetings of Premier Gordon Campbell's first mandate). The most promising involve processes to take seriously the views and expertise of non-cabinet members of the government party in government decision making. A number of such variations are not only possible but have been put into practice at the provincial level. Among the possibilities is attendance and active participation in cabinet and cabinet committee meetings of representatives of the government caucus. Another option, encountered from time to time in some provinces, would require that important legislation, policy initiatives, and spending proposals be routinely subject to a serious vetting – and, if appropriate, amendment or veto – by the government caucus.

In recent years, Alberta, British Columbia, and, briefly, Ontario have experimented with mixed cabinet-caucus policy committees (typically replacing traditional cabinet committees). Some such committees, which exercise genuine decision-making authority, are chaired by private members and it is common for private members to outnumber ministers. Academic analysis of such committees is thin on the ground, so that it is difficult to evaluate their effectiveness and the extent to which they truly represent meaningful change. Still, the attempt to move beyond the self-imposed restraints of Westminster governance, Canadian-style, is noteworthy. It is hard to imagine the powers-that-be in the upper echelons of the Ottawa power structure, be they politicians or bureaucrats, seeing such ideas as anything other than heresy unless of course their political horizons had been broadened and their appreciation of the flexibility of the Westminster system sharpened by some substantial, discomforting shift ... such as the experience of coalition government.

It is worth emphasizing that none of the revisions to cabinet decision-making structures and processes outlined above offend the principles of responsible government, though they may well offend the sensibilities of those with a vested interest in the status quo. Whatever the advice and influence of private members in the process, ministers remain individually and collectively responsible to Parliament for government policy and administration. Odd that the political elite fears for the sanctity of the system if the notion of empowering private members in cabinet processes is broached – won't accountability be compromised? what if there's leaks? – but sees little cause for concern when senior bureaucrats and (especially) political staff play a leading role in cabinet decision making.[9]

Conclusion

In recent decades Canadians have experienced and welcomed major change in their governmental institutions. Think of the Charter of Rights and Freedoms, of the creation of Nunavut, and of the emerging Aboriginal self-government regimes across Canada. Municipal governments large and small across the country have undergone hugely transformative restructuring. Parliament, by contrast, has been all but impervious to significant change. In many quarters the absence of change is laid at the door of responsible government, which is portrayed as an antiquated constitutional straitjacket. For some, this means that real change is impossible. For others, the implication is that responsible government must be jettisoned in favour of a populist, plebiscitary model. Both are wrong.

Reasons for the paralysis that has long characterized Parliament and thwarted serious reform thinking (never mind action) are many. One of the most pernicious is the abysmal lack of understanding of the basic principles that underpin governance in this country. How depressing that so few voices arose to contradict the claim of Conservative politicians and their fellow-travellers in the media that having more seats than any other party (with all of 37 per cent of the vote) meant that the Conservatives had 'won' an unquestioned right to govern regardless of the will of the majority of MPs and that entirely proper attempts to establish a new government according to the precepts of responsible government constituted, in the prime minister's words, an 'undemocratic seizure of power.' (Other Conservatives called it a 'coup.') Such comments betray an abysmally inaccurate view of fundamental constitutional realities. That they were made for partisan purposes does not justify them. They should have been hooted down or, better yet, greeted with the dismissive laughter they deserved. (Bad enough that the Conservatives tried to push an untenable interpretation of the constitution; even worse were their reprehensible efforts to retain power by stirring up anti-Quebec feeling through effectively denying that the democratically elected Bloc Québécois MPs, who proposed to support but not join the coalition, should have the right to participate in the parliamentary process.)

British-style responsible parliamentary government is one of the great political inventions of all time. We're very lucky to have it. Our political class needs to appreciate and act upon its enormous flexibility and adaptability. A Liberal-NDP coalition would not have solved all the pressing problems vexing Canadians, nor would it have transformed the House of Commons into some ideal representative body. It might have proven a disappointment in policy or political terms. But it had the potential to bring new thinking, new life to Parliament. The very existence of a coalition would have demonstrated that we don't have to accept the way things are in Parliament, that it is possible to bring about change to make Parliament more of the democratic, representative institution Canadians deserve.

Michael Valpy writes earlier in this book that, by the end of January 2009, the drama was over. Political dramas can be entertaining or disturbing and this one will doubtless be recounted for years to come. Its lasting significance, I suggest, was the loss of the best opportunity in decades to get on with the essential business of parliamentary reform.

NOTES

1 David E. Smith, *The People's House of Commons: Theories of Democracy in Contention* (Toronto: University of Toronto Press, 2007).
2 Tom Flanagan, 'Only Voters Have the Right to Decide on the Coalition,' *Globe and Mail*, 9 January 2009.
3 Colin Perkel, 'Canadians Need Lesson in Civics, Poll Shows,' Toronto *Star*, 15 December 2008, A2.
4 See Eugene Forsey and Graham Eglington, 'Twenty-Five Fairy Tales about Parliamentary Government,' in Paul W. Fox and Graham White, eds., *Politics: Canada*, 7th ed. (Toronto: McGraw-Hill Ryerson, 1991), 417–22. This interpretation is, of course, mistaken on two counts. Not all government defeats constitute loss of confidence (see Peter Russell's discussion of this point in his chapter), and even if the government loses a confidence vote, the result may be its resignation and replacement with another government.
5 See William Cross, 'And the Future Is: Coalition,' *Globe and Mail*, 26 January 2009.
6 Thomas Axworthy, 'Everything Old Is New Again: Observations on Parliamentary Reform,' Queen's University Centre for the Study of Democracy, 2008; for an overview of his analysis and recommendations, see 'Parliamentary Reform – Everything Old Is New Again,' *Policy Options*, June 2008, 74–9.

7 Australian 'community cabinets' and the other reform possibilities mentioned in subsequent paragraphs are discussed in my *Cabinets and First
Ministers* (Vancouver: UBC Press, 2005).

8 On 'consensus government' in Nunavut, see Ailsa Henderson, *Nunavut: Re-
thinking Political Culture* (Vancouver: UBC Press, 2007), chapter 6; and Kevin
O'Brien, 'Some Thoughts on Consensus Government in Nunavut,' *Canadian
Parliamentary Review*, 26 (winter 2003–4): 6–10.

9 Academics such as Donald Savoie certainly voice concern; see his *Governing
from the Centre: The Concentration of Power in Canadian Politics* (Toronto: University of Toronto Press, 1999) and *Court Government and the Collapse of Accountability in Canada and the United Kingdom* (Toronto: University of Toronto
Press, 2008).

PART FIVE

Tensions in Canada's Democratic Culture

12 Western Canada and the 'Illegitimacy' of the Liberal-NDP Coalition Government

GRACE SKOGSTAD

The parliamentary events of late 2008 and January 2009 exposed a regional divide among Canadians. It was apparent to some degree among the constitutional experts and politicians who disagreed on whether constitutional convention required Governor General Michaëlle Jean to adhere to Prime Minister Stephen Harper's advice to prorogue Parliament or whether it gave her the right to refuse his request and invite the Liberal–New Democratic Party (NDP) coalition to govern. The regional divide was also evident in the debate among Canadian citizens on the appropriate way forward. While Canadians in British Columbia and Ontario split roughly equally on the issue, those living on the prairies and in Quebec were considerably more 'uncomfortable' than they were 'comfortable' with the governor general being the one to decide who would lead the country.[1] In western Canada, most believed that, if the Harper minority Conservative government fell, it should be Canadian voters via the ballot box who determined the government's successor. In another region of Canada, Quebec, Canadians preferred a government consisting of the Liberal, NDP, and Bloc Québécois (BQ) parties to an election.[2]

Why did Canadians in different regions of the country hold different views about the way forward when a newly elected government faces and/or loses a vote of confidence in the House of Commons? This chapter addresses this question of western Canadians. It provides an account of why most in western Canada opposed the coalition and why they preferred an election over an intra-parliamentary transition as the route to installing a government in Ottawa. It also assesses the implications for parliamentary democracy of western Canada's response to the events of late 2008.

Before proceeding further, it is important to justify treating the four western provinces as one region in this analysis. The provinces' political histories differ in some important respects, as do their political cultures and partisan preferences.[3] Alberta has a long tradition of one-party dominance by conservative parties. By contrast, the other three western provinces have all had competitive provincial and federal party systems. British Columbia, Manitoba, and Saskatchewan voters have all elected provincial NDP governments. Internally, Albertans are generally more politically homogeneous than are British Columbians and Manitobans – and, indeed, they were so on the proper course of action in late 2008. Yet, notwithstanding such interprovincial differences, there is compelling evidence that Canadians in western Canada share political attitudes and behaviours that distinguish them from Canadians in other regions.[4]

This chapter makes the following arguments. First, the reactions of many western Canadians – like those of Canadians elsewhere in the country – were based on calculations of self-interest. Simply put, with very strong representation in the Conservative government, western Canada rejected an outcome that would have brought its power to an end. The parliamentary transition to a Liberal-NDP government would have left the region seriously weakened in the governing caucus; most of its MPs would once more be sitting on the opposition benches. Second, and by extension, western Canada's negative response to the coalition government was to a particular coalition. The Liberal-NDP coalition was especially distasteful because its leader had little popular support and its policies were seen as punitive towards the region. Third, the rejection of the Liberal-NDP coalition in western Canada should not be interpreted as a rejection of all coalition governments. Aside from Alberta, western Canadians have been governed by coalitions in their provincial capitals. They don't appear to have any principled opposition to them. Fourth, western Canada's preference for an electoral outcome to end the parliamentary crisis, albeit self-interested, is also rooted in principles of popular or electoral democracy. Championed there to a far greater degree than elsewhere in the country, popular/electoral democracy principles give the people the right to determine who forms the government. They therefore clash with principles of parliamentary democracy under which the people's elected representatives – in the House of Commons – decide not only when the government has lost confidence but also who can replace it. The clash of electoral- and parliamentary-democracy principles suggests that coalition governments are more likely to have legitimacy with Canadian voters, including those in western Canada, if they include the party that has garnered the plurality of votes and have representation from every region of the country. Meeting these conditions for acceptable coalition governments is more likely if the current simple-plurality electoral system is replaced with one that aligns a party's parliamentary representation more closely with its electoral support.

The West Is In and Wants to Stay There

The simplest and arguably most convincing explanation for western Canadians' response to the parliamentary events of late 2008 is self-interest. Canadians in the region stood to lose political power, and they therefore supported an outcome to the parliamentary crisis that would allow them to retain power – or give them a strong likelihood of doing so.

A look at the outcomes of recent elections, as provided in Table 1, shows the partisan self-interest argument to be most compelling with respect to the prairie provinces and slightly less so for British Columbia. Since early 2006, most western Canadians have found themselves in a rare position of exercising political power in the nation's capital. They have arrived there via their own regional protest party. The journey began in Alberta with the Reform Party's inaugural leader, Preston Manning, and subsequently spread to neighbouring western provinces. The ideas of the Reform Party have figured large in the Conservative Party headed by Stephen Harper.[5] And its mantra, 'The West Wants In,' became a reality when the minority Liberal government of Paul Martin was defeated in January 2006. The outcome of the 14 October 2008 election maintained western Canada's position of extraordinary influence on the government side of the House of Commons. The 73 western Canadian Conservative MPs comprise more than half of the 143 Conservative MPs in the House of Commons.

One has to go back a long way to find other Canadian governments in which western Canada enjoyed as much representation and political power. Western Canadians were well represented in Brian Mulroney's two Progressive Conservative governments (1984–93). However, Mulroney had stronger nation-wide support than does Stephen Harper. As a result, western MPs were a smaller part of Mulroney's elected caucuses than they have been of the Harper governments.[6] Western Canada was well represented in the Progressive Conservative minor-

Table 1
Western Canada and MPs in governing/opposition parties

	Government MPs	Opposition MPs
2008 Conservative PM Harper	27 Alberta 13 Sask. 9 Manitoba 22 B.C. (71)	1 Alberta 1 Sask. 5 Manitoba 14 B.C. (21)
2006 Conservative PM Harper	28 Alberta 12 Sask. 8 Manitoba 17 B.C. (65)	0 Alberta 2 Sask. 6 Manitoba 19 B.C. (27)
2004 Liberal PM Martin	2 Alberta 1 Sask. 3 Manitoba 8 B.C. (14)	26 Alberta 13 Sask. 11 Manitoba 27 B.C. (77)
2000 Liberal PM Chrétien	2 Alberta 2 Sask. 5 Manitoba 5 B.C. (14)	24 Alberta 12 Sask. 9 Manitoba 29 B.C. (74)
1997 Liberal PM Chrétien	2 Alberta 1 Sask. 6 Manitoba 6 B.C. (15)	24 Alberta 13 Sask. 8 Manitoba 28 B.C. (73)
1993 Liberal PM Chrétien	4 Alberta 5 Sask. 12 Manitoba 6 B.C. (27)	22 Alberta 9 Sask. 2 Manitoba 26 B.C. (61)
1988 Conservative PM Mulroney	25 Alberta 4 Sask. 7 Manitoba 12 B.C. (48)	1 Alberta 10 Sask. 7 Manitoba 20 B.C. (38)
1984 Conservative PM Mulroney	21 Alberta 9 Sask. 9 Manitoba 19 B.C. (58)	0 Alberta 5 Sask. 5 Manitoba 9 B.C. (19)

ity government elected in 1979 under Joe Clark's leadership but that government was defeated before it could act on its campaign promises.[7] The region also lent its overwhelming support to the majority Diefenbaker Progressive Conservative government (1958–62) and was well represented in its minority government (1962–3). Even during the Diefenbaker governments, however, western Canadian MPs comprised a smaller share of the elected caucus than they have in the Harper minority governments.[8]

With such representation – indeed, one might say disproportionate representation – it is not surprising that Conservative politicians and their supporters reacted with such dismay to opposition parties' announced intention in late November to vote non-confidence in the Harper government and replace it with a formal coalition of Liberal and NDP MPs. The fact that so many of these Conservative Party supporters are concentrated in western Canada gave their response to the late 2008 events the appearance of region-wide discontent.

Partisan loyalties and calculations of self-interest help us understand why western Canadians believed that a new election should decide the successor to a defeated Conservative government. In the current multi-party system, with the Bloc capturing the bulk of Quebec parliamentary seats, a new election would give Canadians on the prairies and in British Columbia a very good chance of being able to send the Conservative Party back to office.

Western Canadians were not the only Canadians to judge the legitimacy of the coalition government on self-interest grounds. Quebec residents did so too. Their support for the Liberal-NDP coalition undoubtedly reflected their belief that a coalition reliant on the Bloc to stay in office would serve their interests well.

Not This Coalition Government

Western Canadians resisted the proposed coalition government not least because they would have little representation in it. Their 21 NDP and Liberal MPs would be a decided minority amidst the coalition's central Canadian and Atlantic base. Beyond this calculation were other reasons. The policies on which parties to the coalition had campaigned in the mid-October 2008 election were viewed as detrimental to the interests of many in western Canada. So was the coalition's dependence upon the support of the Bloc to govern.

The very poor showing in western Canada of the party whose leader would become prime minister in a coalition government undoubtedly owed much to the unpopularity not just of Stéphane Dion but of his party's tax on carbon emissions. During the election campaign, national and provincial Conservative politicians, including the premiers of Saskatchewan and Alberta, compared the carbon tax to the Trudeau Liberal government's 1980 National Energy Program (NEP). Like the NEP, the carbon tax was an effort to transfer wealth out of this region to other parts of the country. Like the NEP, the carbon tax was a federal intrusion into provincial jurisdiction. One important reason, then, to reject the Liberal-NDP coalition was that its policies would be bad for Alberta and Saskatchewan.[9]

Another reason for western Canada to reject the coalition was that it was dependent upon the support of a separatist party. In their concern that the BQ could hold the balance of power as part of the coalition, western Canadians were not alone. A majority of Canadians everywhere except in Quebec were concerned.[10] But western Canadians were especially disturbed. Politicians in this part of the country have long resisted any special status for Quebec. In late 2008 Conservative Party supporters were skilful in characterizing as illegitimate a coalition that relied upon a party that sought the ultimate special status – sovereignty – for Quebec.

Their distaste for the Liberal-NDP coalition as a replacement for the Harper Conservatives should not be taken to mean that western Canadians reject coalition governments outright. With the exception of those in Alberta, western Canadians have had more experience with coalition governments in their provincial capitals than their fellow Canadians in other provinces. Ten of the twelve coalition governments that have existed in Canada have been in British Columbia, Saskatchewan, and Manitoba.[11] Canada's most recent coalition government was an NDP-Liberal coalition in Saskatchewan between 1999 and 2003. The fact that parties who have participated in coalitions have subsequently been elected as majority governments suggests there is no regional antipathy in principle towards coalition governments.

A closer look at these provincial coalitions suggests the criteria by which western Canadians are likely to judge the acceptability of coalition governments. All but one of the provincial coalitions included the party that had garnered the most votes in the previous election and were led by the leader of the most popular party. The 2008 Liberal-NDP coalition failed this important test. It did not include the party that had captured the most votes across the country. Moreover, the coalition's national tally of 114 seats (77 Liberal and 37 NDP MPs) fell well short of the Conservatives' 143 seats. The coalition's share of the popular vote reached majority territory only when the vote of the BQ was added in. The coalition was thus highly vulnerable to charges that it did not reflect the voters' preferences. It was especially vulnerable to this criticism in western Canada, where ideas of electoral democracy are part of the region's history and discourse.

The People Should Decide

As noted above, western Canadians showed a strong preference for allowing the voters to decide what party (or parties) will govern Canada. This preference is consistent with popular-democracy ideas in this region of the country. Popular democracy – also often referred to as direct or electoral democracy – upholds the idea that sovereignty resides with the people and important matters of governing are theirs to decide.[12] Popular democracy and parliamentary democracy are at odds in some important respects. Parliamentary democracy vests the people's delegates or elected representatives, rather than the people themselves, with the right to decide if/when the government of the day has lost the confidence of the people. Popular democracy would strip MPs in the House of Commons of the right to make this decision. It would require an election when a government loses the support of the House and not permit an intra-parliamentary transition of government from one party to others. (See Peter Russell's chapter for a further discussion and critique of this position.)

Principles of popular democracy have a long heritage in western Canada. They began with farmers' protest movements in the early twentieth century and have persisted over the decades. As Jennifer Smith elaborates in her chapter in this book, popular-democracy ideas received a real shot in the arm from the Reform Party of Canada and its leader, Preston Manning. In place of parliamentary democracy and parliamentary debate, Manning advocated popular rule via plebiscites and referenda. Manning's rhetoric of democratizing politics by handing it back to the people resounded more broadly.[13] Before he became prime minister, Paul Martin spoke of the importance of 'giving parliament back to the people.'[14]

Indeed, a steady stream of criticism of Parliament, not only by populist parties but also by academics and the media, has weakened the stature of Parliament. The public often sees Parliament as dysfunctional and MPs as motivated overwhelmingly by partisan self-interest. In this context, Conservative Party politicians and sympathizers had considerable success in depicting as 'opportunistic' the efforts of opposition parties not simply to defeat the governing party but to replace it.

It is important to stress that such suspicions of parliamentarians' motives – not simply in this crisis but more generally – don't mean ignorance of the workings of parliamentary democracy. Western Canadians understand the rules of parliamentary democracy as well or better than those in other provinces.[15] Indeed, the efforts of Conservative politicians and sympathizers to depict the coalition as illegitimate were resisted by some opinion leaders in the region. For example, Edmonton *Journal* veteran columnist Lorne Gunter wrote that Harper was 'wrong' to describe the coalition's behaviour as 'a coup d'état.' Stated Gunter, 'It is part of our parliamentary democracy that opposition parties may attempt to replace a minority government without forcing an election.'[16] Gunter was not alone in western Canada in being careful to distinguish between what was constitutionally possible in Canada and what was politically acceptable to western Canada.

Still, the readiness of Conservative partisans to blur the line between what was constitutionally possible and what was not politically acceptable is worrisome. It is one thing to argue that a coalition of parties with meagre representation in western Canada is not politically acceptable. It is quite another to argue that such a situation is unconstitutional, as did Prime Minister Harper and his former adviser, Tom Flanagan, when they claimed that a coalition headed by a leader who lacked a direct electoral mandate from the people 'had no right to take power.'[17] Such a misinterpretation is troublesome because there are clear limits to reconciling electoral-democracy principles with the workings of parliamentary democracy. If minority governments are likely to prevail in Ottawa for some time, then calling an election every time a minority government loses a vote of confidence is hardly a recipe for stable government. Unstable government is not in the interest of any Canadian, including western Canadians. At the same time, western Canadians (and other Canadians for that matter) cannot be expected to be enthusiastic about coalition governments when they are not represented in them.

Getting to the desired outcome of broadly representative governments, including coalition governments, will probably require electoral reform. Moving away from the 'winner takes all' simple-plurality electoral system to one that aligns votes more closely with parliamentary seats would help to enhance the legitimacy of coalition governments. If Canada's electoral system employed a full proportional-representation (PR) logic – whereby the percentage of seats a party achieves is proportional to its vote – the results of the 2008 general election would have given the Liberals and NDP about thirty-five seats in western Canada. This figure compares with the twenty-one seats they achieved under the current first-past-the-post system. Although without representation in the House of Commons and therefore not in a position to lend tangible support, the Green Party also supported the coalition. Had a system of full PR prevailed, the Greens would have been able to translate their popular vote into five to six seats in western Canada. Although the seat gain would still have left the opposition parties well back of the Conservative Party, the more accurate portrayal of these parties' popularity in western Canada would have had a number of salutary consequences.[18] With more western Canadian representation in their parliamentary caucuses, the Liberals and NDP would be better equipped to understand and respond to the region's concerns. They would also be better positioned to undercut arguments that only one party – the Conservative Party – represents the west. As with the Green Party, voters' realization that their vote 'counts' in a PR system in a way it often does not in the simple-plurality system would possibly also give voters more incentive to vote for minority parties. The impact of electoral reform, then, would be to alter the partisan complexion of western Canada to make it far less monochromic.

Conclusion

The parliamentary crisis – 'of Harper's making'[19] – has exposed the regional fault lines in Canadian politics. Partisans have been quick to exploit these cleavages in their self-interest, no less in western Canada than elsewhere in the country. Such opportunistic behaviour is not surprising; indeed politicians who don't exploit events to their advantage don't survive long. It is therefore important to try to minimize the opportunities for politicians to play the regional card, especially when their doing so undermines constitutional principles of parliamentary democracy. This chapter has proposed electoral reform as one way to undermine the regional-card trump. Although such reform is not on the near national horizon, it is on the provincial agenda in western Canada.

In 2004 British Columbia's Citizen Assembly on Electoral Reform recommended a single-transferable-voting (STV) system to replace the province's simple-plurality electoral system. STV falls short of being a proportional-representation system, but it does aim at translating voters' preferences more accurately into electoral outcomes. The B.C. Legislative Assembly's recommendation failed to get sufficient support from the province's electorate to become law, but the debate surrounding it engendered a similar reform debate and referendum in Ontario in 2007. Although that initiative also failed, electoral-reform discussions are unlikely to move off the political agenda. Indeed, British Columbia will hold a second referendum on the STV electoral system in May 2009. Whatever the outcome, it can be only salutary for parliamentary democracy that Canadians, including those in western Canada, are giving serious contemplation to how we end up with the parliaments we do.

NOTES

I am grateful to Peter Russell, Lorne Sossin, and Nelson Wiseman for their constructive comments on an earlier version of this chapter.

1 The results of the Sun Media-Leger Marketing poll conducted online between 2 and 3 December 2008 are available at: http://www.leger marketing.com/documents/pol/08124ENG.pdf (accessed 25 January 2009).
2 Ibid. Albertans most preferred an election, with 71 per cent opting for it over a coalition. Saskatchewan and Manitoba (as the prairie region) were the second most supportive at 58 per cent and British Columbia followed with 54 per cent. In no other region (Ontario, Quebec, the Maritimes) did a majority opt for an election.
3 For a comprehensive examination of the political cultures of Canadian provinces, see Nelson Wiseman, *In Search of Canadian Political Culture* (Vancouver: UBC Press, 2007).
4 See Loleen Berdahl, 'Regional Distinctions: An Analysis of the Looking West 2004 Survey,' Canada West Foundation, March 2004, http://www. cwf.ca/V2/files/Looking%20West%202004.pdf. Survey data reported in Berdahl demonstrate that a strong plurality of Canadians in the four western provinces share attitudes of regional discontent. Moreover, they see western Canada as a distinct region.
5 The Reform Party joined with dissident Progressive Conservative members in 2000 to form the Canadian Alliance. In 2003 the Canadian Alliance

and Progressive Conservative parties merged to become the Conservative Party of Canada.

6 Following the 1984 and 1988 elections, western Canadian MPs made up 28 per cent and 27 per cent respectively of the 1984 and 1988 Mulroney governments' elected caucuses. They comprised 52 per cent and 50 per cent of the 2006 and 2008 Harper governments' elected caucuses.

7 With 57 Progressive Conservative MPs, western Canada had 42 per cent of its 136 MPs.

8 Western Canadian MPs constituted 65 of the 208 Progressive Conservative seats – 31 per cent – in the 1958–62 Diefenbaker government, and 48 of its 116 seats – 41 per cent – in the 1962–3 minority government.

9 Besides Conservative politicians, Roger Gibbins, president of the Canada West Foundation, argued that the policies of the coalition – including the carbon tax Liberal leader Stéphane Dion had championed during the fall 2008 election campaign – would be bad for Alberta.

10 Sun Media-Leger Marketing poll, 2–3 December 2008.

11 Manitoba has had more coalition governments (five) than any province; British Columbia has had three; Saskatchewan, two; and Ontario, one. See Gregory P. Marchildon, 'Provincial Coalition Governments in Canada: An Interpretive Survey,' in Hans J. Michelmann and Cristine de Clercy, eds., *Continuity and Change in Canadian Politics* (Toronto: University of Toronto Press, 2006), 170–94.

12 See chapter 4 of David E. Smith, *The People's House of Commons* (Toronto: University of Toronto Press, 2007), for a helpful discussion of electoral democracy and its distinction from parliamentary democracy.

13 Quoted in ibid., 60.

14 Quoted in ibid., 31.

15 A poll by Ipso Reid showed that a majority of western Canadians do not believe that the prime minister is directly elected. By contrast, 70 per cent of Canadians believe incorrectly that he is. Western Canadians were also more likely than other Canadians to know that the governor general is the head of state. See 'In Wake of Constitutional Crisis, New Survey Demonstrates That Canadians Lack Basic Understanding of Our Country's Parliamentary System,' http://www.dominion.ca/DominionInstitute December15Factum.pdf.

16 Lorne Gunter, 'A Much Needed Time out on the Hill,' Edmonton *Journal*, 5 December 2008, http://www.edmontonjournal.com/much+needed+ time+Hill/1035308/story.html.

17 Brian Laghi, Steven Chase, Gloria Galloway, and Daniel Leblanc, 'Harper Buys Time, Coalition Firms up,' *Globe and Mail*, 20 November 2008, A1.

18 These effects are among those identified by Alan Cairns in his insightful analyses of the effects of the simple-plurality electoral system on Canadian political parties. See Alan C. Cairns, 'The Electoral System and the Party System in Canada,' *Canadian Journal of Political Science*, 1, no. 1 (1968): 55–80.

19 This description occurs in an editorial in the Edmonton *Journal*, 'Too Much Mystery on the Rideau,' 27 December 2008, http://www.edmontonjournal. com/much+mystery+Rideau/1116981/story.html.

13 Parliamentary Democracy versus Faux Populist Democracy

JENNIFER SMITH

The Conservative government of Prime Minister Stephen Harper has undermined the right conduct of parliamentary democracy, first by taking deliberate steps in the direction of populist democracy and second by creating confusion about the role of the House of Commons in sustaining or dismissing the government of the day. The steps in the direction of populist democracy are the establishment of fixed election dates and the proposal to elect the Senate. The confusion about the role of the House in relation to the minority government that the prime minister leads stems from his own efforts to avoid a vote of want of confidence in his government, a vote that he looked likely to lose. In rationalizing the tactic used to avoid the vote, he sought to narrow the options traditionally held to be available to the House to replace one government with another. If any of these developments endures, to say nothing of all three, the government will have made a change in the country's system of parliamentary democracy by moving it closer to a populist model, although not necessarily a coherent populist model, or so I argue.

In order to make the argument, I examine the roots of democratic populism in the western-based Reform Party that was established in Winnipeg in 1987, and identify the extent to which its successor party, the Conservative Party, has carried forward these populist ideas in the platforms on which it campaigned in the 2006 and 2008 general elections. Next I consider in turn the fixed election date, the proposal to elect the Senate, and the prime minister's view of the House of Commons in the circumstance of minority government. The key question to answer is what these developments mean for the existing system of parliamentary democracy. First, however, it is necessary to begin by defining the main concepts already employed in this brief introduction – parliamentary democracy and populist democracy.

Definitions of Parliamentary Democracy and Populist Democracy

Certainly these concepts are not the same thing. To begin, Canada's version of parliamentary democracy is responsible government. Responsible government is a one-rule system.[1] The rule is that the government must have the confidence of the elected House of Commons – the so-called confidence convention. Whenever there is a vote in the House on important matters like the budget, more members must support the government than oppose it. Armed with this support, the prime minister (the head of government) can properly advise the governor general (the head of state) on the matters at hand.

Canada's parliamentary democracy is embedded in the elegant simplicity of this one-rule system. The democracy *is* the government's need of the confidence of the House. Before moving on to the very different notion of populist democracy, however, it is important to highlight at least two features that flow from the one-rule system of responsible government. One is that the government alone is responsible to the House – and through the House to the people – for its conduct of the nation's business. This is given technical effect by the constitutional requirement that only ministers of the crown can table tax and spending measures in the House.[2] For its part, the House depends on the confidence convention to exact the accountability of the government to itself but it does not thereby participate in the government. A second feature is the constitutionality of the opposition, that is, the opponents of the government in the House. The leader of the strongest opposition party is the *Official* Opposition leader, an idea that signifies the legitimacy of opposition to the government of the day and distinguishes such opposition from opposition to the state itself.[3]

Parliament is comprised of crown, House of Commons, and Senate, but parliamentary democracy is centred in the House, and through the House in the people. By contrast, populist democracy is about a direct connection between the government and the people. It is easy to conceptualize the concept when by 'government' is meant all elected offices, or at least the elected executive (perhaps a president) and the elected legislators (perhaps a Congress). If the people elect these offices, then those who hold them are directly accountable to the people, who use the next election to make that accountability real. It is not so easy,

however, to conceptualize populist democracy within the context of responsible parliamentary government. For that purpose we need some
help from the Reform Party.

The Reform Party of Canada Advances Democratic Populism

Preston Manning, a self-styled populist and the first leader of the Reform Party, characterized the essential assumption of democratic populism in the phrase, 'the common sense of the common people.'[4] He
meant that the ordinary person is not simply driven by the promotion of narrow self-interest but instead, given a chance, can assist in
the crafting of wise public policy. Any populist has to believe this and
Manning does. The rest is technique. How can the common sense of the
common people be harnessed to the conduct of government?

The answer was set out in the Reform Party's statement of principles
which, among other things, highlighted accountability and participation.[5] Accountability is about enabling people to make the government
directly accountable to them, something that is trickier to accomplish
in a parliamentary system than it looks. First, accountability requires
that *all* political offices be elected – hence the need to reform the Senate by electing it – otherwise people have no lever of accountability at
all. Second, accountability requires that those who are elected in fact
participate in government, for if they are shut out of it, then again there
is no lever of accountability for people to pull. From this requirement
flow proposals designed to enhance the role of the ordinary member
of Parliament in the policy-making process, like the liberal use of 'free'
(non-partisan) votes and the establishment of more powerful parliamentary committees. Third, accountability requires transparency so
that the people know the basis on which to judge the elected politicians,
and when. From this requirement flows the proposal that the political
parties issue written statements of their principles to which they can
be held to account at elections. At the same time, there is the demand
that elected politicians place their duty to their constituents ahead of
their duty to their respective parties in the event of a clash of interests
between the two. Finally, and consistent with the value of transparency,
there is the proposal to establish a fixed election date.

Not satisfied with the idea of the people holding their government to
account at elections, the Reform Party also championed the techniques
of direct democracy like the initiative, under which the people themselves propose legislative measures for which there is significant public

support, and the referendum, under which people vote on the public-policy issues of the day.

One striking feature of these proposals is the broadening of the concept of government to include all elected officials rather than merely the government of the day, or even the governing party. Another is the revised understanding of the place of the House of Commons in the responsible-government system. There is no reference in the statement of the Reform Party to the direct responsibility of the government to the House of Commons or any recognition of the House as an intermediary between the government and the people. Further, there is no indication of the role of the House in overturning governments and generating new ones without referring the matter to the people in an election. Finally, there is no separate consideration of the role of the opposition qua opposition. Whatever one thinks about democratic populism, certainly it does not fit the traditional model of responsible parliamentary government.

The Democratic Populism of the Conservative Party of Canada

The Conservative Party, twice-removed heir of the Reform Party, advocated the following proposals in the platform prepared for the general election in January 2006: an effective, independent, and elected Senate; the restoration of representation by population in the House of Commons; a fixed election date every four years, adjusted in the event that a government loses the confidence of the House and advises that an election be held immediately; free votes in Parliament except on the budget and the main estimates; and more power for parliamentary committees to review departmental spending estimates and hold ministers to account.[6] Each one is consistent with the populist effort to tie the elected officials more closely to the voters.

The Conservative-sponsored bill establishing a fixed date for federal elections, introduced in the party's first administration, received royal assent on 3 May 2007.[7] This was the only item of the list that the Conservative government accomplished. In the platform prepared for the general election in October 2008, they set aside the ideas of free votes and more powerful parliamentary committees and instead pared the list of objectives of democratic reform to two items. One is to elect the Senate or, failing that, to abolish it altogether. The other is to increase the assignment of seats in the House to provinces, the population of which has outstripped their existing assignment, in order to secure the principle of representation by population in that body that is required under the constitution.[8] Since there is nothing in this principle that stands in conflict with the system of responsible government, there is no need to deal further with it here. It is now time to consider carefully the significance of the fixed election date, the proposal to elect the Senate, and the new theory of the role of the opposition for the system of responsible government.

Fixed Election Date

The law initially set the date of the general election on the third Monday in October, beginning 19 October 2009, and at four-year intervals thereafter. It is important to stress that nothing in the law compromises – or could compromise – the legal power of the governor general under the constitution to set an election on another date altogether, which she might need to do in the event that a government loses the confidence of the House. In any event, that would require an amendment of the constitution. Should the governor general set an election for a different date, then the law prescribes that the election following it be held on the third Monday in October, four years hence. Touting its achievement, the government said that the previous Liberal government had 'repeatedly abused' the power to set election dates to suit itself, a bad practice that would now end.[9] MPs from all parties supported the initiative and the prime minister was widely praised for his self-sacrifice in restricting his own invaluable electoral-timing options in favour of the fairness of the fixed date for all of the political leaders and parties.[10]

Sceptics who thought that nothing had changed must have felt rewarded when Prime Minister Harper advised Governor General Michaëlle Jean to call an election for 14 October 2008, a full year before the initial fixed election date. Since his government had not lost the confidence of the House, he had to manufacture some other reasons for flouting the spirit of his own democratic reform, and he did, saying that the House was 'dysfunctional' because the opposition parties did not support his government's legislative agenda and that the country needed strong stewardship in tough economic times. Then he added that the law applies to majority governments, not minority governments that the opposition can combine to defeat at any moment.[11]

The prime minister could say anything at all about the fixed-date election law because it in no way affects the legal power of the governor general to call an election on the date that her principal adviser requests her to do. Does that mean it has no significance for responsible government? I argue that it does, not because it stands in the way of an election short of the four-year interval – it obviously does not – but because it will enable an unpopular government led by an unpopular prime minister to stay on longer than he should if he can manage to avoid losing a confidence vote in the House. It is a hook to which a beleaguered government can cling and an incentive to dream up ways around a confidence vote. Such a development is completely opposed to responsible government, the democracy of which centres on the political sensibility of the House to which the government is held responsible. The imposition of artificial deadlines like the four-year interval dulls this sensibility. Indeed, it shifts the centre of gravity from the House, in the circumstance of minority government in which it can be expected to shine, and transfers it to the prime minister, who now is thought to deserve a four-year term, in the pursuit of which he and his successors undoubtedly will explore and use an array of confidence-avoidance stratagems.

The Senate

While the fixed election date is not without subtle peril for the system of responsible government, the elected Senate is a far less subtle one. The reason is simple. Under responsible government, the elected House of Commons is the confidence chamber. The government is responsible to the House, not the appointed Senate. What happens to this critical convention when the Senate is elected, as the current government proposes? The fact of the matter is that no one knows.

Appearing before the special Senate committee on Senate reform that was examining the government's bill to shorten Senate terms to an eight-year, renewable term (subsequently amended to a non-renewable term), Harper said nothing directly about the matter. No one asked him to comment on it anyway. Instead, he argued that the current term of appointment until age seventy-five was unacceptable to the public, being potentially too long, and that appointment itself lacks democratic legitimacy. He stressed the need of the Senate to be democratic and accountable.[12] He did not specify to whom it should be accountable, although logic would dictate the people who elect the senators.

Harper emphasized that his government is taking a step-by-step approach to the reform of the Senate, beginning with the establishment of shorter terms and the election of senators, and then moving to the distribution of seats and the powers of the Senate.[13] The inference to be drawn is that he knows the Senate as currently empowered is too strong to be an elected body. It would be in danger of overpowering the House. The appointed Senate is content to play second fiddle to the House and careful not to use the vast legal powers it possesses under the constitution, like the legislative veto. Elected senators, on the other hand, are unlikely to see things that way, for not only would they be elected and thereby equipped with a mandate, but they would have run in province-wide elections, representing more voters than any of the MPs from the province. Should they choose to flex their democratic muscles, they could easily frustrate the legislative agenda of the government of the day, thereby effectively turning themselves into a confidence chamber in all but name.

As the prime minister stated before the Senate committee, further steps in the government's reform plan include the powers of the Senate, the implication being the desirability of reducing them (there is no room to increase them). Would a reduction in the powers of an elected Senate solve the problem of an elected body becoming a de facto confidence chamber? How significantly would they need to be reduced? The answer is quite significantly, otherwise the Senate would remain an elected rival of the House and a potentially serious problem for any government. The issue of the term of senators is also a factor in the equation.

Let us say that the proposed term of eight years is renewable, and the powers of the Senate are reduced substantially in an effort to ensure that it is second to the House and in no way a confidence chamber. The obvious problem is the inconsistency of an elected, renewable term of eight years, a very strong mandate indeed, and a weak second chamber. They do not go together. What other federal systems with directly elected upper chambers follow such a model? None. The common pattern is to be found in the United States and Australia, the senates of which are nearly as powerful as the lower houses. The reason is not hard to discern. Why would people want to undergo the costly and competitive ordeal of province-wide elections in order to secure a seat in an inferior legislative body? Would they not see such a body as a stepping stone to election to the House, in which case it is a pass-through institution?

Alternatively, let us say that the proposed term of eight years is non-renewable, and the powers of the Senate are substantially reduced to keep it in its place behind the House. Arguably, a non-renewable term is somewhat more in keeping with a secondary legislative body because a non-renewable term blunts the ambition to succeed in the institution. There is nothing for a senator at the end of the eight years except to leave it and abandon politics altogether unless he or she has managed to secure a nomination for election to the House or moves to the provincial or municipal level of political life. The combination of a weak Senate and a non-renewable term is likely to attract political and non-political actors at the end of their careers, or political actors at the beginning of theirs. However that may be, non-renewability plays havoc with the accountability that the prime minister stresses is such an important part of democratic reform. It is impossible for the voters to extract accountability from elected officials who are not permitted to seek re-election.

In sum, should the prime minister's plan succeed, Canadians would find themselves saddled with a Senate nearly as powerful under the constitution as the House of Commons, the senators being elected for a non-renewable term of eight years. There would be a phase-in period owing to the fact that the terms of the existing senators, who are appointed, are grandfathered under the proposed legislation. Nevertheless, possibly the whole Senate would be elected by the time the country sorted out the issue of the Senate's powers, if it gets sorted out. A change in the Senate's powers requires a formal amendment to the constitution, a very difficult thing to achieve however motivated are the premiers by the desire to trim the jib of their Senate rivals. Incidentally, these same premiers are not likely to look kindly on any effort to fix the problem of the lack of accountability that a non-renewable term entails. Why would they want their Senate rivals to be able to reoffer themselves for another term of eight years?

The House of Commons in the Circumstance of Minority Government

The new theory about the role of the House of Commons in sustaining or dismissing the government of the day is an inadvertent by-product of the Conservative government's unexpected (by it) problem in managing its second minority. At the end of November, the Conservative finance minister, Jim Flaherty, tabled an economic and fiscal statement in the House that quickly became a *casus belli* for the opposition parties, who said that it showed no grasp of the gravity of the economic problems facing the country and as well contained poorly timed partisan moves, such as the proposal to eliminate some of the public funding available to the political parties. They planned to defeat the government in the House at the earliest opportunity.

Before the opposition parties were able to negotiate the terms of a coalition to replace the government, the prime minister acted quickly to delay the vote for a week. He then outlined his new theory of the role of the House: '"The opposition has every right to defeat the government, but [Liberal leader] Stéphane Dion does not have the right to take power without an election … Canada's government should be decided by Canadians, not backroom deals. It should be your choice – not theirs."'[14] According to him, then, the House can dismiss a government but not replace it with another one from its own ranks without an election. It was reported that the Conservatives planned to use the week delay to encourage doubts in the mind of the public about the legitimacy of a coalition government, even though experts were already scoffing at the government's parliamentary theory.[15]

The Liberals and the New Democratic Party (NDP), meanwhile, reached an agreement to form a coalition government to replace the Conservatives. The Bloc Québécois (BQ), led by Gilles Duceppe, agreed to support it for at least eighteen months. In a written statement to her, Dion apprized the governor general of the coalition's readiness to replace the Conservative government, should it fall.[16]

In its fight to stay in office, the government ably exploited two undeniable political weaknesses of the proposed coalition. One was Dion's general lack of popularity with the voters – he never did 'catch on' with them. The other was the idea of a coalition dependent upon the support of the BQ, a party dedicated to the independence of Quebec. Nevertheless, the prime minister's claim that really mattered was his denial of the legitimacy of the House to generate an alternate government without an election. But no mere claim could save his government from a defeat in the House. For that, he needed more votes than he had. Once again, he opted for a delay of the vote, this time by requesting the governor general to prorogue Parliament until late January, at which point the government would bring down its budget. She agreed to his request, although apparently took care to remind him that she had the legal authority to turn him down.[17] No Canadian prime minister has ever made such a request to a governor general. Prime Minister Harper ploughed new constitutional ground. It was a successful political gambit, too, because it gave the government time to put together a budget that, with some amendments, the Liberals under their new leader, Michael Ignatieff, were prepared to support. That support spelled the demise of the coalition.

Is the prime minister's contention that the House cannot generate an alternate government without an election simply that? A mere contention? Or is there an argument? For example, before getting prorogation, Harper was quoted as saying that the 'highest principle of Canadian democracy is that if you want to be prime minister, you get your mandate from the Canadian people – not from Quebec separatists!'[18] Setting aside the reference to Quebec separatists, that statement merely begs the question – how? Later he added that the prospect of coalition government would require the support of the people in an election. Evidently the bottom line is that anyone aiming to be prime minister, as the head of either one party or a coalition of parties, needs to win a general election.

This argument fails in the only situation at issue, that is, when no party wins a majority of seats in the election. In that event there is no 'winner' with the kind of claim Harper thinks is necessary. His argument also overlooks the fact that Canadians do not directly vote for the office of prime minister. Instead, a prime minister is elected from one of 308 electoral districts across the country. He does not have a direct mandate from the voters of the country. This is true in all parliamentary systems. Moreover, there are very few non-parliamentary systems in which the executive is elected directly by the voters. For example, in the United States the president is elected by the Electoral College, an indirect form of election. The Electoral College mediates the choices of the voters.

If the test of democracy is the direct election of the chief executive, then very few liberal democracies meet it. (France does – the French president is directly elected by the voters. So does Russia.) And yet this is the idea that Harper appears to advance, as does one of his former campaign managers, Tom Flanagan. Indeed, Flanagan has gone so far as to question the democratic credentials of the system of responsible government under which the government of the day must maintain the support of the House. According to him, the most important decision of modern politics is the choice of 'the executive of the national government' and the citizens must have a 'meaningful voice' in it.[19] It is a curious phrase, the executive of the national government, since under parliamentary terminology the government *is* the executive, the collective executive. Flanagan must mean the prime minister. He also argued that, if defeated on the budget in the House, the Conservatives were entitled to an election because the alternative government, the coalition, was a new development on which the voters had not said their peace. He insisted that the voters, not the House, were entitled to speak first on the fate of the coalition.

The fact of the matter is that, under the system of responsible government, the voters speak first on the composition of the House. Were a coalition government with the support of the House to replace one that could not command such support, the voters would assess the coalition in the next election. So what's the problem here? Is it just a matter of partisans making arguments that suit their side? Or is there something else that troubles people like Flanagan? If there is, it must be that, under the system of responsible government, there is no straight line between the voters on the one hand and the prime minister and the cabinet on the other – or between the voters and the executive. The straight line is between the voters and the members of the House, which in turn sustains or dismisses the executive.

Conclusion

In their effort to bring a measure of populist democracy to the parliamentary system of responsible government, the Conservatives have weakened the democratic element of the system and as well sowed confusion about it. They certainly have not made it more democratic or populist. The fixed election date is not consistent with the confidence convention. The democracy of the confidence convention is that it permits the House at any time to rid the country of an unpopular government that no longer has the confidence of a majority of the MPs. Sometimes the result is another election. At other times the House itself can generate an alternate government without the need of an election. Much depends on the political factors in play at the time. Nevertheless, the action takes place within the horizon of public opinion, and public opinion bears down on the choices that political actors are able to make. Fixed election dates have no place in this scheme of things. They not only weaken the democratic process that I have just described, but as well they can be expected to elicit a raft of self-interested manoeuvres on the part of governments that are determined to get around the constraints that they impose. Already Harper says that that the fixed date applies only to majority governments, even though the law does not say that. Why would anyone think that a majority government that

wants an election earlier than the prescribed fixed date could not manage its own defeat in the House in order to get one?

The proposal of an elected Senate implies an injection of democracy
into the system. However, the current proposal of an eight-year, non-renewable term puts an end to any notion of an elected Senate that is accountable to the voters. Such a lack of accountability does not make for
good populist democracy. In addition, an elected Senate will generate
a host of problems for the system, and no one appears to have thought
through how these problems should be addressed. There is the problem
of two elected chambers interfering with the confidence convention,
since the powerful Canadian Senate, once elected, could wreak havoc
with any government's legislative agenda. There is the problem of a
rivalry between two elected chambers that saps resources better spent
on the conduct of the nation's business. If the devotees of democratic
populism want a government more directly accountable to the voters,
they are unlikely to get it from an elected Senate.

Finally, there is the confusion that the prime minister has caused with
his novel interpretation of the confidence convention, that is, the role of
the House in sustaining or voting down governments. In the event that
the House votes want of confidence in a government, there is no rule
that stipulates the need of an election because the government-in-wait-
ing happens to be formed by MPs from different political parties. That
is simply a claim that the prime minister has made, a claim that suits his
side. The only real issue is time, or whether it is too soon since the last
election to call another one, particularly if there is a viable government-
in-waiting.

My conclusion is that, taken together, the fixed election date, the proposal of an elected Senate, and the prime minister's novel view of the
confidence convention weaken the democracy of responsible government. They damage the system rather than enhance it. Does this mean I
think that democratic populism has nothing to offer the Canadian system of governance? Not at all. There are a couple of elements of democratic populism that could be grafted onto the system of responsible
government, the very ones that the Conservatives campaigned on in
2006 and then dropped from their 2008 campaign platform. One is the
proposal to restrict the need to vote on party lines to budget items, and
hold free votes on the rest. This is a somewhat more radical version of
the proposal of the government of Paul Martin to borrow the British
practice of the three-line whip, in which the governing party demands
outright support on only one of three categories of government meas-

ures (like the budget), less on the second category – and is indifferent on the third category.[20] Flexible voting is not inconsistent with responsible government and at the same time fulfils the populist demand that MPs have the option – at least on some occasions – to vote the interest of the constituency ahead of the interest of the party should the two stand in conflict with one another.

A second proposal that the Conservatives dropped from the 2008 campaign was to enhance the capacity of parliamentary committees to review the spending estimates of departments and to hold ministers to account for those estimates. There are ways of doing this, one of which is to augment the staffs of the committees so that MPs can be properly briefed for the purpose. Another is to develop the practice of enabling governments to make some changes in budgetary measures without thereby jeopardizing their hold on the confidence of the House. Proposals such as these are not only consistent with the existing system of responsible government but might well enhance it. They are a better bet than ill-advised additions that are designed to promote democracy but in fact have the effect of weakening it.

NOTES

1 Peter Aucoin et al., *Responsible Government: Clarifying Essentials, Dispelling Myths and Exploring Change* (Ottawa: Canadian Centre for Management Development, 2004), 20.
2 Constitution Act, 1867, s.54.
3 Jennifer Smith, 'Democracy and the Canadian House of Commons at the Millennium,' *Canadian Public Administration*, 42, no. 4 (1999): 398–421.
4 Preston Manning, *The New Canada* (Toronto: Macmillan Canada, 1992), 25.
5 Ibid., 360–1.
6 Conservative Party of Canada, Federal Election Platform, *Stand up for Canada*, http://www.conservative.ca/media/20060113-Platform.pdf, 44.
7 An Act to Amend the Canada Elections Act, S.C. 2007, c.10.
8 Conservative Party of Canada, *The True North Strong and Free: Stephen Harper's Plan for Canadians*, http://www.conservative.ca/media/20081007-Platform-e.pdf, 26–7.
9 Government of Canada, 'Canada's New Government Delivers on Fixed Date Elections,' 3 May 2007, http://www.democraticreform.gc.ca/eng/media.asp?media_category_id=1&id=1381, 1.

10 Peter Russell, *Two Cheers for Minority Government: The Evolution of Canadian Parliamentary Democracy* (Toronto: Emond/Montgomery, 2008), 141.
11 Sean Kilpatrick, 'Harper Strongly Suggests Fall Election Coming, Dismisses Fixed Election Date,' *Canadian Press*, 27 August 2008, http://canadianpress.google.com/article/ALeqM5jFxzeM7zpCGhxKsRMBHu5Kp1VNGw, 1.
12 Senate of Canada, Proceedings of the Special Senate Committee on Senate Reform, First Session, 39th Parliament, 7 September 2006, http://www.parl.gc.ca/39/1/parlbus/commbus/senate/Com-e/refo-e/pdf/02issue.pdf, 2: 6.
13 Ibid., 2: 18.
14 Brian Laghi et al., 'Harper Buys Time, Coalition Closes in,' *Globe and Mail*, 29 November 2008, A1.
15 Gloria Gallaoway, 'Jean Would Have Little Choice but to Accept Coalition Pact, Experts Say,' *Globe and Mail*, 29 November 2008, A7.
16 Bruce Cheadle, 'Opposition Tells Governor General They're Prepared to Run Canada in a Liberal-led Coalition,' Halifax *Chronicle Herald*, 2 December 2008, A1–A2.
17 Michael Valpy, 'G-G Made Harper Work for Prorogue,' *Globe and Mail*, 6 December 2008, A4.
18 Bruce Cheadle, 'Gov. Gen. Winding Her Way Back to Canada to Deal with Turmoil,' Halifax *Chronicle Herald*, 3 December 2008, A1, A3.
19 Tom Flanagan, 'Only Voters Have the Right to Decide on the Coalition,' *Globe and Mail*, 9 January 2009, A13.
20 Peter Aucoin and Lori Turnbull, 'The Democratic Deficit: Paul Martin and Parliamentary Reform,' *Canadian Public Administration*, 46, no. 4 (2003): 427–49.

14 Ultimately, the System Worked

DAVID R. CAMERON

Ultimately, the system worked. Canada's parliamentary democracy rose to its fundamental task; it held the government to account by requiring it to fashion a policy that would enjoy the confidence of the House. Not only that: it also imposed an astringent discipline on the main opposition party.

Consider where things stood as Canadians sat down to their Christmas dinner in December 2008. An election had produced a minority Parliament with the Conservatives holding the largest number of seats. Governor General Michaëlle Jean had invited the Conservatives to form the new government, which they did, with a Speech from the Throne which suggested an intention to work with the opposition parties to sustain the support of a majority of members of the House of Commons. Then, in a sudden reversal on 27 November, Jim Flaherty, the minister of finance, presented an economic statement that provoked, and was designed to provoke, the opposition parties, and clearly indicated a refusal to engage in the inter-party negotiation and accommodation normally required to sustain the confidence of a minority House. The Liberals, New Democratic Party (NDP), and Bloc Québécois made it clear they would defeat the government on the basis of the measures in the economic statement, and went further, fashioning an alternative government that could be asked to take the place of the Tories if they were defeated. To demonstrate their seriousness, the three parties signed an agreement on 1 December, committing themselves to support a governance arrangement for a year and a half. It would be a Liberal-NDP coalition government, supported in the House by the Bloc.

Prime Minister Stephen Harper at first tried to discredit the opposition parties, arguing that they were seeking to seize power in a kind of illegitimate coup, that he and the Conservatives had won the election and been chosen by the people to rule, and that a defeat in the House of Commons would require new elections. This was all incorrect, but politically effective. There was nothing in the least unconstitutional about the opposition parties' plan: the Conservatives had won the most seats, but only a minority of votes, and Stephen Harper had not been elected by 'the people' – but only by the people in his own riding; and a defeat in the House so soon after an election would properly lead to consultation with the opposition parties to see whether their claim to be able to form a government was credible. Harper's attack, however, successfully focused attention on the hapless leadership of Stéphane Dion, and on the appalling prospect, for most Canadians, of his becoming prime minister so soon after his party had received a drubbing in the general election.

Stephen Harper demonstrated that there was very little he would not do to stay in power. Having miscalculated the resolve of his opponents, whom he had got used to treating with contempt, he engaged in a slash-and-burn strategy, heedless of the damage this would do to his party's electoral prospects in Quebec, and apparently unconcerned about the risk of reawakening dormant national-unity tensions. The contrast in leadership north and south of the 49th parallel could hardly have been starker. While Barack Obama, building his team of rivals, rose to the occasion and gave his people hope, Stephen Harper stooped to conquer, filling a great many Canadians with a feeling of despair and hopelessness. He demonstrated that there was no bridge he would not burn, no low road he would not take, to stay in power. Beyond the deceit and the intentional obfuscation, what could not be forgiven was the prime minister's willingness to conjure up our national-unity demons for the sake of discrediting the proposed coalition. That, surely, was the lowest blow of all. Successive prime ministers of Canada have seen it as their central duty to manage the national-unity file with prudence and care; to light a match near a can of gasoline – to set east against west, and alienate the 38 per cent of Quebec voters who gave their support to the Bloc in the last election – simply for the sake of personal political survival was to scatter this primordial leadership obligation to the four winds.

We Canadians are generally blessed. National-unity issues aside, we live in a country in which the political passions that cripple and sometimes destroy other societies are for the most part cribbed, cabined, and confined. Canadians have a deep respect for the rule of law and Canadian constitutionalism; consider the fact that since 1970 the profoundly divisive question of Quebec's place within or outside Canada has been worked through democratically and peacefully by all participants. We have constructed something of a constitutional garden for ourselves, and, on the whole, we tend it pretty well. It is, however, at moments such as we experienced in November and December 2008 – when our political system is put on the rack – that you can sense the jungle creeping closer. And, in this case, our system was put under such severe stress, not by the economic crisis that is preoccupying the rest of the world, but by the unruly passion for power. Constitutionalism is supposed to regulate political power; there were moments in November and December when the passion for political power sought to regulate constitutionalism.

Realizing that he would face certain defeat in the 8 December confidence vote to which he had committed himself, Stephen Harper then went to the governor general to request prorogation for the sole purpose of avoiding a parliamentary test of confidence he knew he would lose. Putting it mildly, avoiding a Commons vote of confidence is a doubtful ground on which to seek the suspension of the House, and it revealed the length to which Harper was prepared to go to stay in office. In this act, the dramatic policy reversal represented by the budget of 27 January was prefigured, although we didn't fully realize it at the time.

Clearly, the prime minister's request for prorogation in these circumstances put the governor general in the hot seat, and risked putting her office at the centre of a venomous political debate. At their meeting on 4 December, the governor general gave the prime minister what he asked for, although she seems to have made him sweat for it. By granting prorogation, she pushed the affair back into the political arena, and gave all the actors an opportunity to regroup and reflect.

Was it appropriate constitutionally to accede to the prime minister's request in these circumstances? My position at the time was that the decision was constitutional in the sense that Her Excellency acted properly within her sphere of authority; she was entitled to make a choice, and prorogation is what she chose. However, I noted that sometimes legitimate constitutional choices can undermine sensible constitutional norms and prohibitions (such as not using prorogation to evade a confidence vote), and expressed the concern that the decision will establish something of an unfortunate historical precedent, available in the future to a desperate politician seeking desperate measures.

I still believe that that is one of the implications of her decision. But there are others. Prorogation acted as a kind of constitutional time out, giving all of the political parties an opportunity to reflect on what they had been doing and to settle their plans for the future. Two parties were significantly affected in this way, and two were not. The Bloc and the NDP had made their moves before Christmas, when they had signed on to the idea of a coalition. Little changed for them during the weeks that followed. They remained committed to the agreement they had signed on 1 December.

However, the impact of the governor general's decision on the two other parties was profound. It gave the Liberals the impetus to do what they should have done immediately after the last election, namely, remove Stéphane Dion as leader of the Liberal Party. Paul Martin had had the wisdom to step down quickly as leader of the opposition after he lost the election of 2006, which permitted Bill Graham to step in and serve as an effective interim leader. This time round, the Liberals, thinking they would be experiencing normal politics until their leadership convention in May 2009, underestimated the cost of permitting Stéphane Dion to stay on in the interim. Then they compounded the error by allowing Dion to be put forward as the prospective leader of a coalition government. This offered Harper a juicy target to attack. The governor general's time out allowed the Liberals the time they needed to correct this. Recognizing that many Canadians did not want Dion to be their prime minister, the Liberals found a way to make a rapid shift in party leadership, and put Michael Ignatieff in the saddle.

This is one of the ways in which the system ultimately worked. The brutal politics of this period imposed a kind of political accountability on the main opposition party. The Liberals had been decisively rejected in the previous election, and Stéphane Dion's leadership had had a good deal to do with it. The critical events of November and December, and the political space opened up by the governor general's prorogation, made it possible for the Liberals to respond to the discipline of the political marketplace. The accession of Michael Ignatieff to the leadership instantly changed the political calculus, forcing both the Liberals and the Tories to up their game. The rapid and graceful withdrawal of Bob Rae from the leadership race left no opening for Stephen Harper to engage in divisive attacks about the Liberals' unfitness to govern; led by Ignatieff, the Liberals became a credible alternative to the Conservatives.

The unfolding of political events imposed a fearsome accountability on Stephen Harper and the Conservatives as well. Clearly, Harper was able at first to evade the core requirement of responsible government, namely, accountability to the House of Commons, by arranging the prorogation of Parliament. But he was able to evade it only temporarily. Ultimately, he was forced to bend to the will of the House.

The basic question at issue was simple: Where, finally, does power lie in our political system? Stephen Harper is not the first modern Conservative leader who has tried to govern as if he held a majority when he didn't. Joe Clark lost his minority premiership in 1979 because he thought he could govern as if he had a majority, and because he reckoned that, in any case, if he lost the confidence of the House, he would win the ensuing election. Neither his assumption nor his calculation proved to be true, and his seven-month government proved to be one of the briefest on record.

We were on the verge of seeing something like this scenario played out again. The Conservatives' November economic statement contained several poison pills. If, as Harper assumed, the Liberals could be induced to swallow them, he would have demonstrated his mastery of the House, and it would be back to business as usual; in the months running up to the last election, Stéphane Dion felt he had no alternative but to hold his nose and let the Conservatives have their way. With the Liberals in the previous election having had one of their worst showings since confederation, Stephen Harper clearly believed he could rub their noses in the dirt. He was shocked to discover that the Liberals and the other two opposition parties were prepared to defeat him and to replace the Tories with a Liberal-NDP coalition government supported by the Bloc. When his scathing attacks did not dislodge the opposition accord, he, in desperation, sought and obtained the suspension of Parliament for seven weeks.

At last, he recognized reality; the parliamentary time out gave him and his colleagues time to accommodate themselves to it. Having withdrawn the offensive measures, the Conservatives replaced them with a set of initiatives that responded to the demands of the opposition. In so doing, Stephen Harper turned his back on his ideological convictions and left the Conservative agenda in tatters. His reputation as a ruthless, cunning political strategist was sideswiped by a crisis of his own making, and he has grievously damaged his leadership within his own party. Michael Ignatieff warned Harper not to engage in the nasty personal attacks that marked his earlier political strategy, and the prime minister duly heeded this call.

This is accountability – brutal accountability – with a vengeance. That one can almost feel a pang of sympathy for what Stephen Harper is going through brings home the extent to which the game has changed. The ideological shift to the right that he went into politics to achieve has ground to a halt; he has had to acknowledge that the state has a place in the boardrooms of the nation. His strategy for winning over Quebec is in ruins. He has been forced to adopt the policies of his political enemies. And to cap it all off, the Liberal leader has imposed regular parliamentary accountability sessions on his government at which the effectiveness of the implementation of the financial-aid package will be assessed. The House of Commons has shown who's boss.

Classical parliamentary theory holds that the government must retain the confidence of the House of Commons. If the governing party holds a majority and there is party discipline, this core requirement is fulfilled uneventfully; in a minority Parliament, however, this obligation is brought into bold relief. So it is with Canada's 40th Parliament. Despite the Tories' highly debatable avoidance of the 8 December confidence vote, Conservative MPs are today unequivocally responsible to the House of Commons on whose confidence their survival as a government depends, and they know it. Ultimately, the system worked. Parliamentary government demonstrated, once again, its strength, and the political passions that flared up so brightly before Christmas were tamed by the practices and institutions of a constitutional people.

I think of the third verse of the great Welsh hymn, written by John Hughes, *God of Grace and God of Gladness*:

> *Cure Thy children's warring madness,*
> *Bend our pride to Thy control;*
> *Shame our wanton, selfish gladness,*
> *Rich in things and poor in soul.*

> *Grant us wisdom, grant us courage,*
> *Lest we miss Thy kingdom's goal,*
> *Lest we miss Thy kingdom's goal.*

I am not quite prepared to say that Canadian constitutional government is the secular equivalent of the Divine, but in the absence of God's grace, it serves us pretty well.

Contributors

David R. Cameron is professor and chair of the Department of Political Science at the University of Toronto.

The Right Honourable Adrienne Clarkson was the 26th governor general of Canada, from 1999 to 2005.

Adam Dodek is associate professor at the University of Ottawa's Faculty of Law.

C.E.S. (Ned) Franks is professor emeritus at the Queen's University Department of Political Studies and School of Physical and Health Education.

Jean-François Gaudreault-DesBiens is associate dean, Research, and Canada Research Chair in North American and Comparative Juridical and Cultural Identities at the Faculty of Law of the Université de Montréal.

Andrew Heard is associate professor in the Political Science Department at Simon Fraser University.

Jean Leclair is professor at the Université de Montréal's Faculty of Law.

Lawrence LeDuc is professor in the Department of Political Science at the University of Toronto.

Gary Levy is editor of the *Canadian Parliamentary Review* and a former professor of political science at the University of Western Ontario and the University of Ottawa.

Peter H. Russell is professor emeritus at the University of Toronto's Department of Political Science.

Grace Skogstad is professor in the Department of Political Science at the University of Toronto.

Brian Slattery is professor at the Osgoode Hall Law School of York University.

Jennifer Smith is professor in the Department of Political Science at Dalhousie University.

Lorne Sossin is professor and former associate dean at the University of Toronto's Faculty of Law.

Michael Valpy writes for the *Globe and Mail* on public policy, politics, religion spirituality, and ethics, has co-authored two books on the Canadian constitution, and holds an honorary doctorate of journalism from Trent University.

Lorraine E. Weinrib is professor at the University of Toronto's Faculty of Law and Department of Political Science.

Graham White is professor in the Department of Political Science at the University of Toronto.

Index